the
passionate cook

the
passionate cook

THE VERY BEST OF KAREN BARNABY

whitecap

Some of the recipes in this book previously appeared in *Pacific Passions*, *Screamingly Good Food*,
Girls Who Dish, *Girls Who Dish II: Seconds Anyone?*, and *Girls Who Dish: Inspirations*

Edited by Marial Shea
Cover and interior design by Jacqui Thomas
Front cover and interior photographs by Jenn Walton / Digiwerx Studio
Back cover photograph by Clinton Hussey
Food styling by JoAnne M. Strongman

Printed and bound in Canada

National Library of Canada Cataloguing in Publication

Barnaby, Karen
    The passionate cook: the very best of Karen Barnaby.

    Includes index.
    ISBN 1-55285-525-2

    1. Cookery. I. Title.
TX714.B36 2004   641.5   C2004-900369-0

The publisher acknowledges the financial support of the Government of Canada through the Book
Publishing Industry Development Program for our publishing activities.

the passionate cook

Tempest Fugit

I started writing *Pacific Passions* in 1993 on a dinky little laptop computer. At first, it seemed like a snap — writing a cookbook? Sure, no problem! But the actual recipe development and testing, along with the writing, took two years. I can't remember if I didn't receive the writing guidelines or if I somehow missed the information, but I had written the manuscript entirely in capital letters and that had to be changed. When that was done, I had to add in the metric measurements and write intros to all the recipes. Holey moley! I couldn't believe the amount of work. It was almost anti-climatic to hold the actual book in my hand for the first time because I had lived and breathed it for so long. We had become one.

The exciting reality of it all did kick in. I proudly sent copies to all my relatives and gave them away to my friends. I was a published cookbook author! I even got to go on a book tour!

Screamingly Good Food was a different experience, since I was now a "seasoned" author and all. I loved writing that book! I was thrilled with the seasonal concept, the recipes and recounting my own reasons to feast. By comparison, the three Girls Who Dish! books were very easy as well as being snappy and fun. Each author contributed 16 recipes which made for a considerably lighter load.

The recipes I love the most are those that strike a certain chord with me. Great meals with family and friends, special seasonal treats, recipes that remind me of certain times, people or places, or those that just make me giddy with pleasure are the ones I've chosen to include in this book. All of the hits from my cooking classes are here too. It's a wonderful thing to see what I consider my best work all in the same place.

A lot can happen in ten years. But no matter what happened, I never stopped cooking. I'm grateful to have this passion that keeps me motivated to always give. What I receive in return from the people who have supported me through the years is priceless.

— November 2003

Feast for a Fool: My Birthday Feast

My Birthday Ribs

Laotian Charred Tomato Sauce

Sticky Rice

Zebra Cake

Chocolate Milk

For years, my birthday feast was ribs, a spicy Laotian charred tomato sauce, sticky rice, chocolate milk and Zebra Cake. A very adult bottle of nice old vintage port is opened later. The ribs, sticky rice and charred tomato sauce came from the incredible barbecues my Laotian friends have in the summer. The rest came later.

I am very dogmatic about foods that have to be picked up and eaten with your hands, such as ribs, corn or chicken wings: dishes requiring a fork cannot be served with them. These foods are pleasurable to eat with your hands and I don't see the point of putting down a rib, picking up a fork, and eating some macaroni salad. It's just too distracting. Steven and I would have this argument every year during corn season. He would concede, but only once. For my birthday...well, *it's my party* and everyone eats with their hands.

The initial baking makes the ribs tender, then the sauce and barbecuing or broiling crisps them up. I use a specific saté sauce — Tia Chieu Sa-té from Huy Fong Foods Inc. It comes in an 8-oz. (240-mL) plastic bottle with a rooster logo. You will find it in stores that sell Vietnamese products and in well-stocked supermarkets. This is a great sauce on steaks too. The recipe is easily doubled.

My Birthday Ribs   serves 4

3 lbs. (1.4 kg) pork side ribs

salt

3 Tbsp. (45 mL) ketchup

3 Tbsp. (45 mL) oyster sauce

3 Tbsp. (45 mL) saté sauce

1/2 tsp. (2.5 mL) Worcestershire sauce

Preheat the oven to 300°F (150°C). Sprinkle the ribs lightly with salt and place in a single layer in baking pans. Pour in 1/2 inch (1.2 cm) water, cover tightly with aluminum foil and bake for 2 hours. Remove from the oven, uncover and cool.

Preheat the broiler or barbecue to medium. Mix the remaining ingredients together and brush on both sides of the ribs. Broil or grill the ribs until browned and crusty. Cut into single ribs before serving.

Laos has some of the most interesting sauces I have ever come across. These are thick sauces, used as a dip for meat, vegetables or the Lao staple, sticky rice. They sometimes contain fish or meat or can be vegetable-based like this one.

Laotian Charred Tomato Sauce   makes 1 1/2 cups (360 mL)

1/2 lb. (227 g) cherry tomatoes

4 small shallots, unpeeled

6 cloves garlic, unpeeled

3 Thai chilies

1/2 tsp. (2.5 mL) salt

2 tsp. (10 mL) fish sauce

1/2 tsp. (2.5 mL) sugar

1 Tbsp. (15 mL) freshly squeezed lime juice

Heat a large, heavy, preferably cast iron frying pan over medium-low heat. Place the tomatoes, shallots, garlic and chilies in separate piles in the frying pan. Cook the ingredients, turning each one, until the tomatoes and chilies have blackened in spots (the skins might split and this is fine) and the garlic and shallots are completely blackened. As they are done, remove the ingredients to a plate, keeping them separate. Cool. Remove the blackened skins from the garlic and shallots. With a mortar and pestle or in a large bowl with a fork, mash the chilies and salt together. Add the garlic and shallots and mash to a rough paste. Add the tomatoes and mash until well incorporated. Stir in the fish sauce, sugar and lime juice. The sauce will keep for a week, covered and refrigerated.

Sticky Rice

Sticky or glutinous rice is a variety of rice that is high in amylopectin, the component that makes rice sticky. It can be long or short grain. Long-grain is used in Laos and northern Thailand as a daily rice. Viewed side by side with typical long-grain rice, you will see that the glutinous rice is bright white, whereas the other is opaque. Short-grain rice is used in other Asian cultures for desserts and stuffings. Anyone who is familiar with dim sum will know it as the filling of the lotus leaf wrap, along with sausage, dried shrimp, egg yolk and chicken. Sticky rice is not Japanese rice. There is a misconception that the rice used in sushi is glutinous rice. Sushi rice is cooked Japanese rice that has been tossed with a mixture of vinegar, sugar and salt and fanned. This gives it a lustrous sheen and helps it to stick together. I once tried to assist a couple in a Laotian store looking for rice for sushi. They were holding a bag of short-grained glutinous rice. I explained that this rice was not used for sushi and they dismissed me with a bland smile. I had a little chuckle, thinking of how they would be looking at a nice pot of goo and trying to figure out what went wrong.

Two cups of raw rice will be enough for 4–6 people. Wash it several times in cool water and let it soak overnight. A special steaming apparatus that consists of an urn-shaped aluminum pot and a triangular, cone-shaped basket is used to cook the rice. Fill the bottom with a few inches of water and place the soaked rice in the basket. Cover with a lid and steam over high heat until the bottom rice is tender. Hold the basket by the top and deftly jerk it down, flipping the rice over. When the rice has finished steaming, transfer it to lidded baskets for serving. Each diner takes a small handful of rice in the non-dominant hand, pulls off a small clump, and forms it into a tight ball. It is then used to convey food to the mouth. The ball has to be tight, especially when eating from communal dishes. It is a real no-no to leave grains of your rice in the dish. Stores selling Vietnamese, Thai or Laotian ingredients will carry the essentials for making sticky rice as well as beautiful clay mortars with wooden pestles for making the charred tomato sauce.

Zebra Cake   serves 4 to 6

Unfortunately, I cannot give you the recipe for Zebra Cake because it's on the back of the Christie chocolate wafer box and belongs to them. They call it Chocolate Wafer Log, a rather dull name I think when compared to the exciting Zebra Cake. It is thin chocolate wafers, sandwiched together and iced with whipped cream and left to sit overnight. Sitting overnight is what transforms it into a glorious deep brown and white striped cake. And if it's layered up in a round springform pan, it can actually fool people into thinking you spent days slaving over it. But I can tell you why it is my birthday cake. Having cooked professionally for 20 years I always hear, "Oh, I could never cook for you!" People are naturally intimidated, although I appreciate it even when someone will make me a piece of toast! I started making this cake thinking that if anyone ever *wanted* to make my birthday cake, it would be a breeze for them. I have never had any offers, so I continue to make it, as well as my whole dinner, year after year. Wait, one year my dear friend Sjoerd made the cake with a Barbie doll sticking out of it and the cake part a big, flouncy, skirt decorated with Smarties. It was beautiful! The great thing about using chocolate wafers and whipping cream for a cake is it lends itself to construction, like bricks and mortar. I've made round cakes, dog cakes and snake cakes, to name a few, dyed the whipping cream in rainbow colors, decorated it with Easter eggs and Kit Kat bars. With Zebra Cake in your repertoire, there is never a dull moment!

appetizers

Asparagus and goat cheese are a natural combination. David Wood's truffled Salt Spring Island goat cheese makes an even better combination, but the effect can be simulated by scattering droplets of truffle oil over the dish. This sabayon is not difficult and it is a great sauce to have in your repertoire. Try it with salmon.

Warm Asparagus with Cool Goat Cheese Sabayon serves 4 to 6

6 large egg yolks

1/2 cup (120 mL) white wine

6 oz. (170 g) soft unripened goat cheese, at room temperature

1 Tbsp. (15 mL) milk

1 Tbsp. (15 mL) lemon juice

1/2 cup (120 mL) whipping cream

2 Tbsp. (30 mL) minced chives

2 lbs. (900 g) fresh asparagus, woody stems snapped off and, if desired, peeled

Whisk the egg yolks and white wine together in a heat-proof bowl. Place the bowl over, not in, a pot of simmering water. Continue whisking until the mixture becomes thick and triples in volume, about 4–5 minutes. Set the bowl into a larger bowl filled with ice water, or refrigerate until cool, whisking occasionally.

Beat the goat cheese until smooth. Gradually beat in the milk and lemon juice. Fold in the chilled egg yolk mixture. Beat the whipping cream until soft peaks form. Fold into the mixture. Stir in half the chives. Cover and refrigerate. Use the same day.

Tie the asparagus into two bundles with string. Bring a large pot of water to a boil. Salt liberally. Add the asparagus and cook until tender.

Serve the asparagus hot; or serve it cold, first cooling it under cold running water. Drain well, remove the string and arrange on a platter or individual plates. Top with the sauce and sprinkle with the remaining chives. Serve immediately.

Both tangy and slightly sweet, this is a delicious dip. Try it on a sandwich instead of mayonnaise. It can also be reheated over low heat and served as a vegetable with chicken or pork.

Garlicky Goat Cheese and Yam Purée   makes 1³/4 cups (420 mL)

1 yam that weighs around ¹/2 lb. (227 g)

2 bulbs garlic

olive oil for garlic

¹/2 tsp. (2.5 mL)   sea salt

1 Tbsp. (15 mL) lemon juice

5 oz. (140 g) soft, unripened goat cheese

4 Tbsp. (60 mL) extra virgin olive oil

freshly ground black pepper to taste

Preheat the oven to 350°F (175°C). Prick the yam several times with a fork and place in a small baking pan. Make a straight cut, about ¹/2-inch (1.2-cm) deep across the stem end of the garlic bulbs, exposing the cloves. Rub with a little bit of olive oil and wrap securely but loosely in aluminum foil. Place in the pan with the yam. Bake the garlic and yam for 1 hour, until soft. Remove the garlic from the foil and let both cool to room temperature.

Peel the garlic cloves and yam. Transfer to a food processor along with the salt and lemon juice and puree until smooth. Add the goat cheese along with the contents of the container, olive oil and black pepper and pulse to combine. Refrigerate until ready to serve.

This recipe is a combination of inspirations — David Wood's fabulous Salt Spring Island goat cheese and T Tearoom's wonderful teas. Cheese marinated in jasmine, Earl Grey or a fruit tea would be good with fruit, while the nutty flavor of Genmai Cha or the smoky flavor of Lapsang Souchong would be good in a salad.

Tea-Scented Fresh Goat Cheese   serves 4

1 soft unripened goat cheese,
  approximately 4 oz. (113 g)

2 Tbsp. (30 mL) fragrant tea (natural fruit tea,
  Lapsang Souchong, Genmai Cha, jasmine,
  Earl Grey, etc.)

Wrap the cheese in a single layer of cheesecloth with very little overlap.

Place a piece of plastic wrap that is large enough to completely wrap the cheese on your work surface. Spread 1 Tbsp. (15 mL) of the tea in a band lengthwise down the middle of the wrap. Place the curved edge of the cheese in the tea at one end of the wrap and tightly roll the cheese in the wrap, making sure that the tea is covering the side of the cheese all the way around. Place the cheese with one of the flat sides up and sprinkle half the remaining tea over the cheese. Enclose it tightly with the wrap. Repeat on the remaining side. You should end up with a piece of cheese that is almost completely covered in tea, tightly wrapped in plastic. Refrigerate for 24 hours.

Remove the plastic wrap and cheesecloth from the cheese. Wrap in plastic wrap to store the cheese if you are not serving it right away. Like all cheese, this one is better at room temperature.

This combination came to me **while preparing a friend's birthday dinner one year. Artichokes from California are at their peak in February and are a birthday must. I served them as a first course with three different types of mayonnaise — curry, sesame, and honey caper, which was everybody's favorite, hands down.**

Whole Artichokes with Honey Caper Mayonnaise   serves 4

1 lemon, cut in half

4 large, fresh artichokes

1 recipe Honey Caper Mayonnaise
(see page 108)

Have a large bowl of cold water at hand. Squeeze juice from half the lemon into the water.

Trim the artichokes by snapping off the bottom layer of leaves. Cut off the top 1 inch (2.5 cm) of the artichoke with a serrated knife. Trim the points of the bottom leaves with scissors. Rub all the cut surfaces with the other half of the lemon.

Trim the stem and peel it with a vegetable peeler or a small knife. Rub with lemon and drop into the bowl of water. Continue with the remaining artichokes.

Transfer the artichokes to a large pot and cover with cold water. Bring to a boil and cook until the bases are tender when pierced with a knife, 30–40 minutes. Drain and turn the artichokes upside down to cool. Cover and refrigerate until cold, about 1 hour. The artichokes may be prepared a day in advance.

To serve, place each artichoke on a plate and serve with a ramekin of the mayonnaise. Pull off a leaf at a time and dip into the mayonnaise. Pull the leaf through your teeth to extract the tender flesh on the bottom. When you reach the choke, remove the spiky, purple-tinged leaves to expose the fuzzy choke. Scrape out the choke with the tip of a knife or a small spoon. Cut the heart into quarters and enjoy.

When I lived in Toronto, a supplier of excellent wines and olive oils gave me a jar filled with a miraculous eggplant dish that his mother made. It was a perfect blend of sweet, sour and salty, with a creamy texture. I was so impressed that I immediately set to work replicating it and it seemed like that's all we ate that summer—on pasta, with meat and fish, on salads, with cheese, as an appetizer. We fed it to our friends. They started making it . . . and so on. This is one of my favorite dishes of all time. If you can find the Sicilian eggplants that appear in the summer, use them. They are the sweetest.

Caponata   makes about 2 cups (480 mL)

1 lb. (454 g) eggplant

1/4 cup (60 mL) olive oil

1 stalk celery, cut into julienne strips,
   2 inches by 1/4 inch (5 cm by .6 cm)

1 medium onion, cut into 1/2-inch (1.2-cm)
   lengthwise wedges

1 1/2 cups (360 mL) drained, canned plum
   tomatoes, puréed and sieved

8 good-quality green olives, pitted

8 good-quality black olives, pitted

1 Tbsp. (15 mL) small capers, drained

1 1/2 tsp. (7.5 mL) golden raisins

sea salt and freshly ground black pepper

1 tsp. (5 mL) balsamic vinegar

1 1/2 tsp. (7.5 mL) fresh Italian parsley,
   coarsely chopped

1/2 cup (120 mL) fresh basil leaves

Preheat the oven to 350°F (175°C). Prick the eggplant several times with a fork and place on a baking sheet. Bake for 30–45 minutes, until the eggplant is completely soft and collapsing. Remove from the oven and slit the eggplant open on one side. Place in a colander, slit side down, to drain and cool completely.

While the eggplant is cooling, heat the olive oil in a large pot over medium heat. Add the celery and onion and sauté until translucent. Add the tomato purée, olives, capers and raisins. Cook over medium heat for about 10 minutes, stirring occasionally, until it is slightly thickened and the oil starts to separate from the tomato mixture.

When the eggplant has cooled, peel off the skin. Chop the eggplant crosswise into 2-inch (5-cm) pieces. Add to the tomato mixture and simmer for 10 minutes. Season with salt and pepper. Add the balsamic vinegar, parsley and basil and remove from the heat. Keeps for a week in the refrigerator.

This is a good condiment **to have around for spreading on bread or adding to pastas.**

Cracked and Cooked Olive Salad makes 3¹/₂ cups (840 mL)

1 lb. (454 g) whole, good-quality green olives

¹/₃ cup (80 mL) olive oil

2 Tbsp. (30 mL) minced garlic

2 cups (480 mL) well-drained, canned plum tomatoes, finely chopped

1 Tbsp. (15 mL) tomato paste (see page 84)

¹/₂ cup (120 mL) water

4 thin slices lemon, seeds removed

1 tsp. (5 mL) paprika

¹/₂ tsp. (2.5 mL) cayenne pepper

1 tsp. (5 mL) ground coriander seeds

¹/₂ tsp. (2.5 mL) ground cumin seeds

Using the flat of a large heavy knife, whack each olive to split it in half. Remove the pits and discard. Combine the olives, olive oil, garlic, tomatoes, tomato paste and water in a heavy pot. Bring to a boil, turn down to a simmer and simmer for 5 minutes, stirring frequently. Add the lemon slices, paprika, cayenne, coriander and cumin. Simmer, stirring frequently, until the mixture clings to the olives, about 10 minutes. Cool. Cover and refrigerate until ready to serve.

A great and versatile spread that is good on grilled or toasted bread, drizzled on summer tomatoes or as an embellishment for pasta, prawns, swordfish or tuna. Do not use California black olives — they lack the gusto required for this recipe.

Totally Intense Olive Spread makes 1 1/2 cups (360 mL)

1 cup (240 mL) pitted green olives (see Note)

1 cup (240 mL) pitted black olives,
  such as Kalamata

1/4 cup (60 mL) walnut halves, lightly toasted

1/2 cup (120 mL) olive oil

1 Tbsp. (30 mL) lemon juice

1 Tbsp. (30 mL) balsamic vinegar

16 large leaves fresh basil

1/4 cup (60 mL) coarsely chopped parsley

1/4 cup (60 mL) finely diced red onion

1 Tbsp. (30 mL) minced garlic

1/4 tsp. (1.25 mL) hot red pepper sauce

2 tsp. (10 mL) prepared horseradish

1 Tbsp. (30 mL) Dijon mustard

salt and pepper to taste

Place the green and black olives, walnuts and olive oil in the work bowl of a food processor. Pulse until the olives and walnuts are the size of a popcorn kernel. Add the remaining ingredients and pulse a few times to combine. To make it by hand, chop the olives and walnuts until they are the size of a popcorn kernel. Coarsely chop the basil. Place in a bowl and stir in the remaining ingredients. Refrigerate overnight, covered, to let the flavors develop.

NOTE
To pit olives, place them individually on a cutting board and hit them decisively with the flat of a chef's knife to split them. Open them up and remove the pits.

Why fanatic? I peel the chickpeas. It isn't difficult and you don't need a chickpea peeler. Just pop off the skins between your thumb and first finger. The reward: a hummous that is smooth like silk!

Fanatic's Hummous   serves 8

1 28-oz. (796-mL) can chickpeas, drained and rinsed

1/4 cup (60 mL) water

1/2 cup (120 mL) tahini

1/4 –1/2 cup (60–120 mL) freshly squeezed lemon juice

2 cloves garlic, minced

1/2 tsp. (2.5 mL) sea salt

Peel the chickpeas. Place in a food processor or blender with the water and blend until completely smooth. Add the tahini and the smaller amount of lemon juice, garlic and salt. Blend until well combined. Add more lemon juice and salt to your taste. Refrigerate, covered, until serving time.

I'm picky about tzatziki, that's why this recipe is included. It should be nice and thick and not overwhelmed with cucumber. This is great as an all-purpose sauce to go with barbecued lamb, sausages, pork or chicken.

Tzatziki   makes about 3 cups (720 mL)

4 cups (1 L) plain, full fat yogurt

1/2 English cucumber, seeded

4 large garlic cloves, crushed to a paste

1 tsp. (5 mL) good-quality red or white wine vinegar

sea salt to taste

Line a colander with paper towels and set it over a large bowl. Add the yogurt to the colander and let drain, covered and chilled, for 2 – 4 hours until thick. Transfer the yogurt to a bowl.

Grate the cucumbers and squeeze out the water with your hands. Add to a bowl along with the yogurt, garlic and vinegar. Mix well and season to taste. Refrigerate until serving.

Skordalia is great **as a sauce for cod or lamb as well as being a dip.**

Skordalia makes about 4 cups (1 L)

1 lb. (454 g) russet potatoes

5 cloves garlic

1 tsp. (5 mL) sea salt

2 Tbsp. (30 mL) good-quality red wine vinegar

2 Tbsp. (30 mL) fresh lemon juice

3/4–1 cup (180–240 mL) extra virgin olive oil

sea salt and freshly ground black pepper

In a large saucepan bring salted water to a boil. Add the potatoes and cook 15 minutes, or until tender. Drain and cool until they are easy to handle. Peel the potatoes and push them through a ricer into a bowl.

Pound the garlic with salt in a mortar and pestle or mince with the salt until smooth and add to the potatoes. Gradually add the vinegar, lemon juice and 3/4 cup (180 mL) of the oil, stirring constantly as if you were making mayonnaise. Taste and season with salt and freshly ground pepper to taste and add more oil if desired to make a creamy texture.

Brandade is a traditional Provençal dish of salt cod that is served at the grand Christmas Eve dinner or as an appetizer during other times of the year. Salt cod requires advance planning as it has to be soaked a few days beforehand to soften and de-salt it. While using smoked black cod is not authentic, it certainly is delicious and fast. If you are familiar with the Greek taramasalata, you will immediately take a shine to brandade. Serve a plate of raw vegetables—fennel, cucumber, tomatoes, peppers and endive leaves—for dipping into the brandade along with toasted baguette.

Smoked Black Cod Brandade   serves 6 to 8

1½ lbs. (360 g) russet potatoes (2 medium)

4 cups (1 L) water

1 bay leaf

1 Tbsp. (15 mL) salt

10 black peppercorns

1 whole dried chile

1 lb. (454 g) naturally smoked black cod fillet, cut into 4 pieces

¼ cup (60 mL) fruity extra virgin olive oil, warmed

¼ cup (60 mL) milk, warmed

2 cloves garlic, minced and mashed to a paste with ⅛ tsp. (.5 mL) salt

1 Tbsp. (15 mL) lemon juice

salt and freshly ground black pepper to taste

black olives

Cook the potatoes in their skins in abundant boiling water until tender, 30–40 minutes. Drain and cool until easy to handle, but still warm. Peel the potatoes, cut them into chunks and mash by hand until smooth.

While the potatoes are cooking, combine the water, bay leaf, salt, peppercorns and chile in a medium pot. Bring to a boil and add the cod. Cover and turn the heat down to low. Simmer for 10–12 minutes until just cooked through. Remove to a plate with a slotted spoon. Remove the skin and bones from the cod and flake the fish. Add it to the potatoes. With an electric mixer, beat the cod and the potatoes until they start to "mass" together. Slowly beat in the olive oil, milk, garlic paste and lemon juice. Mix until smooth and creamy. Season with salt and pepper (it should be a bit on the salty side).

Serve the brandade warm or at room temperature; do not refrigerate. Spread it out on a large plate and drizzle with a fruity extra virgin olive oil. Garnish with the olives and serve with toasted baguette and vegetables as above, if you wish.

I love this heady combination of flavors **with the smoothness of the cream. Add some boiled, sliced potatoes to the cooking pot for an exotic chowder.**

Clams with Bacon, Olives and Tomatoes   serves 4

1/2 lb. (227 g) sliced bacon, cut into 1/2-inch (1.2-cm) pieces

4 cloves garlic, minced

1/4 cup (60 mL) shallots, finely chopped

1/2 cup (120 mL) dry white wine

1/2 cup (120 mL) drained, canned plum tomatoes, finely chopped

12 large, good-quality green olives, pitted and chopped

1/2 cup (120 mL) whipping cream or crème fraîche (see page 291)

3 lbs. (1.4 kg) Manila clams, scrubbed

2 Tbsp. (30 mL) fresh parsley, finely chopped

In a large pot, cook the bacon on low heat until crisp. Remove the bacon and discard all the fat except 1 Tbsp. (15 mL). Turn the heat to high and add the garlic and shallots. When they sizzle, add the wine, tomatoes, olives, whipping cream or crème fraîche and clams. Cover tightly and steam until the clams open, shaking the pot occasionally. When the clams have opened, add the bacon and parsley and shake to mix. Serve in heated bowls.

This is also very good with mussels and can be served with steamed rice for a main course. It is quickly assembled and cooked—bonus!

Clams Steamed in Spicy Coconut Lime Broth serves 4

1 14-oz. (398-mL) can unsweetened coconut milk

1/2 cup (120 mL) canned or bottled clam nectar

1 cup (240 mL) canned plum tomatoes, well drained and finely diced

1 Tbsp. (15 mL) fresh cilantro leaves

2 green onions, thinly sliced

1 Tbsp. (15 mL) fresh ginger, grated

1/4 tsp. (1.2 mL) turmeric

1 jalapeño pepper, finely chopped

2 Tbsp. (30 mL) freshly squeezed lime juice

1 lime, thinly sliced

3 lbs. (1.4 kg) fresh Manila clams, scrubbed

In a large pot combine all the ingredients except the clams. Bring to a boil and add the clams. Cover and cook until the clams open, shaking the pot occasionally. Ladle the clams and broth into heated bowls and serve.

This is a little bit different **because mussels are seldom served out of the shell.**

Mussels Saganaki   serves 4

3 lbs. (1.4 kg) mussels, cleaned and debearded

2 Tbsp. (30 mL) extra virgin olive oil

1 cup (240 mL) diced red bell pepper

1 jalapeño pepper, seeded and minced

2 cloves garlic, minced

1½ cups (360 mL) canned Italian plum tomatoes, chopped, with juice

1 tsp. (5 mL) oregano

2 Tbsp. (30 mL) ouzo

½ lb. (227 g) feta, cut into ½-inch (1.2-cm) cubes

extra virgin olive oil

Place mussels and ½ inch (1.2 cm) of water in a large pot. Cover and steam mussels until they open. Cool until the mussels are easy to handle and remove mussels from their shells. Strain and save the liquid.

Heat olive oil over medium heat in a large skillet. Add the peppers and cook until soft. Add the garlic and cook for a minute. Add the tomatoes, oregano and mussel liquid. Lower heat and simmer for 10 minutes until slightly thickened. Add mussels and ouzo, and simmer another three to four minutes. Add the feta and simmer over medium heat until the feta begins to melt. It should not disintegrate completely. Just before removing from heat, drizzle with olive oil, then serve.

What makes this mussel preparation unique is the crumbled tortillas that add texture and flavor to the sauce. Making this dish is actually an excuse for me to eat the sauce all by itself. I like to slurp it back with a spoon and share most of my mussels. Serve with bread, warm tortillas or corn chips. Chipotle chiles en adobo are available in large supermarkets and stores selling Latin American ingredients.

Spicy Steamed Mussels with Tortilla Crumbs   serves 4 to 6

3 lbs. (1.4 kg) fresh mussels

1 Tbsp. (15 mL) olive oil

1/2 tsp. (2.5 mL) whole cumin seeds

6 cloves garlic, minced

1/2 cup (120 mL) finely diced onion

1 28-oz. (796-mL) can plum tomatoes, well drained

1/2 cup (120 mL) dry red wine

2 canned chipotle chiles en adobo, finely chopped

1 large pinch allspice

2 fresh or frozen corn tortillas, crumbled into coarse crumbs

1/4 cup (60 mL) coarsely chopped cilantro

4 thin slices lime

Check over the mussels, removing any bits of beard. Tap any mussels that are open and isolate them from the rest. If they do not close within a few minutes, discard them.

Heat the oil in a large, wide, heavy pot over medium-high heat. Add the cumin seeds. When they darken a shade, stir in the garlic and onion and cook until the onion browns lightly. Add the tomatoes, wine, chiles and allspice. Simmer over low heat for 10 minutes. The sauce may be prepared up to several hours in advance to this point.

Bring the sauce to a full boil and add the tortillas and mussels. Cover with a lid and steam until the mussels open, 5–10 minutes. Add the cilantro and lime and shake the pot to distribute the cilantro. Serve immediately in heated bowls.

This is stunningly good. I got the idea after eating in Japanese restaurants where oysters and sea urchin roe were broiled under a topping of plain mayonnaise.

Baked Oysters with Wasabi Mayonnaise   serves 6 as an appetizer, 3 to 4 as a main course

1 cup (240 mL) mayonnaise (commercially prepared)

1 Tbsp. (15 mL) prepared wasabi paste

24 freshly shucked oysters on the half-shell

1 Tbsp. (15 mL) toasted sesame seeds

2 green onions, finely chopped

Combine the mayonnaise and wasabi paste until well blended.

Choose a large, rimmed pan to cook the oysters on. Crumple a piece of aluminum foil twice as large as the pan you are using to broil the oysters in and then stretch it out to fit the pan. You want the little hills and valleys of the foil to hold the oysters securely, so don't smooth it out. Spread about 1 tsp. (5 mL) of the mayonnaise over each oyster, sprinkle with the sesame seeds and arrange on the pan. The oysters may be prepared up to an hour in advance. Cover and refrigerate.

Preheat the broiler. Broil the oysters until the mayonnaise picks up brown spots, 3–4 minutes. Sprinkle with the green onion and serve on the half-shell.

Irresistible and super spicy! **My favorite way of eating oysters.**

Peppered Oysters with Roasted Corn and Tomato Relish   serves 4 to 6

1 qt. (1 L) medium shucked oysters with their juice

2 bay leaves

2 Tbsp. (30 mL) black peppercorns

8 cloves roasted garlic, mashed to a paste

1/4 tsp. (1.2 mL) ground allspice

1 Tbsp. (15 mL) lemon juice

Roasted Corn and Tomato Relish

1 ear fresh corn

4 ripe plum tomatoes, peeled, seeded and finely chopped

2 thinly sliced green onions

2 Tbsp. (30 mL) coarsely chopped cilantro leaves

salt and pepper

In a large frying pan, bring the oyster juice and bay leaves to a boil. Add the oysters and cook until their edges curl. Drain in a sieve that has been placed over a bowl to catch the juice.

While the oysters are draining, dry-roast the peppercorns over medium heat until they start to smell fragrant. Grind to a powder in a coffee grinder.

Return the oyster juice and bay leaves to the frying pan. Add the pepper, garlic and allspice. Bring to a boil and cook, stirring frequently, until the mixture becomes pasty. Return the oysters to the pan and coat thoroughly with the mixture. Stir in the lemon juice. Serve at room temperature or chilled, with the corn and tomato relish.

Roasted Corn and Tomato Relish

Preheat the oven to 400°F (200°C). Cut the corn kernels from the ear. Spread them out on a baking pan and roast for 10–15 minutes, stirring occasionally, until the corn picks up a few brown spots. Remove from the oven and cool.

Combine the corn with the remaining ingredients and season with salt and pepper. Serve with the oysters.

When my first book, <u>Pacific Passions</u> came out, many people asked, "Are the flaming prawns in it?"
"Next book," I would say. From <u>Screamingly Good Food</u>, these are the flaming prawns, one of the most
popular dishes at the Fish House in Stanley Park.

Flaming Prawns!   serves 4 as an appetizer, 2 as a main course

1 Tbsp. (15 mL) olive oil

1 tsp. (5 mL) garlic, minced

24 large prawns, peeled and deveined

1/2 cup (120 mL) coarsely chopped roasted
  sweet red peppers

1/2 cup (120 mL) coarsely chopped, well-
  drained canned Italian plum tomatoes

1/2 cup (120 mL) crumbled feta cheese

1/4 cup (60 mL) fresh basil leaves

1 oz. (30 mL) ouzo, in a shot glass or
  small glass

1/2 lemon, seeds removed

In a large frying pan, heat the olive oil over high heat. Add the garlic, and when it sizzles, add the prawns and stir-fry until they turn pink. Add the roasted peppers and tomatoes and stir-fry until the prawns are cooked through.

While the prawns are cooking, heat a heavy, preferably cast iron frying pan over high heat. Have a wooden board ready to place the frying pan on and, at the table (or wherever you are going to flame the prawns), have the ouzo and lemon ready.

Add the feta and basil to the prawns and stir to combine. Scoop the mixture to one side of the hot frying pan and place the pan on the board. Carry the board to the table and advise everyone to stay well back. Pour the ouzo into the empty side of the pan and ignite immediately with a long match. Squeeze the lemon over the prawns to douse the flames, then give the prawns a stir. If pyrotechnics are not your style, just add the ouzo to the prawns after they have finished cooking. This, however, lacks drama. Serve with pasta, rice or bread to mop up the juices.

Lapsang Souchong is a delicious, smoked Taiwanese tea. I have loved its flavor since my teens, and became interested again in its potential when I had an especially good one at a Vancouver institution called T that deals exclusively in quality teas. The charming proprietors sent me home with a bag and this is what I came up with. This salmon is sweet, smoky and very delicious.

Salmon Marinated in Lapsang Souchong Tea   serves 6 as an appetizer, 2 as a main course

1 tsp. (5 mL) sea salt

2 tsp. (10 mL) sugar

1 lb. (454 g) boneless, skinless salmon fillet

1/4 cup (60 mL) Lapsang Souchong tea leaves

1 Tbsp. (15 mL) vegetable oil

Wrap the salmon in a double layer of cheesecloth.

Mix the salt and sugar together and sprinkle both sides of the fillet. Sprinkle both sides of the fillet with the tea, pressing it gently onto the fish. Cover and refrigerate overnight.

Scrape the tea from the salmon. In a heavy, nonstick frying pan, heat the vegetable oil over medium-low heat. Place the salmon fillet in the pan and cook until the outside is brown and crispy, about 3 – 4 minutes on each side. Remove from the heat and let sit for a minute before serving.

This tastes and smells just like pastrami, **but with a salmon flavor. Serve it as an appetizer, on top of scrambled eggs or as the obvious — a sandwich on light sour rye bread.**

Salmon Pastrami   makes 1 1/2 lbs. (680 g)

10 medium cloves garlic, peeled and sliced

1 celery stalk, chopped

1/3 cup (80 mL) sea salt

1/4 cup (60 mL) granulated sugar

2 Tbsp. (30 mL) black peppercorns

1 Tbsp. (15 mL) coriander seeds

1 Tbsp. (15 mL) yellow mustard seeds

10 whole cloves

6 bay leaves

1 whole dried chili pepper

1/8 tsp. (.5 mL) cinnamon

2 tsp. (10 mL) paprika

2 Tbsp. (30 mL) Worcestershire sauce

2 tsp. (10 mL) liquid smoke

1 boneless salmon fillet with the skin on, 1 3/4 – 2 lbs. (800 – 900 g)

Combine the garlic, celery stalk, salt and sugar in the work bowl of a food processor. Coarsely grind the peppercorns, coriander seeds, mustard seeds, cloves, bay leaves and chili pepper. Add to the salt mixture with the cinnamon, paprika, Worcestershire sauce and liquid smoke. Process until the garlic is finely chopped and the whole mixture is evenly wet.

Prick the skin side of the salmon filet about 40 times with a pin. Spread a third of the mixture over the skin and the remaining mixture on the top of the filet. Wrap securely with plastic wrap and place on a tray. Cover with another tray and weight down with tinned goods or bottles of water. Refrigerate for 4 days.

Unwrap the salmon and scrape off the marinade. Wash under cold water and pat dry. To serve, slice the salmon extremely thinly on the diagonal, with the grain.

THE COFFEE GRINDER
One of my best kitchen "friends" is a cannister-type coffee grinder. I use it for grinding whole spices, turning lemon grass or sesame seeds into powder and chopping small quantities of nuts.

My friend Vanipha taught me how to make spring rolls and many other Thai and Laotian dishes. Besides running her own restaurant, she also supplied spring rolls to other restaurants and caterers. Some days, she would have orders for 1,000 spring rolls. (They have to be rolled by hand — so let this be an inspiration to you.) Spring rolls are a labor of love, but just think of how impressed everyone will be. If you prefer, you can make them without the prawns.

Prawn Spring Rolls   makes 32 spring rolls

4 cloud ear mushrooms, soaked in hot water until soft (optional)

3/4 cup (180 mL) coarsely chopped bamboo shoots

1/2 cup (120 mL) coarsely chopped water chestnuts

2 Tbsp. (30 mL) vegetable oil

3 medium cloves garlic, minced

3 cups (720 mL) green cabbage, thinly sliced and chopped into fine pieces

1 cup (240 mL) grated carrot

4 thinly sliced green onions

3 Tbsp. (45 mL) oyster sauce

1/2 tsp. (2.5 mL) freshly ground black pepper

3 2-oz. (50-g) packages cellophane noodles, soaked in hot water until softened, then drained

36 8 by 8-inch (20-cm) frozen spring roll wrappers

4 Tbsp. (60 mL) all-purpose flour

2 Tbsp. (30 mL) water

Remove and discard the woody stems from the cloud ear mushrooms and coarsely chop the mushrooms. In the work bowl of a food processor pulse the mushrooms, bamboo shoots and water chestnuts until everything is finely chopped. (Or finely chop by hand.) Squeeze the mixture with your hands to remove as much water as possible.

In a wok or large frying pan, heat the vegetable oil over high heat. Add the garlic and stir-fry until it turns golden. Add the cabbage and carrot. Stir-fry until the cabbage is tender-crisp. Add the green onions, oyster sauce and black pepper and stir-fry for another minute. Remove from the heat and spread out on a pan to cool.

Chop the cellophane noodles into 1-inch (2.5-cm) pieces and add to the cooled vegetable mixture. Refrigerate until cold.

Gently peel the spring roll wrappers apart and cover with a damp cloth. Stir the flour and water together to form a smooth paste. You are now ready to roll the spring rolls.

16 large prawns or shrimp, peeled and cut in
half lengthwise

vegetable oil for frying the spring rolls

1 recipe Sweet and Sour Dipping Sauce
(see page 167)

PREPARING SPRING ROLLS

Although the instructions for rolling may seem
complicated at first, you will understand them
completely after rolling the first spring roll. It
is important that the spring rolls be tightly but
gently rolled. If not, oil will seep in during the
frying and make them greasy.

The filling must be moist but not wet. If there
is water collecting around the filling, place it
in a sieve and gently squeeze out the water.
Leave the filling in the sieve while you are
rolling the spring rolls. This is important
because if the wrappers get wet, the spring
rolls will burst during frying. Fry the spring
rolls within half an hour after making them.

Place a wrapper on a flat surface with one of the points
facing towards you. Place about 2 Tbsp. (30 mL) of the
filling slightly above the middle of the wrapper. Make
a neat cylinder about 4 inches (10 cm) long out of the
filling. Fold the point closest to you over the filling to
slightly below the point that is farthest away from you.
Fold both right and left points firmly over the filling and
roll once away from you. Tuck a prawn half into the right-
hand side of the fold (if you are right-handed). Dab some
of the flour and water paste on the top point and continue
rolling up, gently but firmly, until you reach the top.
Continue rolling spring rolls with the remaining filling.

In a large heavy skillet, heat 3 inches (7.5 cm) of vegetable oil to 325°F (165°C). Fry the spring rolls without
overcrowding the pan until golden brown on all sides.
Remove from the oil and drain on absorbent paper.
Keep warm in a low oven while frying the remaining
spring rolls.

This is an excellent party dish. You can lay out all of the ingredients and instruct your guests how to roll their own! It takes a bit of practice to roll these. What you are aiming for is an even, tight roll. Make sure that all the ingredients are well tucked into the lettuce and somen noodles or errant pieces of cucumber will poke through the rice papers.

Shrimp Salad Rolls   makes 24 rolls

24 8-inch (20-cm) rice papers

12 large leaves of leaf lettuce, cut in half lengthwise

1/4 lb. (113 g) somen noodles, cooked and cooled

3 cups (720 mL) baby shrimp, thawed and well drained

1 cup (240 mL) mint leaves, packed

1 small bunch cilantro, coarse stems removed

1/2 English cucumber, seeded and coarsely julienned

12 green onions, split in half lengthwise and cut into 1-inch (2.5-cm) pieces

1 recipe Sweet and Sour dipping sauce (see page 167)

1/4 cup (60 mL) finely chopped roasted peanuts

Have a large bowl of hot water handy to dip the rice papers into. Take a sheet of rice paper and quickly dip it into the hot water and place it on a flat surface. Dip as many papers as you have room for.

When the papers have become pliable, place the filling ingredients close to the bottom of the papers in this order: lettuce, then a small pile of somen noodles, shrimp, a few mint leaves and a few sprigs of cilantro, the cucumber and some green onion.

Smear a bit of rice noodles at the top of the paper. This will help the roll stick together. Pick up the bottom edge and fold it over the filling. Fold the sides over the filling. Roll from the bottom, gently but firmly. Continue with the remaining rice papers and filling. Place the dipping sauce in bowls and sprinkle with the peanuts. Serve immediately with the dipping sauce.

This is a variation on a traditional Thai salad **known as <u>lap</u>.** The toasted rice powder binds the dressing to the ingredients. Serve with leaf lettuce and thinly sliced cucumber to wrap around the salad and convey it to waiting mouths.

Lamb Salad with Crushed Peanuts and Lime Dressing   serves 4

2 Tbsp. (30 mL) fresh lime juice

1/4 tsp. (1.2 mL) sugar

1/4 tsp. (1.2 mL) salt

1 tsp. (5 mL) fish sauce

2–4 fresh Thai chiles, thinly sliced

1/4 cup (60 mL) roasted, unsalted peanuts

2 4-oz. (113-g) lamb loins

1 tsp. (5 mL) vegetable oil

salt to taste

2 green onions, sliced into thin rounds

1/2 cup (120 mL) coarsely chopped cilantro

1/2 cup (120 mL) coarsely chopped mint

1 Tbsp. (15 mL) toasted rice powder (see Note)

Combine the lime juice, sugar, salt, fish sauce and chiles in a small bowl. Place the peanuts in a heavy plastic bag and crush with a rolling pin into pieces. You want to obtain different textures in the crushed peanuts, from pasty to crunchy. Set aside.

Cut the lamb loins in half lengthwise. Toss with the oil and salt. Heat a heavy, preferably cast iron, pan over high heat. Place the lamb loins in the pan and sear on all sides until rare. You may do this on a barbecue if you wish. Remove from the heat and cool slightly. Place the green onions, cilantro and mint in a bowl. Thinly slice the lamb loins and add to the bowl. Add the dressing, peanuts and toasted rice powder. Toss well and serve immediately.

NOTE
To make toasted rice powder, dry-roast a cup (240 mL) of long grain glutinous rice (or plain long grain rice) in a frying pan, stirring occasionally until dark brown. Pour into a bowl to cool. Grind to a coarse powder in a coffee grinder and store in a covered jar.

Lamb is not usually a traditional meat for satay, **but I like to mix things up a bit!**

Lemon Grass Lamb Satay   makes 20 skewers

2 Tbsp. (30 mL) finely chopped lemon grass

1 Tbsp. (15 mL) minced shallots

2 tsp. (10 mL) minced garlic

1 Tbsp. (15 mL) ground coriander seeds

1½ tsp. (7.5 mL) curry powder

1 Tbsp. (15 mL) sugar

¼ tsp. (1.25 mL) sea salt

½ cup (120 mL) coconut milk

1 lb. (454 g) lamb loin, trimmed and thinly sliced with the grain into 20 strips

20 bamboo skewers, soaked in water

Peanut Sauce
makes approximately 3 cups (720 mL)

1 Tbsp. (15 mL) finely chopped garlic

2 Tbsp. (30 mL) vegetable oil

2 Tbsp. (30 mL) red curry paste

4 cups (1 L) coconut milk

2 stalks lemon grass, trimmed and cut into 2-inch (5-cm) pieces

1 cup (240 mL) roasted unsalted peanuts, ground almost to a paste

4 Tbsp. (60 mL) lime juice

1 Tbsp. (15 mL) sugar

2 Tbsp. (30 mL) fish sauce

In a blender or food processor, grind the lemon grass, shallots, garlic, coriander, curry, sugar and salt. Add the coconut milk and pulse to combine. Mix well with the lamb and marinate for 1 hour.

Thread the meat strips on skewers and grill or broil until cooked through. Serve with Peanut Sauce.

Peanut Sauce
In a pot over medium heat, sauté the garlic in the oil to pale gold. Add the curry paste and cook over low heat until it starts to look dry. Add the coconut milk and lemon grass. Bring to a boil and whisk in the peanuts. Turn down to a simmer and cook, stirring frequently until the oil rises to the top of the sauce. Remove from the heat and cool. Stir in the lime juice, sugar and fish sauce.

These are impressive and very easy to make. You need the porcelain spoons that are half the size of the ones used for soup. They're generally easy to find in Chinese grocery stores. If you don't have or want to get the spoons, you can simply roll dumplings into balls.

Pork and Shiitake Mushroom Spoon Dumplings   makes about 36

10 medium dried shiitake mushrooms

2 lbs. (900 g) ground pork

2 Tbsp. (30 mL) soy sauce

1 tsp. (5 mL) sea salt

1 tsp. (5 mL) sugar

1 Tbsp. (15 mL) cornstarch

4 Tbsp. (60 mL) finely chopped green onion

2 Tbsp. (30 mL) finely chopped cilantro

1/2 cup (120 mL) panko

1 tsp. (5 mL) roasted sesame oil

2 eggs

finely chopped green onion

soy sauce

Place the shiitake mushrooms in a bowl and cover them with boiling water. Let the mushrooms stand until they are completely soft, about 1/2 hour. Squeeze the water out of the mushrooms with your hands, remove the tough stems and discard. Finely mince the caps.

Combine the mushrooms with the remaining ingredients (except green onion and soy sauce) and mix until everything is well combined. Pile onto small porcelain soup spoons, rounding the tops. Place in a steamer and steam for 10 minutes until cooked through. Sprinkle with the green onion and drizzle with soy sauce.

This pâté has an intriguing, earthy flavor that comes from the fermented black beans. Serve it thinly sliced with good bread or melba toast, hot Chinese mustard, pickled ginger and hoisin sauce.

Chinatown Pâté with Fermented Black Beans   makes 1 loaf, about 2 lbs. (900 g)

2 Tbsp. (30 mL) vegetable oil

2 Tbsp. (30 mL) finely chopped garlic

1/2 cup (120 mL) fermented black beans, rinsed and drained

1 1/2 lbs. (680 g) pork shoulder, finely ground

1 lb. (454 g) salt pork, finely ground

1/2 cup (120 mL) white wine

3 large eggs

1 Tbsp. (15 mL) Szechuan peppercorns, coarsely ground

1 tsp. (5 mL) black pepper

Heat the oil in a small frying pan over high heat and fry the garlic until it sizzles. Add the black beans and when they sizzle, remove from the heat.

Combine all the ingredients, including the garlic and black beans, in a large bowl. Beat well until everything is thoroughly mixed. Cover and refrigerate overnight.

Preheat the oven to 350°F (175°C). Pack the pâté mixture into an 8- by 5-inch (20- by 12.5-cm) loaf pan. Cover securely with tin foil and place in a larger, deeper pan. Pour hot water into the larger pan so that it comes 2 inches (5 cm) up the sides of the loaf pan. Place in the oven and bake for 1 hour and 40 minutes, or until a thermometer inserted in the middle of the loaf reads 165°F (75°C).

Remove from the oven and let the pâté cool completely in the water bath. Place a loaf pan of the same size on top of the pâté and place some heavy cans inside the pan. Refrigerate for at least 2 days before serving.

Nice to serve as a nibble **before a Chinese-style meal.**

Five Spice Sesame Walnuts   makes 3½ cups (840 mL)

3 Tbsp. (45 mL) sugar

½ tsp. (2.5 mL) cayenne

½ tsp. (2.5 mL) salt

1½ tsp. (7.5 mL) five spice powder

1 egg white

3 cups (720 mL) raw walnut halves

½ cup (120 mL) sesame seeds

Preheat the oven to 350°F (175°C). Combine the sugar, cayenne, salt and five spice powder. Beat the egg white with a whisk until foamy but not stiff. Add the walnuts and sesame seeds to the egg white, stirring to coat. Add the spice mixture and stir until evenly blended. Spread out in a single layer on a parchment-lined baking sheet and bake for 10 minutes. Stir the nuts with a spoon and bake for 5–10 minutes longer, until lightly browned. Cool completely. Keeps for 2 weeks at room temperature, tightly covered.

This is something I came up with one Christmas. The coconut adds a Far Eastern flair. It is an easy and much-appreciated gift. I use T Tearoom's Herbal Spice Chai, but you can use any chai without tea leaves, or chai masala purchased in East Indian grocery stores.

Chai Spiced Nuts   makes 3 1/2 cups (840 mL)

3 Tbsp. (45 mL) sugar

1/2 tsp. (2.5 mL) cayenne

1/2 tsp. (2.5 mL) sea salt

1 1/2 tsp. (7.5 mL) Herbal Spice Chai, ground

1 egg white

1 cup (240 mL) whole raw almonds

1 cup (240 mL) whole raw cashews

1 cup (240 mL) whole raw pecan halves

1/2 cup (120 mL) unsweetened, shredded coconut

Preheat the oven to 350°F (175°C).

Combine the sugar, cayenne, salt and chai. In a separate bowl, beat the egg white with a whisk until foamy but not stiff. Add the nuts and coconut. Stir to coat with the egg white. Add the chai mixture and stir until evenly blended. Spread out in a single layer on a parchment-lined baking sheet and bake for 10 minutes. Stir the nuts with a spoon and bake for 10 minutes longer. Cool completely in the pan. Keeps for 2 weeks at room temperature, tightly covered.

soup

Visions of a Rich Brown Soup Danced in My Head

When I was around nine, my mother taught me how to make omelettes and bake bread. The "Galloping Gourmet" taught me how to chop when I was ten, via TV. I read my mother's cookbooks avidly and tried different things — I fondly remember a meatloaf roulade with a Cheddar cheese filling. My sister Jennifer had brought a friend home for dinner who was totally intimidated by this meatloaf creation. She looked miserable when confronted with it on her plate, and I could tell that she thought we were pretty weird because of the strange food we were eating. I thought it was a triumph of high cuisine.

The first foray out of recipe land was a disaster. I somehow got it into my head that I wanted to make an oxtail soup. I imagined at as being rich, decadent and sumptuous. I actually bought the oxtails with my allowance and came home full of excitement and hope. Visions of a rich brown soup danced in my head. I brewed up the oxtails, added barley and vegetables and, for some reason that is lost to me now, a handful of pickling spices. Of course, I didn't realize that the oxtails would take hours to cook, barley would expand about three times and that pickling spices were not a common soup seasoning. I ended up with a pale barley sludge with tough bits of meat and the overpowering flavor and crunch of pickling spice. Everybody had a small, small bowl, saying it was not that bad, but I knew it was real bad. I persevered and continued to follow recipes to which I made slight changes until I felt comfortable enough to go solo.

In Italian, this is known as Pasta e Fusioli. Parmesan rinds are what is left when you can grate no more cheese from a piece of Parmesan. They are a great addition to almost any soup. Save the rinds in the freezer.

Romano Bean Soup with Pasta serves 6 to 8

3/4 cup (180 mL) dried Romano beans or
  1 28-oz (796-mL) can Romano beans

1/2 cup (120 mL) carrots, finely chopped

1/2 cup (120 mL) onion, finely chopped

1/2 cup (120 mL) celery, finely chopped

2 medium cloves garlic, minced

2 Tbsp. (30 mL) olive oil

10 cups (2.5 L) beef or chicken stock
  (see page 46)

1 28-oz (796-mL) can tomatoes, drained
  and sieved

1 slice prosciutto, 1/4-inch (.6-cm) thick

1 Parmesan rind

sea salt and freshly ground black pepper

1/2 lb. (227 g) short, tubular, dried pasta

If you are using dried beans, place them in a large pot and cover with water. Bring to a boil and skim off any foam that rises to the top. Turn down to a simmer and cook until tender, about 2 hours. Drain. If you are using canned beans, drain well and rinse under cold water.

In a large heavy pot over medium heat, sauté the chopped carrots, onion, celery and garlic in the olive oil until lightly browned. Add the stock, tomatoes, prosciutto and Parmesan rind. Simmer for 1 hour. Season lightly with salt. Add the beans and cook for 1 hour longer. The soup should be thick. Season with salt and pepper.

Bring a large pot of water to a boil. Add the pasta and salt liberally. It should taste like seawater. Cook, stirring occasionally, until the pasta is tender but still firm to the bite, 8–10 minutes. Drain and stir into the soup. Serve immediately in heated bowls.

Most cities, large and small, now have bakeries which make traditional Italian breads. It is well worth seeking out their soulful breads. This feeds a crowd and is better the day after it is made.

Winter Bread Soup   makes 24 cups (6 L)

1 cup (240 mL) dried navy beans

3 Tbsp. (45 mL) olive oil

1 cup (240 mL) peeled and diced carrots

1 cup (240 mL) diced onions

1 cup (240 mL) diced celery

1 Tbsp. (15 mL) finely chopped parsley

4 cloves garlic, finely minced

16 cups (4 L) chicken stock (see page 46) or water

1 28-oz. (796-mL) can plum tomatoes with juice, finely chopped

1 cup (240 mL) each peeled and diced parsnips and turnips

2 cups (480 mL) peeled and diced sweet potatoes

2 cups (480 mL) finely chopped green or savoy cabbage

1 bunch green kale, stem and central rib removed, finely chopped

2 large Parmesan or grana padano rinds (optional)

1 bay leaf

6 cups (1.5 L) stale, good-quality bread, crusts removed and diced

sea salt and freshly ground black pepper

Place the navy beans in a large pot, cover with cold water and bring to a boil. Cook for 1–2 hours, replenishing the water as necessary until the beans are tender. Drain and set aside.

In a very large pot, heat the olive oil over medium heat. Sauté the carrots, onions, celery, parsley and garlic until lightly browned. Add the chicken stock or water and the tomatoes. Bring to a boil and add the remaining vegetables, cheese rinds, bay leaf and the cooked navy beans. Season lightly with salt and simmer for 1/2 hour.

Add the bread and cook for 1 hour longer, or until the bread has dissolved. Season with the salt and pepper. This is a rather thick soup. Add more stock or water if you like it a bit thinner.

This easy and delicious soup **may be garnished with yogurt if you like.**

Chickpea, Rice and Spinach Soup with Lemon and Mint   serves 4

6 cups (1.5 L) chicken stock (see page 46)

1 15-oz. (420-mL) can chickpeas, drained and rinsed

1 cup (240 mL) cooked rice

4 cloves garlic, minced

1/2 tsp. (2.5 mL) turmeric

1/2 tsp. (2.5 mL) whole cumin seeds

1/2 lb. (227 g) fresh spinach, stems removed and washed

2 large eggs

1/2 cup (120 mL) freshly squeezed lemon juice

sea salt and freshly ground black pepper

2 Tbsp. (30 mL) fresh mint, finely chopped

Combine the chicken stock, chickpeas, rice, garlic, turmeric and cumin in a large pot. Bring to a boil and simmer for 15–20 minutes. Finely chop the spinach and add it to the soup. Beat the eggs and lemon juice together. Whisk 1 cup (240 mL) of the hot soup into the egg mixture. Over low heat, slowly whisk the egg mixture into the soup. Do not let it boil. Stir until the soup is piping hot. Season with salt and pepper. Ladle into warm bowls and garnish with mint.

If you like punchy flavors, **serve this soup with a salad tossed with crumbled blue cheese.**

Potato Soup with Horseradish and Caraway   serves 4 to 6

4 Tbsp. (60 mL) unsalted butter

3 medium onions, thinly sliced

2 lbs. (900 g) Yukon Gold or russet potatoes,
  peeled and thinly sliced

10 cups (2.5 L) water or chicken stock
  (see page 46)

pinch sea salt

2 Tbsp. (30 mL) prepared horseradish

2 tsp. (10 mL) caraway seeds

sea salt and freshly ground black pepper

1/2 cup (120 mL) 18% or light cream (optional)

Heat the butter in a large pot and sauté the onions over medium-low heat until very soft but not browned. Add the potatoes, water or stock and a bit of salt. Bring to a boil, then turn the heat to low and simmer until the potatoes are very soft, 30–40 minutes.

Remove the soup from the heat and purée in a food processor, blender or food mill until smooth. Add the horseradish, caraway seeds and salt and pepper. (The soup can be made up to 2 days in advance. Cool, cover and refrigerate until ready to use.)

When ready to serve, reheat gently to the boiling point. If desired, stir in the cream before serving.

THE EASY WAY TO PURÉE
This is the easy way to purée. Strain the solids from the soup and return the liquid to the cooking pot. Purée the solids with a food mill, blender or food processor, using a bit of the liquid to keep the mixture blending smoothly. Return the purée to the liquid and stir well. This is especially fast and easy when working with large batches.

A lovely salmon-pink color, **this can be served hot or cold.**

Sweet Red Pepper "Vichyssoise"   *serves 6*

1 Tbsp. (15 mL) unsalted butter

4 large leeks, white part only, cleaned and thinly sliced (see page 162)

1 medium onion, thinly sliced

1 lb. (454 g) russet potatoes, peeled and thickly sliced

5 cups (1.2 L) chicken stock (see page 46)

sea salt to taste

1 lb. (454 g) sweet red peppers, roasted, seeded and peeled

2 cups (480 mL) milk

2 cups (480 mL) half-and-half cream

1 cup (240 mL) sour cream

2 Tbsp. (30 mL) freshly squeezed lemon juice

Melt the butter over medium heat in a large pot. Add the leeks and onion and sauté until soft but not brown. Add the potatoes, chicken stock and salt. Turn down to a simmer and cook, partially covered, until the potatoes are very tender, 20 – 30 minutes. Add all the roasted sweet red peppers except one.

In batches, purée the soup in a blender or food processor, then strain through a sieve to make it perfectly smooth. Return it to the pot, add the milk and cream and bring to a boil. Finely chop the reserved sweet red pepper and add it to the soup. Remove from the heat and stir in the sour cream and lemon juice. If you want to serve it cold, add the sour cream and lemon juice after the soup has chilled for 2 – 24 hours. Adjust the seasoning and serve.

I like to make a plain chicken stock with very little seasoning in it, so it can be used in many different dishes. It is worth your while to make a lot and freeze it in convenient portions in zip-lock bags.

Chicken Stock   makes 8 to 10 cups (2 to 2.5 L)

5 lbs. (2.25 kg) chicken bones

2 small onions, peeled and cut in half

2 small carrots, peeled and cut in half

2 celery stalks, cut in half

1 head garlic, cut in half crosswise

water

Put the chicken bones in a large stock pot. Cover with water and bring to a boil. Drain the bones in a colander and rinse with cold water. Return to the pot and add the remaining ingredients. Add water to cover by 4 inches (10 cm). Bring to a boil, turn down to a simmer and cook for 6 hours, skimming the top of fat. Add water periodically to return it to its original level. Strain through a cheesecloth-lined colander and cool. It will keep for 2–3 days refrigerated. Freeze for longer storage.

STOCK OR BROTH?

My friend Steven was in our local supermarket seeking frozen chicken stock. He asked one of the clerks if such a thing was to be had and she replied, deadly serious, "What part of the chicken is that from?" He came home with canned low-sodium chicken broth. Canned chicken broth is fine to use in place of chicken stock in stir-fries, sautés, soups and pasta sauces. If a dish has no other thickening agent, such as flour, cornstarch or potatoes, and requires reducing the liquids to thicken it, use homemade or a reliable frozen chicken stock. Canned broth will not thicken as it reduces, though its flavor will become concentrated. That is why low-sodium chicken broth is advised.

This is a soup that everyone loves. It's fast to make once the ingredients are assembled. I keep galangal and kaffir lime leaves in my freezer so they'll always be on hand. You can freeze lemon grass too!

Thai Coconut Chicken Soup (Tom Ka Gai)   serves 4

1/2 lb. (227 g) boneless chicken breast meat

5 thin slices galangal

6 kaffir lime leaves

3 cups (720 mL) coconut milk

1 stalk of lemon grass, trimmed and outer leaves removed, chopped into 1-inch (2.5-cm) pieces

2 Thai chillies, seeded, stemmed and finely sliced, or to taste

2 Tbsp. (30 mL) fish sauce

2 limes

sugar and sea salt

1/4 cup (60 mL) chopped fresh cilantro

Cut the chicken into bite-sized pieces. Put the chicken, galangal, lime leaves and coconut milk in a pan and bring to a boil, stirring occasionally so the chicken doesn't clump together. Simmer for 15 minutes or until chicken is done.

Add the chilies, fish sauce, juice from one of the limes and sugar and salt to taste. Turn the heat to low. Stir well, and then taste. It will probably taste milky. If so, adjust with lime juice, salt and sugar. Continue until it doesn't taste milky any more, but not so much that it tastes like lime. It should be a balance of tart, sweet and salty. Ladle into bowls and garnish with the cilantro.

A lovely, hot-weather main course, served with corn chips. For a very smooth-textured soup, you can strain the purée through a sieve. Press on the solids to extract all the liquid, then discard the solids.

Chilled Corn and Chicken Soup with Tomato and Cilantro   serves 4

1 lb. (454 g) boneless, skinless chicken breasts

7 cups (1.7 L) chicken stock (see page 46)

4 leeks, white part only, cleaned and finely sliced (see page 162)

1/2 lb. (227 g) large, new red potatoes, peeled and diced

4 cups (1 L) fresh or frozen corn kernels

1 tsp. (5 mL) whole cumin seeds

1/4 tsp. (1.25 mL) cayenne pepper

sea salt and freshly ground black pepper

1 medium ripe tomato, finely diced

1 avocado, peeled, pitted and finely diced

1 Tbsp. (15 mL) fresh cilantro, coarsely chopped

2 tsp. (10 mL) lime juice

sea salt and freshly ground black pepper

1/2 cup (120 mL) yogurt

Place the chicken in a single layer in a pot or frying pan. Cover with chicken stock by 1 inch (2.5 cm). Bring to a simmer and cook 10 minutes. Remove from the heat and let stand, covered, until cool. Drain, cover and refrigerate the chicken, reserving the stock.

In a large pot, combine the remaining chicken stock, reserved stock, leeks, potatoes, corn, cumin, cayenne, salt and pepper. Bring to a boil and simmer for 15–20 minutes, until the potatoes are very tender. In a blender or food processor, purée 2/3 of the soup in batches until smooth. Place the purée in a large bowl and add the remaining soup. Taste and correct the seasoning. Refrigerate the soup until cold or for up to 1 day.

Shred the cooked chicken. Combine the tomato, avocado, cilantro and lime juice. Season with salt and pepper.

Whisk the yogurt into the chilled soup. If the soup seems too thick, thin it with cold water. Taste and adjust the seasoning. Ladle the soup into bowls and top with the tomato mixture and the chicken.

What makes this chowder really good is the sweet and tender Manila clams that grow so plentifully in this area. I prefer not to put bacon in chowder. Instead, I like to use a local delicacy called Indian Candy. Indian Candy is made from sugar-cured salmon bellies that are cut into strips and smoked until they are almost dry. If it is available in your area, add a small handful, finely chopped, when you are sautéeing the onions and celery.

Clam Chowder   serves 6

4 lbs. (1.8 kg) fresh clams, in their shells

4 Tbsp. (60 mL) unsalted butter

1/2 cup (120 mL) diced onion

1/2 cup (120 mL) diced celery

4 Tbsp. (60 mL) all-purpose flour

2 cups (480 mL) clam nectar, heated

sea salt and freshly ground black pepper to taste

2 cups (480 mL) peeled diced potatoes, cooked until tender and drained

1 cup (240 mL) whipping cream

Scrub the clams and place in a large pot. Steam over high heat, shaking the pot occasionally, until the clams open. Drain the clams, reserving the juice. Strain the juice. Remove the clams from the shells and chop coarsely.

Melt the butter over low heat in a large heavy pot. Sauté the onion and celery until they are translucent. Add the flour and stir for a few minutes. Slowly whisk in the heated clam nectar and the reserved liquid from the drained clams, ensuring that there are no lumps. Bring to a boil then reduce to a simmer. Cook for 20 minutes. Season with salt and pepper.

When ready to serve, add the potatoes and heat through. Add the cream and the reserved chopped clams. Bring to a simmer and serve.

This is quite fine without the cheese, **but the cheese does make it excessively special! The smoked paprika gives the chowder a nice, smoky flavor, but if you can't find it, a mild, good quality Hungarian paprika will do.**

Halibut, Corn and Cheddar Chowder   serves 6 to 8

6 Tbsp. (90 mL) unsalted butter

1 cup (240 mL) finely chopped onion

1 cup (240 mL) finely chopped celery

3 Tbsp. (45 mL) flour

2 tsp. (10 mL) smoked or mild paprika

3 cups (720 mL) clam nectar or fish stock

1/2 cup (120 mL) finely chopped red bell
   pepper

2 cups (480 mL) homogenized milk

sea salt and freshly ground black pepper
   to taste

2 lbs. (900 g) boneless, skinless halibut, cut
   into bite-sized pieces

1 cup (240 mL) corn kernels

1 cup (240 mL) shredded sharp Cheddar
   cheese

1 Tbsp. (15 mL) minced parsley

1 Tbsp. (15 mL) minced chives

In a large pot over medium heat melt the butter. Add the onion and celery and cook until softened. Add the flour and paprika, stirring for 1 minute. Slowly whisk in the clam nectar or fish stock until smooth. Bring to a boil then turn down to a simmer. Add the red pepper. Cook, stirring frequently for 10 minutes.

Add the milk and bring to a simmer. Season to taste and add the halibut and corn. Simmer for 5 minutes or until the halibut is cooked through. Stir in the cheese, parsley and chives. Serve immediately.

Eat this on a cold rainy day **with a still-warm loaf of soda bread and you will feel contentment right down to your toes.**

Purist's Oyster Stew   serves 4

1 pint (475 mL) shucked oysters with their juice

2 cups (480 mL) homogenized milk

1½ cups (360 mL) half-and-half cream

a few drops Tabasco sauce

a few drops Worcestershire sauce

sea salt and freshly ground black pepper

unsalted butter

If the oysters are large, cut them into quarters.

Heat the milk and cream in a saucepan until just steaming. In another pan, heat the oysters with their juice just until their edges curl up. Pour the steaming milk and cream over the oysters and heat until very hot but not boiling.

Season to taste with Tabasco and Worcestershire sauce, salt and pepper. Serve in large heated bowls, with a piece of butter floating on top.

The inspiration for this soup came from the Portuguese soup called <u>Caldo Verde</u>, which uses smoked Portuguese chourico sausage instead of the oysters. I think this version is almost as good as the original.

Potato, Kale and Oyster Soup   serves 6 to 8

4 Tbsp. (60 mL) vegetable oil

3 medium onions, thinly sliced

2 lbs. (900 g) potatoes, peeled and thinly sliced (russets or Yukon Golds are a good choice)

10 cups (2.5 L) chicken stock (see page 46) or water

1 tsp. (5 mL) sea salt

1 lb. (454 g) kale, washed (stems removed)

1 qt. (1 L) oysters, cut into bite-sized pieces if large

freshly ground black pepper

Heat the oil in a large pot, and sauté the onions until soft but not browned. Add the potatoes, chicken stock or water and salt. Bring to a boil. Turn the heat down to a simmer and cook until the potatoes are very tender, about 1 hour.

Purée the soup in a food processor, blender or food mill and return to the pot. Bring to a simmer. Thinly shred the kale — the thinner, the better. Add to the soup and simmer for 20 minutes.

Just before serving, add the oysters and their juice to the simmering soup and stir for a few minutes. Season with the black pepper (I like to use a lot!). Serve immediately.

salads

If arugula is unavailable, you can substitute watercress or escarole in this recipe.

Arugula Salad with Warm Bacon and Apple Vinaigrette   serves 4

2 large bunches arugula, trimmed, washed and dried

2 Tbsp. (30 mL) apple cider vinegar

1/4 tsp. (1.25 mL) sea salt

1/4 tsp. (1.25 mL) freshly ground black pepper

3 Tbsp. (60 mL) vegetable oil

8 slices bacon

1 small apple, peeled, cored and thinly sliced

Place the arugula in a large bowl. Add the apple cider vinegar, salt and pepper and toss well. Set aside.

Heat the vegetable oil in a frying pan on medium heat. Add the bacon and cook until just crisp. Add the apple slices and heat through.

Pour immediately over the arugula and toss well. Divide among 4 heated plates and serve immediately.

If you have access to a farmers' or specialty market you may find that they carry many different varieties of beets. Yellow, white, Chioggia and Easter egg beets are more commonly available now and make a nice change from the purple variety.

Beet Salad with Mint and Feta Cheese   serves 6

1 lb. (454 g) small beets

6 Tbsp. (90 mL) blackberry or apple cider vinegar

2 Tbsp. (30 mL) honey

1/2 tsp. (2.5 mL) sea salt

1 small onion, thinly sliced

3 Tbsp. (45 mL) coarsely chopped mint

1/4 lb. (113 g) feta cheese, crumbled

Place the beets in a pot and cover with water. Bring to a boil, then turn down to a simmer. Cook the beets until they can be pierced easily with the tip of a sharp knife, about 30–40 minutes. Drain.

Combine the vinegar, honey, salt and onion in a wide, shallow bowl. When the beets are cool enough to handle, slip off the skins and cut into 3/8-inch (1-cm) slices. Add to the vinegar mixture and stir well. (The beets may be covered and refrigerated overnight at this point.) Marinate until just before serving. Drain half the dressing from the beets and onions and place them on a plate. Sprinkle with half the mint. Scatter the feta over the beets and sprinkle with the remaining mint.

This salad is good **with any simply prepared meat, fish or fowl. Try it with Graham's Grilled Flank Steak with Cumin Aioli, page 145.**

Chopped Summer Salad with Mint and Parmesan Dressing   serves 4 to 6

1 clove garlic, minced

1/2 tsp. (2.5 mL) salt

2 tsp. (10 mL) Dijon mustard

1 Tbsp. (15 mL) white wine vinegar

5 Tbsp. (75 mL) vegetable oil

3 Tbsp. (45 mL) olive oil

1 1/2 cups (360 mL) peeled, seeded cucumber, diced into 1/2-inch (1.2-cm) cubes

1 head of romaine lettuce, washed, dried and cut into 1/2-inch (1.2-cm) squares

1 cup (240 mL) radishes, diced into 1/2-inch (1.2-cm) cubes

2 cups (480 mL) tomatoes, diced into 1/2-inch (1.2-cm) cubes

1 cup (240 mL) yellow pepper, cut into 1/2-inch (1.2-cm) squares

1/4 cup (60 mL) finely diced red onion

1/2 cup (120 mL) freshly grated Parmesan cheese

1/2 cup (120 mL) fresh mint, coarsely chopped

In a small bowl, whisk the garlic, salt, Dijon mustard and vinegar together. Slowly whisk in the vegetable and olive oils. Mix all the vegetables together in a large bowl. Pour the dressing over the vegetables and toss well. Add the Parmesan cheese and mint and toss again.

I was smitten by this salad **and contemplated putting it on the menu. After much deliberation, I realized that I could never get away with it—it was too old and too new at the same time. But in my mind, it will always be high fashion.**

Iceberg Wedges with Blue Cheese Dressing   serves 8

4 oz. (113 g) blue cheese, crumbled

1 cup (240 mL) sour cream

1/4 cup (60 mL) mayonnaise

2 tsp. (10 mL) minced garlic

1 Tbsp. (15 mL) red wine vinegar

sea salt and freshly ground black pepper

1 head iceberg lettuce, cut into 8 wedges

Mix all the ingredients except the lettuce in a bowl. Cover and refrigerate overnight or for up to one week. Taste and adjust the seasoning. Place the iceberg wedges on chilled individual plates. Spoon the dressing over the lettuce before serving, or pass the dressing separately.

This salad is a great combination of colors and tastes. It is especially good with pork and chicken.

Red Lettuce with Roasted Peppers, Feta and Marjoram Vinaigrette   serves 6

1 head red leaf lettuce

1 small head radicchio

2 Tbsp. (30 mL) red wine vinegar

2 Tbsp. (30 mL) finely chopped shallots

1/2 tsp. (2.5 mL) sea salt

2 tsp. (10 mL) honey

2 tsp. (10 mL) finely chopped fresh marjoram, or 3/4 tsp. (3.75 mL) dried marjoram

2/3 cup (160 mL) extra virgin olive oil

1/2 tsp. (2.5 mL) freshly ground black pepper

3 red peppers, roasted, peeled and cut into 1-inch (2.5-cm) strips

1/2 lb. (227 g) feta cheese, crumbled

Wash and dry the lettuce. Core and separate the radicchio leaves. Arrange on a platter or individual plates. Cover with a damp cloth and refrigerate until serving time.

Whisk the vinegar, shallots, salt, honey and marjoram together. Slowly beat in the olive oil and pepper.

To serve, scatter the peppers and feta over the salad. Whisk the dressing to recombine the ingredients and drizzle over the salad. Serve immediately.

I like to add a drizzle of truffle oil to this salad for a true taste experience. It is very good, truffled or not, with roasted lamb rack or leg. Le Puy lentils are the best as they retain their shape when cooked.

Warm Lentil and Chicory Salad with Bacon Dressing   serves 6

1/2 lb. (227 g) Le Puy lentils (see page 205)

1 large shallot, finely diced

2 Tbsp. (30 mL) red wine vinegar

1 tsp. (5 mL) Dijon mustard

3/4 tsp. (3.75 mL) sea salt

1/2 cup (120 mL) olive oil

1/4 lb. (113 g) sliced bacon, cut into 1-inch (2.5-cm) pieces

2 Tbsp. (30 mL) fresh parsley, chopped

1 large head chicory, washed, dried and torn into 1-inch (2.5-cm) pieces

Pick over the lentils and remove any stones or chaff. Rinse well. Place in a large pot and cover generously with water. Bring to a boil and skim off any foam that rises to the top. Turn down to a simmer and cook until the lentils are tender but not mushy.

While the lentils are cooking, make the vinaigrette. Combine the shallot, vinegar, Dijon mustard and salt in a bowl. Mix well. Slowly beat in the olive oil. Fry the bacon over medium heat until crisp and brown. Discard most of the fat. Keep the bacon in the frying pan.

Drain the lentils and combine with 2/3 of the vinaigrette and the parsley. Set aside for an hour or so.

When you are ready to serve the salad, toss the chicory with the remaining dressing and divide among 6 plates. Add the lentils to the bacon in the pan and heat quickly over high heat. Spoon the lentils over the greens and serve immediately.

Chopped salads, as the name suggests, incorporate a number of ingredients chopped into small, manageable pieces. With each forkful, you get a variety of textures and flavors. You can toss everything in a bowl or create rows of the components on top of the lettuce and then toss at the table. A perfect summer meal with a loaf of bread. Use cooked turkey instead of the chicken if you wish.

Chopped Chicken Salad with Creamy Basil Dressing   serves 4

1/2 cup (120 mL) mayonnaise

1/4 cup (60 mL) yogurt

1 Tbsp. (15 mL) lemon juice

2 tsp. (10 mL) Dijon mustard

1/2 tsp. (2.5 mL) sea salt

1/2 cup (120 mL) fresh basil, finely chopped

1 clove garlic, minced

1 large head romaine lettuce, washed, dried and cut into 1/2-inch (1.2-cm) squares

1 cup (240 mL) cucumber, peeled, seeded and cut into 1/2-inch (1.2-cm) cubes

1 1/2 cups (360 mL) tomatoes, cut into 1/2-inch (1.2-cm) cubes

2 green onions, thinly sliced

1/2 cup (120 mL) celery hearts, cut into 1/2-inch (1.2-cm) squares

1 cup (240 mL) tart apple, diced into 1/2-inch (1.2-cm) cubes and tossed with 1 Tbsp. (15 mL) lemon juice

3 cups (720 mL) cooked chicken, cut into 1/2-inch (1.2-cm) cubes

1 cup (240 mL) grated Asiago cheese

Stir the mayonnaise, yogurt, lemon juice, Dijon mustard, salt, basil and garlic together. Refrigerate for 1 hour to develop the flavors.

Place the lettuce in a serving bowl and arrange the remaining ingredients in rows, spokes or willy-nilly over the lettuce. Pour the dressing over the salad and toss well.

Tea-Scented Fresh Goat Cheese   page 12

Clams Steamed in Spicy Coconut Lime Broth page 22

Pork and Shiitake Mushroom Spoon Dumplings page 35

Chilled Corn and Chicken Soup with Tomato and Cilantro   page 48

Whatever happened to Green Goddess dressing? It was one of the first California food waves to make a splash. I just loved it, and would reach for the comfortably shaped bottle to pour over my salad, leaving the Catalina, Thousand Islands and Italian forlornly sitting on the table. I made the dressing occasionally in my early twenties, but somewhere, the spark died. I realize now that it was replaced by quiche, carrot cake and cheesecake — the romantic foodstuffs of the late 1970s. Now I have come to understand that the Goddess lives — especially when she's Green.

Clubhouse Chicken Salad with Green Goddess Dressing   serves 4

1 cup (240 mL) mayonnaise, homemade or store-bought

1 cup (240 mL) sour cream

1 2-oz. (57-g) can anchovies, well drained

1 Tbsp. (15 mL) lime juice

3 Tbsp. (45 mL) white wine vinegar

1 Tbsp. (15 mL) finely chopped fresh tarragon

1/4 cup (60 mL) finely chopped fresh chives

1/2 cup (120 mL) finely chopped parsley

1/2 tsp. (2.5 mL) salt

1/2 tsp. (2.5 mL) freshly ground black pepper

1 large head romaine lettuce, washed, dried, and torn into bite-sized pieces

2 cups (480 mL) freshly cooked chicken, cut into bite-sized cubes

3 large ripe tomatoes, cut into 1/2-inch (1.2-cm) cubes

1 avocado, pitted, peeled and cut into 1/4-inch (.6-cm) cubes

6 slices lean bacon, cooked until crisp and crumbled

To make the dressing, combine the mayonnaise, sour cream, anchovies, lime juice, vinegar, tarragon, chives, parsley, salt and pepper in the workbowl of a food processor or blender. Process until smooth. This dressing keeps for 2 weeks, covered and refrigerated.

Arrange the lettuce on a large platter. Scatter the chicken over the lettuce, then the tomatoes, avocado and bacon. Serve the dressing on the side.

This is one of my favorite salads. I can eat it all by itself with a bowl of basmati rice. If you're not feeling that austere, serve it with simple meat dishes or as part of a Thai or Indian feast.

Cucumber Salad with Peanuts, Coconut and Lime   serves 4

2 Tbsp. (30 mL) dried unsweetened shredded coconut

4 Tbsp. (60 mL) boiling water

1½ cups (360 mL) English cucumber, diced into ¼-inch (.6-cm) cubes

2 small chilies, finely chopped

½ cup (120 mL) freshly roasted peanuts

2 Tbsp. (30 mL) lime juice

½ tsp. (2.5 mL) sugar

½ tsp. (2.5 mL) sea salt

1 Tbsp. (15 mL) vegetable oil

¼ tsp. (1.25 mL) whole black mustard seeds

In a small bowl, combine the coconut and boiling water. Let sit until cool. Mix with the cucumber, chilies and peanuts. Mix the lime juice, sugar and salt together. Just before serving, heat the oil over high heat in a small frying pan. Add the mustard seeds. When they pop, add them to the lime juice mixture. Toss with the cucumber mixture and serve immediately.

I was taught how to make this salad many moons ago, in Ottawa. It traditionally has a spice mixture called za'atar added to it, made of sumac, thyme and sesame seeds. If you know of a store that sells Middle Eastern foods, obtain some za'atar and add a few spoonfuls to the salad. Za'atar is also delicious eaten with bread that has been dipped in olive oil.

Lebanese Bread Salad   serves 6 to 8

1 small sweet green or red pepper, cored and cut into 1/2-inch (1.2-cm) dice

1/3 English cucumber, cut into 1/2-inch (1.2-cm) dice

1 cup (240 mL) green onion, thinly sliced

1 1/2 cups (360 mL) fresh parsley, coarsely chopped

1/4 cup (60 mL) fresh mint leaves, coarsely chopped

2 cloves garlic, minced and crushed to a paste with 1/2 tsp. (2.5 mL) salt

1/4 cup (60 mL) lemon juice

1/2 cup (120 mL) olive oil

1 large pinch ground cinnamon

1 large pinch ground allspice

sea salt to taste

3 medium, ripe tomatoes, cut into 1/2-inch (1.2-cm) dice

4 small pita breads, separated into halves, lightly toasted and broken into 1/2-inch (1.2-cm) pieces

In a large bowl, combine the pepper, cucumber, green onion, parsley and mint. Mix together the garlic paste, lemon juice, olive oil, cinnamon and allspice. Set aside. When ready to serve, toss the salad with the dressing. Check for salt. Add the tomatoes and pita and toss again.

This is a fantastic summer salad **and is also great the next day. Serve it with grilled chicken or as part of an antipasto plate.**

Grilled Eggplant Salad with Yogurt Dressing serves 6 to 8

3 cups (720 mL) plain yogurt

4 small eggplants, about 3 lbs. (1.4 kg)

olive oil

1/4 cup (60 mL) water

1/2 tsp. (2.5 mL) sea salt

1/4 tsp. (1.25 mL) freshly ground black pepper

1/4 cup (60 mL) fresh basil leaves, chopped

1/4 cup (60 mL) fresh mint leaves, chopped

2 cloves garlic, minced

1 large tomato, finely diced

Place the yogurt in a sieve lined with a coffee filter or a double layer of cheesecloth and let it drain over a bowl for 2 hours. Top and tail the eggplants and cut into 3/4-inch (2-cm) slices.

Preheat the barbecue or broiler to medium. Lightly brush both sides of the eggplant slices with olive oil and grill or broil until golden brown on both sides and completely tender, about 4–5 minutes per side. Remove from the heat and arrange attractively on a platter to cool.

When the yogurt has finished draining, place in a bowl and stir in the water, then add the salt, pepper, basil, mint and garlic. Drizzle the dressing over the eggplant and scatter the diced tomatoes over the top.

Although you can drain the yogurt **a couple of days in advance, the dish is best assembled just before serving.**

Grilled Zucchini with Yogurt, Mint and Feta Cheese   serves 8

1 1/2 cups (360 mL) plain natural yogurt

8 small zucchini, about 2 lbs. (900 g)

2 Tbsp. (30 mL) olive oil

salt to taste

2 Tbsp. (30 mL) water

1 clove garlic, minced

1/4 tsp. (1.25 mL) sea salt

1/2 cup (120 mL) crumbled feta cheese

1/2 cup (120 mL) fresh mint leaves, coarsely chopped

Line a sieve with a double layer of paper towels. Add the yogurt and let it drain for 1 1/2 hours. Transfer to a bowl, cover and refrigerate until ready to use. Discard the liquid.

Preheat the barbecue or broiler to high. Trim the zucchini, cut it in half lengthwise and toss with the olive oil and salt. Grill or broil the zucchini, turning once, until tender and browned. Transfer to a colander, cut side down, to drain and cool.

Combine the yogurt with the water, garlic and 1/4 tsp. (1.25 mL) salt. Transfer the cooled zucchini to a serving platter. Drizzle the yogurt mixture over the zucchini; sprinkle with the feta cheese and mint.

I love this interpretation of tabouli. **If you want a regular tabouli, rinse** $1/2$ **cup (120 mL) fine bulgar in a sieve, drain well and add to the salad just before tossing with the dressing.**

Pine Nut and Parsley Salad   serves 8

2 Tbsp. (30 mL) vegetable oil

1 cup (240 mL) pine nuts

1 cup (240 mL) fresh mint leaves, coarsely chopped

2 cups (480 mL) fresh parsley, finely chopped

$1/3$ cup (80 mL) tomatoes, seeded and finely chopped

$1/3$ cup (80 mL) English cucumber, seeded and finely diced

$1/4$ cup (60 mL) green onion, thinly sliced

2 Tbsp. (30 mL) freshly squeezed lemon juice

$1/2$ tsp. (2.5 mL) sea salt

$1/2$ tsp. (2.5 mL) garlic, finely chopped

5 Tbsp. (75 mL) olive oil

$1/4$ tsp. (1.25 mL) ground cinnamon

$1/2$ tsp. (2.5 mL) ground allspice

In a small frying pan, heat the vegetable oil over low heat. Add the pine nuts and sauté, stirring constantly until pale gold. Remove from the heat and drain off the oil through a sieve. Cool.

Combine the mint, parsley, tomatoes, cucumber and green onion. For the dressing, combine the lemon juice, salt and garlic in a small bowl. Stir well. Slowly beat in the olive oil. Stir in the cinnamon and allspice. The vegetables may be prepared 4–6 hours in advance. Cover and refrigerate. Just before serving, toss with the pine nuts and dressing.

STORING PARSLEY
To store parsley, wash the bunch in cold water and spin it dry. Pluck the tiny clusters of leaves with a bit of the tiny stem from each larger stem and place them in a plastic container. Poke holes in the lid, cover and store in the fridge. The parsley will last at least 2 weeks and up to 4, and it will be ready to use whenever you need it.

This salad is a Vietnamese interpretation of what I suppose is a French potato salad. When we worked at the David Wood Food Shop in Toronto, Thao, a co-worker, used to make it for the deli. When we asked her what the salad was called she said, "French Food," and the name has stuck to it ever since. You can cook the carrots and beets in water instead of roasting them, but the flavor won't be as sweet.

French Food   serves 4 to 6

1 lb. (454 g) new potatoes, about 4

6 oz. (170 g) baby beets, about 10 walnut-sized beets

6 oz. (170 g) small carrots, about 3

2 eggs, hard-cooked

1/2 cup (120 mL) celery hearts, thinly sliced

2 green onions, thinly sliced

3 Tbsp. (45 mL) fresh cilantro, coarsely chopped

3 Tbsp. (45 mL) fresh mint leaves, coarsely chopped

1 Tbsp. (15 mL) vegetable oil

2 cloves garlic, minced

2 Tbsp. (30 mL) fish sauce

1 1/2 tsp. (7.5 mL) sugar

5 Tbsp. (75 mL) lime juice

1/4 tsp. (1.25 mL) sea salt

1/2 tsp. (2.5 mL) black pepper

Preheat the oven to 350°F (175°C). Place the potatoes in a pot and cover with water. Bring to a boil and cook until the potatoes are tender, about 20 minutes. Drain and cool.

Lightly oil the beets and carrots. Place in separate areas on a baking sheet and roast for about 45 minutes or until they are tender. Remove from the oven and let stand until cool enough to handle.

Peel the potatoes and cut into 1-inch (2.5-cm) cubes. Place in a large bowl. Peel the carrots and slice into thin rounds. Add them to the potatoes. Peel the beets, cut into 1/2-inch (1.2-cm) cubes and reserve. Peel and coarsely chop the hard-cooked eggs. Add to the potatoes and carrots. Add the celery hearts, green onion, cilantro and mint.

Heat the vegetable oil in a very small pan over medium heat. Add the garlic and cook until it just starts to turn golden. Remove from the heat.

In a small bowl, combine the fish sauce, sugar, lime juice, salt and pepper. Stir well to dissolve the salt and sugar. Add the garlic and vegetable oil. Pour over the salad and mix well. Add the beets and mix again. Let stand for an hour or so before serving.

Baked Onion Salad with Cracked Black Pepper   serves 4 to 6

4 large white onions, about 1 1/2 lbs. (675 g)

5 Tbsp. (75 mL) olive oil

2 tsp. (10 mL) cracked black pepper

1 Tbsp. (15 mL) balsamic vinegar

1/2 tsp. (2.5 mL) salt

1 Tbsp. (15 mL) water

1 Tbsp. (15 mL) chopped parsley

Preheat the oven to 300°F (150°C).

Trim the ends from the onions but do not peel. Cut the onions into 1/2-inch (1.2-cm) slices. Oil a baking sheet with some of the olive oil and place the onion slices close together on the baking sheet. Brush lightly with some of the olive oil and cover loosely with aluminum foil. Bake for 1/2 hour. Remove the aluminum foil and bake for another 1/2 hour. Carefully turn the onion slices over and bake for 1/2 hour more. The onion should be a deep brown but not burned. Cool slightly before removing the skin and any dried-out rings. Place on a serving plate.

Beat the cracked black pepper, balsamic vinegar, salt, water and the remaining olive oil together. Drizzle over the onion and sprinkle with the chopped parsley. Serve at room temperature.

A delicious combination of flavors! The pears would sit nicely beside pork or chicken and could even be served as an unusual dessert. Parmesan or Asiago cheese may be substituted.

Pear Salad with Basil and Pecorino Cheese   serves 4

3 ripe pears (Bartletts are a good choice)

2 Tbsp. (30 mL) balsamic vinegar

1 tsp. (5 mL) honey

3 Tbsp. (45 mL) olive oil

1/4 tsp. (1.25 mL) coarsely ground black pepper

1/2 cup (120 mL) loosely packed Pecorino Romano shavings (see Note)

1/4 cup (60 mL) fresh basil leaves, torn into small pieces

Peel and core the pears. Cut each into 8 wedges. Mix the balsamic vinegar with the honey, add the pears and toss to coat them with the mixture. Arrange the pears on a serving platter and drizzle with the olive oil. Scatter with the black pepper, the cheese shavings and the basil.

NOTE
Make cheese shavings by drawing a vegetable peeler across a wedge of cheese.

In the sixties, Dijon mustard was an exotic ingredient, **onion flakes were commonplace (still are) and Miracle Whip ruled (still does!). So, while this is not exactly my mother's original potato salad, it has the same sentimental value—and it has my mother's approval.**

Inspired by My Mother's Potato Salad   serves 4 to 6

1½ lbs. (680 g) medium russet potatoes, skin on

4 large eggs, hard-cooked

1 cup (240 mL) prepared mayonnaise

½ cup (120 mL) sour cream

2 Tbsp. (30 mL) Dijon mustard

½ cup (120 mL) finely chopped celery

½ cup (120 mL) finely sliced green onion

sea salt and freshly ground black pepper

Cook the potatoes in boiling water until tender, 30–40 minutes. Drain and let cool completely.

Remove and discard the skin from the potatoes and grate coarsely into a bowl. Peel the eggs and grate over the potatoes.

Combine the remaining ingredients and season with salt and pepper. Pour over the potatoes and eggs and mix well. Cover and refrigerate for 1 hour before serving.

This is good **to rest simply cooked fish or chicken upon.**

Lemon Orzo and Warm Spinach "Salad" *serves 4*

2/3 cup (160 mL) orzo

2 Tbsp. (30 mL) unsalted butter

2 Tbsp. (30 mL) thinly sliced green onion, white part

1 clove garlic, minced

1 tsp. (5 mL) finely grated lemon rind

1 Tbsp. (15 mL) lemon juice

1 small bunch spinach, washed, trimmed and dried

sea salt and freshly ground black pepper

Bring a large pot of water to a boil. Add the orzo and salt the water liberally. It should taste like sea water. Cook until the orzo is tender, 8–10 minutes. Drain and return to the pot.

While the orzo is cooking, melt the butter over low heat in a small frying pan. Add the onion and garlic and cook until the onion is translucent. Pour over the cooked orzo along with the lemon rind and lemon juice. Add the spinach and toss well. The spinach will wilt slightly. Season to taste and serve.

For an easy meal, start with Potato Soup with Horseradish and Caraway, page 44, and move on to this salad, served with light rye or sourdough bread.

Spinach and Smoked Salmon with Sweet and Sour Cream Dressing serves 4

1 large bunch spinach, about 12 oz. (350 g), stemmed, washed and dried

3 oz. (85 g) sliced smoked salmon, cut into thin strips

3 Tbsp. (45 mL) cider vinegar

2 tsp. (10 mL) sugar

1/2 tsp. (2.5 mL) sea salt

1/2 cup (120 mL) whipping cream

2 Tbsp. (30 mL) vegetable oil

3/4 cup (180 mL) red onion, sliced into thin half moons, loosely packed

Place the spinach and smoked salmon in a large bowl.

Combine the vinegar, sugar, salt and cream. In a non-corrodible pan, heat the vegetable oil over medium heat. Add the onion and stir to coat with the oil. Add the cream mixture and bring to a boil. Reduce until the dressing thickens slightly. Remove from the heat and pour immediately over the spinach and smoked salmon. Toss well and serve on warm plates.

The tomatoes look "tired" as a result of being salted, **not because they are old! Salting draws out water to leave a true tomato flavor. A great accompaniment to grilled or roasted chicken.**

"Tired" Tomato Salad   serves 4

1 lb. (454 g) ripe, summer tomatoes, about 4

1 1/2 tsp. (7.5 mL) sea salt

3 Tbsp. (45 mL) red wine vinegar

4 Tbsp. (60 mL) olive oil

1 Tbsp. (15 mL) fresh parsley, coarsely chopped

freshly ground black pepper to taste

Core the tomatoes and cut them into 8 wedges each. Place the tomato wedges in a bowl and add the salt, vinegar and 2 Tbsp. (30 mL) of the olive oil. Mix gently and allow to stand for 2–4 hours.

Just before serving, drain the tomatoes in a colander and discard the juice. Mix with the remaining olive oil, parsley and pepper.

An absolutely great vinaigrette. In a restaurant situation it is easy to smoke the tomatoes over alder chips, but it is a somewhat messy and smoky process to go through at home. I have cheated here and used canned tomatoes and liquid smoke with no apologies. The results are superb.

Smoked Tomato Vinaigrette   makes 1¹/4 cups (310 mL)

6 canned plum tomatoes, well drained

2 tsp. (10 mL) cider vinegar

¹/8 tsp. (.5 mL) freshly ground black pepper

¹/4 tsp. (1.25 mL) liquid smoke

1 medium clove garlic, minced

¹/2 tsp. (2.5 mL) sea salt

¹/2 cup (120 mL) olive oil

Combine the tomatoes, vinegar, pepper and liquid smoke in a food processor or blender. Mash the garlic to a paste with some of the salt. Add the garlic along with the remaining salt to the ingredients and blend until puréed. With the motor on, add the olive oil in a slow steady stream. Store covered and refrigerated for up to 3 weeks.

USE THIS VINAIGRETTE
AS A SALAD DRESSING OR:

– with grilled oyster mushrooms

– as a marinade for chicken

– on a pasta salad made with orzo,
  prawns and roasted red peppers

– with salmon, snapper or halibut

– with grilled calamari

– tossed with warm, cooked black beans

– with freshly cooked green beans or corn

pizza,
pasta
and
risotto

This dough can be jazzed up by the addition of fresh herbs, such as rosemary or thyme. For the sake of convenience, the dough can be left in the fridge to rise for up to 8 hours. I like to put it in a large, oiled plastic bag and tie the top securely. This will prevent it from escaping and taking over the fridge.

Basic Pizza Dough   makes 1 16-inch (40-cm) pizza

1¹/2 cups (360 mL) lukewarm water

1 tsp. (5 mL) granulated sugar

1 Tbsp. (15 mL) yeast

¹/4 cup (60 mL) olive oil

¹/2 tsp. (2.5 mL) sea salt

2¹/2–3 cups (600–720 mL) unbleached white flour, plus more for kneading

Combine the water and sugar in a large bowl. Sprinkle the yeast over the surface and let work for 10 minutes.

Stir in the olive oil and salt. Beat in the flour 1 cup (240 mL) at a time until the dough is too hard to beat. Sprinkle about 1 cup (240 mL) of flour onto a flat surface. Scrape the dough out of the bowl and knead it, adding flour as necessary until the dough is smooth and resilient to the touch, about 10 minutes.

Place the dough in a large bowl and pour a bit of olive oil over it. Roll the dough around the bowl to coat it thoroughly with the oil. Cover loosely with plastic wrap or a clean cloth and let rise in a warm place until doubled in bulk, about 2 hours.

Punch down the dough. Lightly oil a 16-inch (40-cm) pizza pan. Roll out and press the dough onto the pan. Proceed with your favorite topping and bake.

As a lover of beet greens, I've always searched for new ways to use them. This shows them off beautifully. A hearty green, such as Swiss chard or mustard greens, can be substituted if you like.

Beet Green Pizza with Garlic and Mozzarella makes 1 16-inch (40-cm) pizza

1 recipe Basic Pizza Dough (see page 76)

1 lb. (454 g) beet greens with stems removed, washed and drained

4 Tbsp. (60 mL) olive oil

2 medium cloves garlic, minced

sea salt and freshly ground black pepper

12 oz. (340 g) full-fat mozzarella cheese, grated

While the pizza dough is rising, prepare the topping. Steam the beet greens in a large lidded pot over high heat, stirring occasionally until they are tender, 3–5 minutes. Drain and spread on a tray to cool. When they are cool enough to handle, squeeze the water out with your hands and chop finely.

Heat the olive oil over medium heat and sauté the garlic until light golden. Add the beet greens and toss to coat with the olive oil and garlic. Season with the salt and pepper and remove from the heat.

Preheat the oven to 400°F (200°C). Press the pizza dough into a 16-inch (40-cm) pizza pan. Spread the beet greens evenly over the dough. Bake for about 10 minutes, until the pizza can be slipped off the pan easily. Sprinkle the pizza with mozzarella cheese and transfer the pizza directly onto the oven rack. Bake until golden brown on the bottom, about 15–20 minutes. Remove from the oven and let rest 10 minutes before cutting.

This pizza illustrates that the simplest ingredients, **thoughtfully combined, can create the best possible things to eat. For the best impression, eat it by itself while watching the sunset.**

Fresh Manila Clam Pizza   makes 1 16-inch (40-cm) pizza

1 recipe Basic Pizza Dough (see page 76)

2 lbs. (900 g) manila clams, scrubbed

1/4 cup (60 mL) water

1/4 cup (60 mL) olive oil

2 medium cloves garlic, minced

1/4 cup (60 mL) white wine

2 Tbsp. (30 mL) parsley, finely chopped

1/8 tsp. (.5 mL) chili flakes

4 Tbsp. (60 mL) freshly grated Parmesan cheese

While the pizza dough is rising, prepare the topping. Place the clams and water in a pot with a tight-fitting lid. Cook over high heat until the clams open. Remove from the heat. When the clams are cool enough to handle, remove them from their shells and swish them around in the clam liquor to remove any sand. Chop the clams coarsely. Strain the liquor through a coffee filter or paper towels to remove any sand. Reserve the clams and liquor.

Heat the olive oil over medium heat and sauté the garlic until golden. Add the white wine and cook until it is reduced by half. Add the clam liquor and cook until reduced by half. Remove from the heat and add the parsley and chili flakes.

Preheat the oven to 400°F (200°C). Press the pizza dough into an oiled pizza pan, making deep indentations with your fingers. Place in the oven and bake for 10 minutes, until the dough will slide easily off the pan. Spread the clam liquor mixture evenly over the dough. Slide directly onto the oven rack and bake for about 15 minutes, until the bottom of the pizza is lightly browned.

Spread the clams and Parmesan cheese over the crust and bake for 5 minutes more. Remove from the oven and let rest for 5 minutes before cutting.

I love the balance of flavors and textures in this flatbread. The sweet eggplant carries the salty olives and the slightly charred mushrooms.

Grilled Mushroom, Eggplant and Olive Flatbread serves 4 to 6

3 Tbsp. (45 mL) extra virgin olive oil

2 lbs. (900 g) eggplant, peeled and cut into 3/4-inch (2-cm) slices

3/4 lb. (340 g) oyster mushrooms, thick stems removed

1/8 tsp. (.5 mL) sea salt

1/2 lb. (227 g) green Colossal olives, pitted and coarsely chopped

3 cloves garlic, minced

1–2 dried hot chili peppers, finely chopped

1 tsp. (5 mL) fresh thyme leaves

salt and freshly ground black pepper to taste

cornmeal, for sprinkling on the baking sheet

1 recipe Basic Pizza Dough (see page 76)

Preheat the barbecue to medium–high. Using 2 Tbsp. (30 mL) of the olive oil, brush the eggplant slices on both sides. Grill each side, turning once, until golden brown and tender. (Or broil the eggplant in the oven on baking sheets until golden brown on both sides.) Let cool.

Toss the oyster mushrooms with the remaining 1 Tbsp. (15 mL) olive oil and 1/8 tsp. (.5 mL) salt. Place them in a single layer on the grill, pressing down lightly with a lifter. Grill until well marked; flip over and grill on the other side. Let cool. (The mushrooms can also be broiled. Heat a sturdy baking sheet under the broiler for 5 minutes before adding the mushrooms. Distribute the mushrooms over the baking sheet and press with a lifter. Broil, turning once to brown the other side.)

Cut the eggplant and mushrooms into 1/2-inch (1.2-cm) pieces. Combine with the olives, garlic, chili, thyme and salt and pepper. Mix gently.

Preheat the oven to 400°F (200°C). Lightly sprinkle a 12- x 17-inch (30- x 43-cm) baking sheet with cornmeal. Roll the pizza dough evenly onto the baking sheet, pressing it into the corners. Spread the topping on the dough in an even layer. Bake in the middle of the oven for 10–15 minutes, until the crust is firm. Slip the dough from the pan directly onto the oven rack and bake for 10–15 minutes longer until the bottom crust is golden brown. Turn off the oven, open the door and let sit for 5 minutes before serving.

It Still Holds True

We learn the pleasures of celebrations and feasting at an early age. A feast usually involves a ritualized event, and for many of us Christmas is our first such memory. Birthdays are another. Your parents might take you to a favorite place or have your favorite cake and food. My mother always made party sandwiches for mine, with chocolate milk, chocolate cake and vanilla ice cream. I was especially fascinated by the pinwheel sandwiches made from Cheez Whiz with the pimento-stuffed olive in the middle. There were other times that I knew were special and profound. I didn't have the words at the time to express what I felt, but raspberries from the lady up the street who had raspberry bushes, avocados with lime and sugar in late winter, and rhubarb compote every spring made me associate certain foods with certain times of the year. The eating of them seemed unique and special, and now, with an adult view of the past, I know that they truly were. This association has been my ally in creating my own feasts and reasons to feast.

We notice the rain making patterns on the window, the quality of sunlight on certain days. When we have the first great tomato of the season, when the scent in the air changes, the first meal of the year we eat outside, when the last leaf falls — events that make us go "ahh" and "aha." A spectrum of sights, sounds, smells, thoughts and feelings becomes a part of who we are — inspiration and doing, cooking and eating.

You don't need a group for a feast or celebration. You could be all alone, tucked into the couch, well blanketed, content, and feeling almost wicked because you are eating only for yourself. It is a grand moment of individual feasting and celebration. Two people often eat together, celebrating something special or simply indulging in foods that they really enjoy.

By following the seasons, we'll always have what is best to eat, simply because it is in season. There are no recipes for fresh tomatoes in winter or oysters in summer. Why? Tomatoes just don't taste right and oysters are milky and spawning. Salmon and halibut have their season (although salmon is farmed in the winter) and so does corn. Consider halibut cheeks, asparagus and artichokes in the spring. Local prawns, zucchini, fresh basil and eggplant in the summer. This is the time of year to cook lightly and simply, have barbecues and a multitude of salads. Corn, potatoes and apples in the fall. This is another transitional season, when you can begin to cook with a bolder stroke. Cabbage, oysters and beets in winter. Hot and steamy bowls of sausage with polenta, roast duck and mashed potatoes. Eating and cooking seasonally gives me a reason to celebrate each ingredient as it arrives, fresh, full of flavor and potential.

I must admit that I don't follow this to the letter. What we cook and eat depends on our mood, the people we are serving, our preferences, and how much effort we want to expend. Whatever you decide to do, enjoyment should be the motivating factor. Seasonal transitions are not dates on a calendar either — only you know when a season changes.

This is a favorite combination—sweet, savory and sharp.

Penne with Beets, Bacon and Blue Cheese   serves 4

2 bunches walnut-sized beets with greens, about 10 in total

1/4 lb. (113 g) good-quality slab bacon, cut into 1/4-inch (.6-cm) dice

4 cloves garlic, minced

4 Tbsp. (60 mL) olive oil

1 lb. (454 g) dry penne

4 Tbsp. (60 mL) blue cheese, crumbled

sea salt and freshly ground black pepper

Trim and peel the beets. Discard the stems and wash the greens. Cut the greens into thin strips and cut the beets into 1/4-inch (.6-cm) dice.

Cook the bacon over low heat until it is crisp. Remove from the pan with a slotted spoon to drain on paper towels. Discard the bacon fat. Add the garlic and olive oil to the same pan. Cook over medium heat until the garlic is pale gold. Add the bacon and remove from the heat.

Bring a large pot of water to a boil. Add the beets to the boiling water and salt liberally. It should taste like seawater. Cook for 10 minutes. Add the penne and cook, stirring occasionally, until the pasta is very firm, about 6 minutes. Add the beet greens and continue cooking until the pasta is tender but still firm to the bite, 3–4 minutes longer. Drain the pasta and return to the pot. Add the bacon and garlic mixture and stir over low heat to coat the pasta with the sauce. Stir in the blue cheese. Season with salt and pepper. Serve immediately in heated bowls.

HOW CAN I STOP PASTA FROM STICKING TOGETHER? I've never understood adding oil to pasta water. Think about it — the oil floats on top of the water. How does it get near the pasta? The main reason pasta sticks is because the pot is too small. Pasta needs a lot of water to cook properly, 5–6 quarts (5–6 L) per pound (454 g) of pasta. The water has to boil rapidly, so if you have a burner that is stronger than the rest, use it. A tall, narrow pot is better than a short, wide pot because the heat will be distributed up through the water, which keeps it boiling rapidly. After adding the pasta to the boiling water, stir it up from the bottom as soon as it starts to bend and stir occasionally while it is cooking. Stay away from those pots that have strainer baskets included. They prevent the water from boiling rapidly enough to cook pasta properly.

The perfect spring pasta. **If you wish, add some fresh peas with the artichokes and asparagus.**

Penne with Fresh Artichokes, Asparagus, Spinach and Prosciutto   serves 4

2 large, fresh artichokes, trimmed down to their hearts

3/4 lb. (340 g) fat asparagus, woody ends snapped off

1/2 lb. (227 g) fresh spinach, stemmed, washed and drained

4 Tbsp. (60 mL) olive oil

4 cloves garlic, thinly sliced

4 thin slices prosciutto

1/2 cup (120 mL) chicken stock (see page 46)

1/2 cup (120 mL) white wine

1/8 tsp. (.5 mL) sea salt

1 lb. (454 g) penne

1/2 cup (120 mL) freshly grated Parmesan cheese or grana padano

2 Tbsp. (30 mL) fresh chives, finely chopped

freshly ground black pepper to taste

Cut each artichoke heart into eight wedges. Cut the asparagus into 1 1/2-inch (3.8-cm) diagonal pieces. Cut the spinach into very thin strips and set aside.

Heat the olive oil in a large frying pan over medium heat. Add the garlic and prosciutto and sauté just until the garlic begins to turn golden. Add the artichoke pieces and asparagus and cook for a moment. Add the chicken stock, wine and salt. Cook over high heat until the liquid is reduced by half and the artichokes are tender. Remove from the heat.

While you are preparing the sauce, bring a large pot of water to a boil. Salt liberally. It should taste like seawater. Add the penne and cook, stirring occasionally, until the pasta is cooked but still firm to the bite. Drain the pasta and quickly reheat the sauce. Add the pasta to the sauce along with the spinach. Toss and stir until the spinach wilts. Add the grated cheese, chives and pepper. Stir a few more times to incorporate the ingredients and serve immediately in heated bowls.

This has a subtle sweet-and-sour flavor that is utterly delicious. You can use cauliflower, broken into small florets, in place of the squash. Try serving this pasta with grated Pecorino Romano instead of Parmesan. It is a robustly flavored grating cheese found in large supermarkets and Italian delicatessens.

Penne with Butternut Squash, Capers and Raisins   serves 4 to 6

1½ cups (360 mL) butternut squash, peeled and diced into 3/8-inch (1-cm) cubes

6 Tbsp. (90 mL) olive oil

2 medium cloves garlic, minced

¼ cup (60 mL) finely diced onion

1 dried red chili pepper, crumbled

1 28-oz. (796-mL) can plum tomatoes, coarsely chopped, with their juice

2 Tbsp. (30 mL) golden raisins

1 Tbsp. (15 mL) capers

sea salt and freshly ground black pepper

1 lb. (454 g) dried penne

½ cup (120 mL) grated Parmesan cheese

Bring a small pot of water to a boil. Add a pinch of salt and the butternut squash. Cook until tender but not mushy, about 10–15 minutes. Drain.

Heat the olive oil in a saucepan over medium heat. Sauté the garlic, onion and chili pepper until the garlic turns a pale golden color. Add the tomatoes, raisins and capers. Bring to a boil, then reduce the heat to a simmer. Cook until the sauce reduces by half and is thick, about 20–30 minutes. Season with salt and pepper. Add the squash and remove from the heat.

Bring a large pot of water to a boil. Add the penne and salt liberally — it should taste like sea water. Cook until tender but firm. Quickly reheat the sauce. Drain the penne and return to the pot. Add the sauce and stir over high heat to coat the pasta with the sauce. Serve immediately in heated bowls with Parmesan cheese.

You can use a full-fat plain mozzarella or fontina cheese in place of the smoked mozzarella.

Bow Ties with Spicy Sausage and Smoked Mozzarella   serves 4

1 lb. (454 g) hot Italian sausage

1 Tbsp. (15 mL) olive oil

1 medium onion, thinly sliced

2 cloves garlic, minced

1 Tbsp. (15 mL) tomato paste

¼ cup (60 mL) dry white wine

2 cups (480 mL) chicken stock (see page 46)

sea salt and freshly ground black pepper

1 lb. (454 g) dried bow-tie pasta

½ lb. (227 g) smoked mozzarella, cut into
   small cubes

1 Tbsp. (15 mL) fresh parsley, finely chopped

Bring a large pot of water to a boil. Meanwhile, prepare the sauce. Remove the casings from the sausages and crumble into small pieces. In a large pot, heat the olive oil over medium heat. Add the onion and garlic and sauté until the onion is soft. Add the sausage and cook until it is lightly browned on the outside. Dissolve the tomato paste in the white wine and add to the sausage mixture. Turn the heat to high and boil for a minute. Add the chicken stock and boil until the mixture is reduced by half. Season with salt and pepper. Remove from the heat.

Add the bow ties to the boiling water and salt liberally. It should taste like seawater. Cook, stirring occasionally, until the pasta is tender but still firm to the bite, 8–10 minutes. Drain the pasta and return to the pot. Add the sauce and stir over low heat to coat the pasta with the sauce. Stir in the smoked mozzarella and parsley. Transfer to heated bowls and serve.

TOMATO PASTE

After opening a small can of tomato paste, put it in the freezer. When frozen, open the closed end with a can opener, and leave the bottom lid on it. To use the tomato paste, push the tomato paste out, using the lid and slice it off. One quarter inch (.6 cm) is about 1 Tbsp. (15 mL) of tomato paste. Store the can in a plastic bag.

You can add fresh basil, **parsley or mint to this pasta if you like.**

Fusilli with Zucchini and Lemon   serves 4

2 Tbsp. (30 mL) olive oil

4 medium zucchini, cut into 2- by ½-inch
  (5- by 1.2-cm) sticks

1 Tbsp. (15 mL) unsalted butter

2 cloves garlic, minced

½ cup (120 mL) dry white wine

1 cup (240 mL) chicken stock (see page 46)

½ cup (120 mL) whipping cream or
  half-and-half cream

2 tsp. (10 mL) lemon zest

sea salt and freshly ground black pepper

1 lb. (454 g) dry fusilli

¼ cup (60 mL) freshly grated Parmesan
  cheese

Heat the olive oil over high heat in a large, heavy frying pan. Add the zucchini in a single layer, in batches if necessary, and fry until it is browned on the bottom. Transfer to a plate.

Melt the butter over medium heat in a large pot. Add the garlic and sauté for a minute. Add the white wine and chicken stock and reduce by half over high heat. Add the whipping cream or half-and-half and boil until slightly thickened. Add the lemon zest and season with salt and pepper.

Bring a large pot of water to a boil. Add the fusilli to the boiling water and salt liberally. It should taste like seawater. Cook, stirring occasionally, until the pasta is tender but still firm to the bite, 8–10 minutes. Drain and return the pasta to the cooking pot. Add the sauce and zucchini and stir over high heat until piping hot. Stir in the Parmesan cheese. Serve immediately in heated bowls.

This sauce is great **served over penne, rigatoni and fusilli as well.**

Fettuccine with Sausage, Porcini Mushrooms and Green Olives   serves 4

1 oz. (28 g) dried porcini mushrooms

1/2 cup (120 mL) boiling water

1 Tbsp. (15 mL) olive oil

1/2 lb. (227 g) sweet Italian sausage, thinly sliced

4 Tbsp. (60 mL) unsalted butter

1 clove garlic, minced

1/4 lb. (113 g) cultivated mushrooms, thinly sliced

1/2 cup (120 mL) chicken stock (see page 46)

1 Tbsp. (15 mL) fresh parsley, finely chopped

1/2 cup (120 mL) large green olives, pitted and thinly sliced

1 lb. (454 g) dried fettuccine

sea salt and freshly ground black pepper

Place the porcini mushrooms in a small bowl and cover with the boiling water. Let the mushrooms soak for half an hour. Remove the porcini mushrooms from the liquid and check for dirt. Coarsely chop. Strain the soaking liquid through a coffee filter to remove any sand and reserve.

Heat the olive oil in a large frying pan over high heat. Add the sausage and cook, stirring frequently, over medium heat until the sausage is browned. Remove the sausage from the pan and add the butter. When it sizzles, add the garlic, cultivated and porcini mushrooms and sauté until the mushrooms throw off their liquid, about 5 minutes. Add the sausage, the reserved porcini soaking water and the chicken stock. Bring to a boil and cook until the liquid thickens slightly, 3–5 minutes. Add the parsley and olives and remove from the heat.

Bring a large pot of water to a boil and salt liberally. It should taste like seawater. Add the fettuccine and cook, stirring occasionally, until the pasta is tender but still firm to the bite, 8–10 minutes. Drain the pasta and return to the pot. Add the sauce and stir over low heat to coat the pasta. Transfer to heated bowls and serve.

This is a perfect way **to show off the first asparagus of spring.**

Fettuccine with Asparagus and Lemon   serves 4 as an appetizer, 2 as a main course

4 Tbsp. (60 mL) unsalted butter

1 1/2 cups (360 mL) whipping cream

2 Tbsp. (60 mL) lemon juice

finely grated zest of 4 lemons

sea salt and freshly ground black pepper

1 lb. (454 g) fresh fettuccine or 1/2 lb. (227 g) dried

1/2 lb. (227 g) fresh asparagus, trimmed and cut into 1-inch (2.5-cm) pieces on the diagonal

1/2 cup (125 mL) freshly grated Parmesan cheese

Combine the butter and whipping cream in a heavy saucepan. Bring to a boil and add the lemon juice and zest. Continue boiling until the cream is reduced by one-third. Season with salt and pepper and remove from the heat.

Bring a large pot of water to a boil. Salt liberally — it should taste like sea water. If you are using fresh pasta, add the asparagus to the water with the pasta. If using dried pasta, add the asparagus 2 minutes before the pasta is done. Drain the pasta and asparagus.

Reheat the sauce and add the pasta and asparagus, turning it to coat well with the sauce. Add the Parmesan cheese and stir until the cheese is incorporated. Serve immediately in heated bowls.

My friend Steven is a wonderful cook — especially of familiar and comforting things. His spaghetti and meatballs proves it.

Steven's Spaghetti and Meatballs *serves 4 to 6*

⅓ cup (80 mL) milk

3 1-inch (2.5-cm) slices white bread, crusts removed and torn into pieces

1 large egg

1 lb. (454 g) lean ground beef

1 lb. (454 g) ground pork

1 cup (240 mL) freshly grated Parmesan cheese

1 tsp. (5 mL) sea salt

¼ tsp. (1.25 mL) freshly ground black pepper

¼ cup (60 mL) fresh parsley, chopped

4 28-oz. (796-mL) cans Italian plum tomatoes, drained

4 Tbsp. (60 mL) olive oil

3 Tbsp. (45 mL) prosciutto, finely chopped

1 Tbsp. (15 mL) garlic, finely chopped

⅔ cup (160 mL) onion, finely diced

1 Tbsp. (15 mL) tomato paste (see page 84)

1 tsp. (5 mL) sea salt

¼ tsp. (1.25 mL) freshly ground black pepper

1 lb. (454 g) dried spaghetti

Heat the milk in a small pot until simmering. Add the bread, remove from the heat and stir until the bread becomes a paste. Cool. In a large bowl, combine the egg, beef, pork, Parmesan cheese, salt, pepper, parsley and the cooled bread paste. Mix well until it is thoroughly combined. Shape the mixture into 2-inch (5-cm) balls. You should have about 24 meatballs, give or take a few.

In a blender or food processor, purée the tomatoes, in batches if necessary. Press the tomato purée through a sieve to remove the seeds.

In a large heavy pot, heat the olive oil over medium. Add the prosciutto and cook until it darkens. Add the garlic and cook for a few moments, stirring. Add the onion and cook until it is translucent, 3–4 minutes. Add the tomato purée, paste, salt and pepper. Bring to a boil, then reduce to a simmer. Cook, stirring frequently, for 30 minutes.

While the sauce simmers, place the meatballs 1 inch (2.5 cm) apart on a baking sheet with a rim. Preheat the broiler and place the baking sheet 4–6 inches (10–15 cm) from the heat source. Broil until the meatballs are lightly browned on top. Turn the meatballs over and broil until lightly browned on the other side. Add the meatballs to the sauce and simmer for about 30 minutes longer, or until the sauce heavily coats the back of a spoon.

Bring a large pot of water to a boil. Salt liberally. Add the pasta and cook until it is tender but still firm to the bite. Drain. Divide the pasta among heated bowls and ladle the sauce and meatballs over each portion. Serve immediately.

Pork and shellfish may seem like a novel combination, **but it has ancient roots in Portugal and Spain. History aside, it is utterly delicious.**

Spaghetti with Prawns and Chorizo Sausage   serves 4 to 6

20 large prawns

12 oz. (340 g) raw, unsmoked chorizo sausage

3 Tbsp. (45 mL) extra virgin olive oil

1/4 cup (60 mL) finely diced onion

3 medium cloves garlic, minced

1/2 cup (120 mL) white wine

2 28-oz. (796-mL) cans plum tomatoes, drained, puréed and sieved to remove the seeds

dried chili flakes to taste

sea salt and freshly ground black pepper

1 lb. (454 g) dried spaghetti

Peel the prawns and reserve the shells. You may leave the prawns whole (nice to look at) or cut them in half crosswise (easier to eat). Refrigerate the prawns. Place the shells in a small pot. Cover with 2 cups (480 mL) of water and bring to a boil. Reduce the heat and simmer 20 minutes. Remove from the heat and strain, reserving the stock.

While the prawn stock is simmering, remove the sausages from their casings and crumble. Heat the oil in a pot over medium heat and sauté the onion and garlic until the garlic starts to turn golden. Add the crumbled sausage and cook until the sausage loses its raw appearance. Add the white wine and prawn stock. Cook at a rapid boil, watching the sauce carefully. As soon as you see the oil starting to float on top of the sauce, remove from the heat. Add the tomatoes and turn the heat down to medium low. Simmer the sauce until it heavily coats the back of a spoon, 15–20 minutes. Season to taste with the chili flakes, salt and pepper. Remove from the heat.

Bring a large pot of water to a boil, salt well (it should taste like sea water) and add the spaghetti. Cook until tender but firm to the bite. A few minutes before the pasta is done, reheat the sauce. Drain the pasta and return it to the pot it was cooked in, add the sauce and the prawns, and stir for a few minutes on low heat until the prawns are cooked through. Serve immediately in heated bowls.

This cooking-class favorite is a great way of using our local hand-peeled shrimp. Its spicy sweet-sour flavor has universal appeal. Many people have confessed to making extra so they can eat it cold out of the fridge the next day!

Shrimp Pad Thai   serves 4

½ lb. (227 g) medium-width dried rice noodles (no wider than ¼ inch/.6 cm)

2 Tbsp. (30 mL) oyster sauce

4 Tbsp. (60 mL) ketchup

2 Tbsp. (30 mL) molasses

2 Tbsp. (30 mL) sugar

2 Tbsp. (30 mL) fish sauce

4 Tbsp. (60 mL) water

1 tsp. (5 mL) dried chili flakes

¼ cup (60 mL) vegetable oil

6 cloves garlic, minced

2 eggs

1½ cups (360 mL) cooked shrimp

2 cups (480 mL) bean sprouts

2 cups (480 mL) Chinese chives or green onions cut into 1-inch (2.5-cm) lengths

2 Tbsp. (30 mL) chopped roasted peanuts

cilantro sprigs

Place the rice noodles in a bowl and cover with warm water for 30 minutes. Combine the oyster sauce, ketchup, molasses, sugar, fish sauce, water and chili flakes in a small bowl and set aside.

Heat the vegetable oil in a wok or large frying pan over high heat. Stir-fry the garlic until golden. Add the eggs and scramble until dry. Drain the noodles and add them to the pan. Stir-fry until the noodles soften, become shiny and start sticking together in a mass. This is crucial to the texture of the finished dish. Add the shrimp, bean sprouts, chives or green onions and the sauce. Cook until the sauce is absorbed. Turn out onto a platter and garnish with the peanuts and cilantro.

For some, macaroni and cheese is the ultimate in comfort food. One of my dear friend Bob's favorite comfort dinners is this macaroni and cheese with baked potatoes and sour cream on the side. Not your everyday kind of dinner, mind you, but fitting when extra special cheering up is required!

Macaroni and Cheese serves 6

3 cups (720 mL) elbow macaroni

4 cups (1 L) homogenized milk

4 Tbsp. (60 mL) butter

4 Tbsp. (60 mL) all-purpose flour

1 tsp. (5 mL) sea salt

4 cups (1 L) grated aged Cheddar, loosely packed

1½ cups (360 mL) grated aged gouda, loosely packed

2 cups (480 mL) grated medium gouda, loosely packed

4 Tbsp. (60 mL) unsalted butter

2 cups (480 mL) soft white breadcrumbs

Bring a large pot of water to a boil and salt liberally. Cook the elbow macaroni until tender and drain. Cool under cold running water. Drain and set aside.

Scald the milk. Melt the butter over medium heat. Add the flour and stir for a few minutes. Slowly whisk in the milk and bring to a boil. Reduce the heat to a simmer and cook for 10 minutes, stirring occasionally. Remove from the heat and whisk in the salt, Cheddar and aged gouda. Fold in the cooked macaroni.

Butter a 2-quart (2-L) casserole dish. Add half the macaroni and cheese mixture. Cover with the grated medium gouda. Add the rest of the macaroni and cheese. (The casserole can be made up to this point a day in advance. Cover and refrigerate overnight. Increase the baking time to 1 hour and 15 minutes.)

Melt the butter for the crumb topping. Toss with the breadcrumbs. Sprinkle on top of the macaroni and cheese. Bake in a preheated 350°F (175°C) oven for 40 minutes until browned and bubbly.

This pasta captures the essence of late summer. Tomatoes, prawns and basil are at their best and the bocconcini is ripe on the vine. Ha!

Seashell Pasta with Tomatoes, Bocconcini, Prawns and Basil
serves 4 as a main course, 6 as an appetizer

1½ lbs. (680 g) ripe plum tomatoes

2 cloves garlic, cut in half and lightly crushed

⅓ cup (80 mL) extra virgin olive oil

¾ tsp. (3.75 mL) sea salt

½ tsp. (2.5 mL) coarsely and freshly ground black pepper

2 good-quality bocconcini

½ cup (120 mL) fresh basil leaves, loosely packed

1 lb. (454 g) large prawns or shrimp, peeled and deveined

1 lb. (454 g) medium-sized seashell pasta

Peel and seed the tomatoes. Dice them and place in a bowl.

Skewer the garlic on a toothpick (this will make it easier to retrieve later) and add to the tomatoes. Mix in the olive oil, salt and pepper. Dice the bocconcini. Tear the basil into small pieces. Add these to the tomatoes and stir well. Let the whole mixture marinate for at least an hour, or up to 4 hours.

Cut the prawns or shrimp into 3 pieces crosswise and refrigerate until ready to serve.

Bring a large pot of water to a boil. Salt liberally — it should taste like seawater — and add the pasta. Cook until tender but firm to the bite. Drain and return to the pot over medium heat. Remove the garlic from the tomatoes. Add the prawns and the tomato sauce to the pasta. Stir gently until the prawn pieces are cooked through and the bocconcini starts to melt. Serve immediately in warm bowls.

The sweetness of the corn **and the saltiness of the clams sing out in harmony.**

Linguine with Manila Clams and Corn   serves 2 as a main course, 4 as an appetizer

1½ lbs. (680 g) Manila clams, scrubbed

2 Tbsp. (30 mL) water

⅓ cup (80 mL) olive oil

2 medium cloves garlic, peeled and thinly sliced

½ cup (120 mL) white wine

1 Tbsp. (15 mL) finely chopped parsley

⅛ tsp. (.5 mL) chili flakes or to taste

½ lb. (227 g) dried linguine

1 ear of corn, kernels cut off, about ½ cup (125 mL)

4 Tbsp. (60 mL) freshly grated Parmesan cheese

Place the clams and water in a pot with a tight-fitting lid. Cook over high heat until the clams open. Remove from the heat. When the clams are cool enough to handle, remove them from their shells and swish them around in the clam liquor to remove any sand. Chop the clams coarsely. Strain the liquor through a coffee filter or paper towels to remove any sand and reserve.

Heat the olive oil over medium heat and sauté the sliced garlic until golden. Add the white wine and cook until reduced by half. Add the clam liquor and reduce by half again. Remove from the heat and stir in the clams, parsley and chili flakes.

Bring a large pot of water to a boil. Salt liberally—it should taste like sea water—and add the linguine. When the water returns to a boil add the corn cob and corn kernels. Cook until the pasta is tender but firm to the bite. Drain and return the pasta to the pot, discarding the corn cob. Quickly reheat the sauce and toss with the pasta over low heat until evenly coated. Add the Parmesan cheese and toss a few more times. Serve immediately in heated bowls.

Don't save this for surf and turf, **page 146; it is divine any time!**

White Clam Linguine   serves 2 to 3 by itself, 4 with a steak

2 lbs. (900 g) Manila clams

4 Tbsp. (60 mL) olive oil

3 cloves garlic, minced

2 Tbsp. (30 mL) finely chopped parsley

1 dried hot chili pepper, crumbled

½ cup (120 mL) dry white wine

1 lb. (454 g) dried linguine

2 Tbsp. (30 mL) unsalted butter

¼ cup (60 mL) freshly grated Parmesan cheese

Wash the clams thoroughly, discarding any that do not close. Place them in a large pot, cover with a lid and steam over high heat until they open, shaking the pot to redistribute them. Remove the clams with a slotted spoon into a strainer over a bowl. Line a sieve with a double layer of paper towels, strain the clam juice and reserve.

Remove the clams from their shells and chop coarsely. Place in a bowl and cover until ready to use.

In a heavy-bottomed pot, heat the olive oil over medium heat. Add the garlic and sauté until it just turns golden. Add the parsley, chili pepper and wine and let it boil away for a minute. Add the strained clam juice and boil for 1 minute longer. Remove from the heat.

Bring a large pot of water to a boil. Add the linguine to the boiling water and salt liberally. It should taste like seawater. Cook, stirring occasionally, until the pasta is very firm to the bite, about 8 minutes. Drain the pasta and return to the cooking pot. Add the clam juice mixture, the reserved clams and the butter. Stir over medium heat until piping hot and the pasta has reached its desired state of tenderness, 1–2 minutes. Stir in the Parmesan cheese. Serve immediately in heated bowls or alongside steaks.

A beautiful, golden-colored risotto; the lemon zest punctuates its sweetness with bursts of flavor.

Butternut Squash Risotto   serves 4 to 6

8 cups (2 L) chicken stock (see page 46)
or water

4 Tbsp. (60 mL) unsalted butter

½ cup (120 mL) finely diced onion

2 cups (480 mL) butternut squash, peeled
and diced into ½-inch (1-cm) pieces

2 cups (480 mL) arborio rice

sea salt and freshly ground black pepper

zest of half a lemon

½ cup (120 mL) freshly grated Parmesan
cheese

Heat the stock or water to a simmer. Melt the butter over medium heat in a large pot and sauté the onion until translucent. Stir in the squash, coating it with the butter and onions. Add the rice and stir for a few minutes. Pour in a ladleful of stock or water and stir until the liquid is absorbed and a loose, creamy film forms around the rice. Continue adding the stock, one ladleful at a time, until the rice is half-cooked. Season with salt. Continue adding stock until the rice is tender but still firm to the bite. Adjust the seasoning. Stir in the lemon zest and Parmesan cheese and serve immediately in heated bowls.

The inspiration for this risotto **came from a late spring cruise through Chinatown, wondering what to have for dinner.**

Fava Bean, Asparagus and Pea Shoot Risotto   serves 4 to 6

1½ lbs. (680 g) fresh fava beans, removed from their pods and peeled

8 cups (2 L) chicken stock (see page 46) or water

4 Tbsp. (60 mL) unsalted butter

½ cup (120 mL) finely diced onions

2 cups (480 mL) arborio rice

salt to taste

½ lb. (225 g) fresh asparagus, trimmed and cut into 1-inch (2.5-cm) pieces on the diagonal

1 cup (240 mL) fresh pea shoots, packed

Parmesan cheese

sea salt and freshly ground black pepper to taste

Bring a small pot of water to a boil. Add the fava beans and cook for 4–5 minutes until bright green. Drain and set aside.

Heat the stock or water to a simmer. Melt the butter over medium heat in a large pot and sauté the onion until translucent. Stir in the rice, coating it with the butter and onions. Add a ladleful of stock or water and stir until the liquid is absorbed and a loose, creamy film forms around the rice. Add the fava beans. Continue stirring in the stock, one ladleful at a time, until the rice is half-cooked. Season with the salt and add more stock until the rice is tender but still firm to the bite.

Five minutes before the risotto is done, add the asparagus. When the risotto is done, add the pea shoots and Parmesan cheese. Adjust the seasoning with salt and pepper. Serve immediately in heated bowls.

A great accompaniment to fish, especially the Sablefish Osso Buco, page 124. Saffron is hand-gathered from crocuses. You may think it is expensive, but a little goes a long way. In fact, it is best to be prudent when using saffron. Too much will completely overwhelm a dish.

Saffron Risotto   serves 6

6 cups (1.5 L) chicken stock (see page 46) or water

1/4 cup (60 mL) unsalted butter

1/4 cup (60 mL) finely diced onion

2 cups (480 mL) arborio rice

1/16 tsp. (.25 mL) saffron, steeped in 2 Tbsp. (30 mL) boiling water

sea salt and freshly ground black pepper

1/4 cup (60 mL) Parmesan cheese, grated

Heat the stock or water to a simmer. Melt the butter in a large, heavy saucepan over medium heat and sauté the onion until translucent. Mix in the rice, stirring to coat with the butter and onions. Add a ladleful of stock and stir until the stock is absorbed and a loose, creamy film forms around the rice. Continue adding the stock, one ladleful at a time, until the rice is half-cooked. Add half the saffron water and season with salt. Continue adding stock until the rice is tender but still firm to the bite. Add more saffron water if you feel that it is necessary and adjust the seasoning with salt and pepper. Stir in the Parmesan cheese and serve immediately in heated bowls.

fish

fish

If you have never had grilled calamari, this dish will be a revelation. Or, instead of using the fennel seed dressing, try the Smoked Tomato Vinaigrette, page 74, sprinkled with 3 Tbsp. (45 mL) chopped parsley, 1 tsp. (5 mL) minced garlic and the zest of a lemon.

Grilled Calamari with Fennel and Red Pepper Vinaigrette   serves 6

1 Tbsp. (15 mL) red wine vinegar

¼ tsp. (1.25 mL) sea salt

½ cup (120 mL) olive oil

1 red pepper, roasted, peeled, seeded and diced

1½ tsp. (7.5 mL) fennel or anise seeds

2 Tbsp. (30 mL) finely chopped parsley

1 medium clove garlic, minced

finely chopped zest of 1 lemon

2 lbs. (900 g) small calamari, cleaned

sea salt and freshly ground black pepper

1 Tbsp. (15 mL) olive oil

To make the vinaigrette, stir the vinegar and salt together. Slowly beat in the olive oil. Add the red pepper. In a small, heavy frying pan over medium heat, toast the fennel or anise seeds, shaking the pan constantly until the seeds turn a shade darker. Add to the vinaigrette.

Combine the parsley, garlic and lemon zest in a small bowl and set aside.

Preheat the barbecue on its highest setting. Toss the calamari with the salt, pepper and olive oil and place them on the grill. When they are marked by the grill, turn them over and mark on the other side. Place the calamari on a heated platter, pour the vinaigrette over them and sprinkle with the parsley mixture. Serve immediately.

Erin's parents own a beautiful cottage in Washington State **where we go for mini vacations. Erin always wants oysters, so I like to make a different oyster dish every time. This received 5 stars.**

Oysters Baked in Garlic and Sherry for Erin   serves 4 as a main course

3/4 qt. (720 mL) small, shucked oysters

1 cup (240 mL) unsalted butter

1/3 cup (80 mL) sweet sherry

4 cloves garlic, minced

1/4 tsp. (1.25 mL) sea salt

2 tsp. (10 mL) coarsely crushed black pepper

6 cups (1.5 L) breadcrumbs (use day-old white bread)

Preheat the oven to 400°F (200°C). Place the oysters in a single layer in a 9- by 13-inch (23- by 33-cm) baking dish. In a pot over low heat, melt the butter. Add the sherry, garlic, salt and pepper. Add the breadcrumbs and toss until well coated. Spread the breadcrumbs evenly over the oysters. Do not pack them down. Bake for 20 minutes in the middle of the oven. Turn on the broiler and broil until the top is golden brown, 3–4 minutes.

I like teaching this dish **because the sceptical looks on people's faces change to smiles of bliss very quickly.**

Oyster Pie   serves 4

½ lb. (227 g) fresh spinach, stems removed, washed

2 Tbsp. (30 mL) unsalted butter

1 cup (240 mL) onion, finely diced

½ cup (120 mL) fennel bulb, finely diced

1 cup (240 mL) dry white wine

2 cups (480 mL) whipping cream

1 tsp. (5 mL) sea salt

2 tsp. (10 mL) fresh tarragon, finely chopped

1 Tbsp. (15 mL) fresh lemon juice

2½ lbs. (1.1 kg) russet potatoes, peeled and cut into 1-inch (2.5-cm) chunks

½ cup (120 mL) buttermilk, warmed

2 Tbsp. (30 mL) unsalted butter at room temperature

1 Tbsp. (15 mL) prepared horseradish

sea salt and freshly ground black pepper

24 shucked medium oysters

½ cup (120 mL) fine dry breadcrumbs

paprika

In a large pot, steam the spinach, using only the water clinging to its leaves. Drain and place on a plate to cool. Squeeze the water out of the spinach and chop coarsely. Set aside.

In a large pot, melt the butter over medium heat. Add the onion and fennel and sauté until the onion is translucent. Add the white wine, turn the heat to high and boil until the wine is reduced by half. Add the whipping cream and boil until the mixture is reduced to 1½ cups (360 mL). Stir in the salt, tarragon and lemon juice. Remove from the heat.

Cover the potatoes with water, bring to a boil and cook until very tender, 15–20 minutes. Drain and return to the pot. Mash the potatoes until smooth. Beat in the buttermilk, then the butter and horseradish. Season with salt and pepper.

Preheat the oven to 425°F (220°C). Place the oysters in an 8-inch-square (20-cm) baking dish and sprinkle with the breadcrumbs. Stir the spinach into the sauce and pour over the oysters. Spoon the mashed potatoes over the sauce and sprinkle lightly with paprika. Place in the oven and bake for 20–30 minutes, until the mixture is bubbling and the potatoes are lightly browned.

I only started to eat oyster stuffing when I moved to the West Coast and was sorry I hadn't had it before. Like most dishes with cooked oysters, the meat almost disappears, leaving its intense briny flavor behind. I like a lot of black pepper in this, but adjust it to your taste. You can serve it with any large roasted bird, but it is especially good with Oxtails Braised in Red Wine, page 147.

Oyster Stuffing   serves 6 to 8

1/3 cup (80 mL) unsalted butter

2 cups (480 mL) finely diced onion

1 cup (240 mL) finely diced celery

2 tsp. (10 mL) fresh thyme leaves

3/4 cup (180 mL) chicken stock (see page 46), plus more if needed

1 pt. (475 mL) shucked oysters, cut into quarters

1 tsp. (5 mL) black pepper

8 cups (2 L) firm white bread, crusts removed, cut into 1/2-inch (1.2-cm) cubes

sea salt to taste

In a frying pan, melt the butter over low heat. Add the onion, celery and thyme. Cook until the onion is translucent. Add the chicken stock and bring to a boil. Add the oysters and pepper and remove from the heat. Pour the mixture over the bread cubes and toss well. The stuffing should be moist but not soggy. Add more chicken stock if it seems too dry. Season with salt.

Preheat the oven to 350°F (175°C). Transfer the stuffing to a 9- by 13-inch (23- by 33-cm) baking dish. Cover with aluminum foil and bake for half an hour. Remove the foil and bake for 15–20 minutes longer, until the top is brown and crusty.

Roasting Peppers
If you have a gas stove, turn a burner on high and place the pepper directly on the flame. Turn the pepper with tongs to blacken the skin on all sides. On an electric stove, preheat the broiler to high. Place the pepper on a baking sheet as close to the element as possible, turning it with tongs to blacken the skin on all sides. Cool, slip off the skin and remove the seeds and core.

*If you thought cod was a dull fish, **this will change your mind. It changed mine.***

Pancetta-Wrapped Cod with Smoked Tomato Vinaigrette   serves 6

6 5- to 6-oz. (150- to 180-g) fillets of ling cod
or true cod

sea salt and freshly ground black pepper

12 thin slices pancetta

1 Tbsp. (15 mL) vegetable oil

1 recipe Smoked Tomato Vinaigrette
(see page 74)

Lightly salt and pepper both sides of the cod. Place the pancetta on one side of the cod.

Preheat the oven to 350°F (175°C). Heat the vegetable oil in a large frying pan over medium heat. Slip in the cod, pancetta side down. Fry until the pancetta is lightly browned. Flip the cod over and fry until the bottom is lightly browned.

Transfer to a baking sheet, pancetta-side up, and bake until the cod just turns opaque, 5–7 minutes. Don't overcook the cod — it turns to cotton if you do.

Serve on warm plates or a platter, drizzled with or surrounded by the vinaigrette.

Feast of the Snow Crab

My ex-husband, Steven, suffered from pre-Christmas blues and wanted something festive for dinner. Veal was mentioned as a possibility, but I would have to drive halfway across town to get it. I opted for crab, which was only two blocks away. It was Christmas Eve and there were four-foot-high drifts of snow in the backyard. This is very unusual for Vancouver—it only happens every 60 years or so.

The crabs were cooked and taken from the pot. We decided to have them chilled and I had prepared a lemony mayonnaise. A moment of madness possessed us and we ran out to the backyard with a flashlight to place the crabs in the snow. We almost choked we were laughing so hard, and the dog Ginger couldn't figure out whether to wag or sulk. We watched the crabs steaming serenely in the snow, in the weak spotlight made by the flashlight, and were awed by the reverence of the occasion. Snow Crab was born and Steven's funk disappeared! It may never snow like that on Christmas Eve here again, but we will have the memory of Snow Crab on Christmas Eve forever. If you don't have a snow bank, the fridge will do.

Chilled crab is an easy way to eat crab. Extracting a small mountain of meat and piling it onto a piece of toasted baguette with a slathering of fresh Lemon Mayonnaise, page 108, is one of the moments that life is all about. You can take your time with it and not worry about it getting cold. Large crabs, 1 3/4–2 lbs. (800–900 g), are ideal for eating as there is a bigger meat reward for the amount of cracking required.

Add a Greek salad and call it dinner! **Gremolata is the classic combination of lemon zest, parsley and garlic that is sprinkled over osso buco. It goes equally well with fish.**

Gremolata Crumbed Cod with Skordalia   serves 4

½ cup (120 mL) fresh breadcrumbs

½ cup (120 mL) chopped fresh parsley

2 tsp. (10 mL) grated lemon rind

½ tsp. (2.5 mL) finely chopped garlic

4 Tbsp. (60 mL) extra virgin olive oil

sea salt and freshly ground black pepper

4 6-oz. (170-g) boneless, skinless cod fillets

1 recipe Skordalia (see page 19)

Preheat the oven to 400°F (200°C). Combine the bread-crumbs, parsley, lemon rind, garlic, olive oil and salt and pepper to taste. Pat evenly on the top of each of the cod fillets. Place on a baking sheet and cook for 15 minutes until the fish is cooked through and the crumbs are golden. Serve with the skordalia.

COOKED AND CHILLED DUNGENESS CRAB

If you have some snow available, be sure to use it for chilling the crab. And be sure to serve crab with plenty of mayonnaise.

Choose 1 crab per person. Have your fish merchant tear off the backs and clean out the insides for you. You will not need the backs, unless you want to cook them and place them back on top for presentation. When you get home, check the crabs to make sure the lungs (these are the spongy "fingers" on the top of the body) have been removed, and rinse under cold water. Bring to a boil a pot of water that is large enough to hold the crabs. Salt liberally. It should taste like seawater. Add the crabs and cook for 5 minutes after the water comes to a boil. Remove from the pot and cool. Refrigerate for at least 1 hour until thoroughly chilled. The crab is best eaten as soon as possible. Do not refrigerate overnight.

Lemon Mayonnaise makes 1½ cups (360 mL)

3 large egg yolks

½ tsp. (2.5 mL) salt

½ cup (120 mL) olive oil

½ cup (120 mL) vegetable oil

2 Tbsp. (30 mL) lemon juice

Place the egg yolks and salt in a food processor or blender. With the motor on, slowly dribble the olive and vegetable oils into the egg yolks. If the mixture seems too thick at any point, add a bit of water. When all of the oil has been incorporated and the mixture is emulsified, add the lemon juice. To make by hand, whisk the egg yolks and salt together in a medium-sized bowl. Whisking constantly, add the oils, drop by drop until it is all incorporated and the mixture is emulsified. Whisk in the lemon juice. Cover and refrigerate for up to three days.

NOTE
If using raw eggs makes you uncomfortable, stir the lemon juice into 1¼ cups (300 mL) prepared mayonnaise.

VARIATION
Honey Caper Mayonnaise
To make this variation, add 1 Tbsp. (15 mL) fragrant honey and 2 tsp. (10 mL) small capers at the same time as the lemon juice.

Macaroni and Cheese   page 91

Salmon Bake with Sour Cream, Bacon and New Red Potatoes   page 138

Miso Sablefish with Waldorf Salad   page 128

Dungeness crab was another glorious reward **for moving west. While I enjoy it chilled with a lemony mayonnaise, this recipe is for those of you who, like me, feel that digging into a drippy, savory crab transcends all other eating experiences.**

Herb and Parmesan Roasted Dungeness Crab   serves 4 as an appetizer, or 2 as a main course

2 2-lb. (900-g) Dungeness crabs, cooked and cleaned

1½ tsp. (7.5 mL) fennel seeds, coarsely crushed

½ cup (120 mL) coarsely chopped parsley

½ cup (120 mL) coarsely chopped fresh basil leaves

4 cloves garlic, minced

¼ tsp. (1.25 mL) cayenne pepper

2 tsp. (10 mL) paprika

½ tsp. (2.5 mL) sea salt

1 tsp. (5 mL) freshly ground black pepper

⅓ cup (80 mL) extra virgin olive oil

½ cup (120 mL) freshly grated Parmesan cheese

Pull the top shells from the crabs and remove the gills and the soft matter in the middle. Cut the crabs in half and crack the legs.

Combine the fennel, parsley, basil, garlic, cayenne, paprika, salt, pepper and olive oil. Place the crab in a shallow baking dish that holds them comfortably in a single layer. Pour the herb mixture over the crab and toss to coat them well. Cover and refrigerate for 2 hours.

Preheat the oven to 400°F (200°C). Sprinkle the crab with the Parmesan cheese and roast on the top rack of the oven until golden brown, about 10 minutes. Serve immediately.

You can make this with salmon **or any firm-fleshed fish.**

Halibut and Bacon Skewers with Honeyed Mayonnaise   serves 4

juice of 1 lemon

¼ cup (60 mL) olive oil

2 small onions

¼ lb. (113 g) small mushrooms

1½ lbs. (680 g) halibut fillets, cut into
    1½-inch (3.75-cm) cubes

¼ lb. (113 g) sliced bacon

8 cherry tomatoes

sea salt and freshly ground black pepper

2 tsp. (10 mL) honey

1 egg yolk

1 Tbsp. (15 mL) Dijon mustard

1 Tbsp. (15 mL) lemon juice

½ cup (120 mL) extra virgin olive oil

sea salt and freshly ground black pepper

Combine the lemon juice and olive oil. Cut the onions into wedges and place them in a bowl with the mushrooms. Toss with half the lemon mixture and season to taste. Add the remaining lemon mixture to the halibut and season to taste. Cut the bacon in half crosswise and roll up loosely.

For the sauce, combine the honey, egg yolk, mustard and lemon juice until smooth. Season to taste. Slowly beat in the oil to form an emulsion. You can do this by hand or with a hand blender, blender or food processor.

Close to serving time, thread the fish, onions and mushrooms onto skewers, adding the bacon rolls and tomatoes here and there. Grill for 10 minutes or so over medium-high heat until the halibut flakes. Serve with the sauce.

You can use asparagus **instead of beans for this handsome hot-weather dish. The halibut may be grilled if you don't want to turn on the oven. The warm salad is delicious with salmon and cod as well.**

Halibut with Warm Bean and Tomato Salad   serves 4

½ lb. (227 g) green beans, trimmed

½ lb. (227 g) yellow beans, trimmed

1 Tbsp. (15 mL) olive oil

4 6-oz. (170-g) halibut fillets

sea salt and freshly ground black pepper

4 tsp. (20 mL) balsamic vinegar

1½ tsp. (7.5 mL) sugar

½ cup (120 mL) red onion, thinly sliced

3 ripe plum tomatoes, cut into ½-inch (1.2-cm) cubes

3 Tbsp. (45 mL) fresh basil, coarsely chopped

salt and pepper to taste

Bring a large pot of water to a boil and salt liberally. Add the beans and cook until they are tender-crisp, 3–5 minutes. Drain and cool under cold water. Pat dry.

Preheat the oven to 400°F (200°C). In a heavy, ovenproof frying pan, heat the olive oil over high heat. Season the halibut fillets with salt and pepper and cook in the hot oil for about 3 minutes, until the bottom is browned. Place the pan in the oven and cook the fish until just opaque, about 8 minutes. Place the fish on a heated plate. Cover and keep warm.

Add the beans to the frying pan and sauté over medium heat until the beans are heated through. Add the balsamic vinegar and sugar and stir to combine. Stir in the onion, tomatoes and basil. Season with salt and pepper. Spoon the bean and tomato mixture around the halibut fillets and serve immediately.

You can use the chutney **on top of cod, salmon or boneless, skinless chicken breasts.**

Halibut with Coconut Cilantro Chutney   *serves 6*

1 cup (240 mL) shredded dried unsweetened coconut

½ cup (120 mL) cilantro leaves, packed

4 Tbsp. (60 mL) water

1 hot chili, chopped

1 ½-inch (1.2-cm) slice ginger, peeled and smashed

1 clove garlic, chopped

6 Tbsp. (90 mL) yogurt

1 Tbsp. (15 mL) lemon juice

sea salt to taste

6 6-oz. (170-g) halibut fillets, about 1 inch (2.5 cm) thick

Preheat the oven to 400°F (200°C).

In a food processor, blend the coconut, cilantro, water, chili, ginger and garlic to a paste. Add the yogurt, lemon juice and salt. Pulse to combine and transfer to a bowl.

Lay the halibut on a baking pan and coat the top of the fillets with the chutney. Bake for 8–12 minutes, depending on the thickness, until the halibut is just opaque in the center.

You can use finely chopped, sweet mango chutney **in place of the apple butter.**

Halibut with Curried Apple Butter   serves 4

¼ cup (60 mL) apple butter

¼ cup (60 mL) mayonnaise

1 Tbsp. (15 mL) minced green onion

½ tsp. (2.5 mL) good quality curry powder

sea salt and freshly ground black pepper

4 6-oz. (170-g) halibut fillets

Preheat oven to 400°F (200°C). In small bowl, combine the apple butter, mayonnaise, onion and curry powder. Season to taste and mix until well blended. Line a baking sheet with aluminum foil. Smooth the apple butter mixture on the tops of the halibut. Bake for 10–15 minutes until the fish just flakes when tested with a fork.

A little bit cheeky and a whole lot good. I've contemplated using sour cream and onion flavored chips, but haven't got around to it yet. One of the best things about this (besides eating it) is squishing the bag of potato chips to turn them into crumbs. This is one of the most requested recipes at the Fish House in Stanley Park.

Halibut and "Chips"   serves 6

1/2 cup (120 mL) prepared mayonnaise

1 Tbsp. (15 mL) Dijon mustard

1/4 tsp. (1.25 mL) garlic powder

1 1/4 tsp. (6.25 mL) lemon juice

1 3 1/2-oz. (100-g) bag plain potato chips

1 cup (240 mL) panko (Japanese-style breadcrumbs)

6 6-oz. (170-g) halibut fillets

Preheat the oven to 350°F (175°C).

Combine the mayonnaise, mustard, garlic powder and lemon juice in a shallow bowl. Mix well.

Coarsely crush the potato chips by squashing them in the bag. Add the panko and shake well. Spread out onto a plate. Dip the halibut fillets into the mayonnaise mixture, coating them on all sides. Dip all sides into the potato chip mixture, patting gently to help the coating adhere. Place in a single layer on a baking sheet and bake for 15–20 minutes, until the halibut is cooked through and the crust is golden brown. Serve with lemon wedges, cocktail sauce or malt vinegar.

This is an interpretation of a dish we used to eat in a small Middle Eastern café that also made excellent falafels. They used sole, and cod or snapper would be a good choice too. Serve with pita bread and Chopped Summer Salad with Mint and Parmesan Dressing, page 56, or Lebanese Bread Salad, page 63. This is great for a buffet.

Baked Halibut with Lemon, Tahini and Pine Nuts   serves 6

2 lbs. (900 g) halibut fillets

1/2 tsp. (2.5 mL) sea salt

1/2 tsp. (2.5 mL) pepper

pinch of cayenne

2 Tbsp. (30 mL) lemon juice

3 Tbsp. (45 mL) olive oil

2 onions, thinly sliced into half-moons

1/2 cup (120 mL) tahini

2 cloves garlic, crushed to a paste with
    1/2 tsp. (2.5 mL) salt

1/2 cup (120 mL) lemon juice

1/2 cup (120 mL) cold water

2 Tbsp. (30 mL) pine nuts

1 Tbsp. (15 mL) fresh parsley, coarsely
    chopped

Cut the fish into 2-inch (5-cm) chunks and toss with the salt, pepper, cayenne and 2 Tbsp. (30 mL) lemon juice. Cover and refrigerate for 1 hour.

In a large, preferably nonstick frying pan, heat the olive oil over medium-low heat. Add the onion and cook until soft and a deep golden brown, about 15 minutes. Remove from the heat and set aside to drain on paper towels.

Place the tahini in a bowl. Slowly whisk in the garlic paste, lemon juice and water until smooth and creamy. Set aside.

Preheat the oven to 375°F (190°C). Lightly oil a baking dish that will hold the fish in one layer. Place the fish in the dish, cover tightly with aluminum foil and bake for 10 minutes. Remove the foil and bake for 5–10 minutes longer, until the fish is just cooked through.

Spread the tahini sauce over the fish. Sprinkle with the onion, pine nuts and parsley. Serve warm or at room temperature.

Fresh halibut has a limited run, confined to the summer months. To fully savor its wonderful texture and sweet flavor, I like to pair it with sauces that won't interfere with that experience.

Pan-Roasted Halibut with Lentil and Tomato Vinaigrette   serves 6

1 cup (240 mL) small brown lentils

1 small onion studded with a clove

1 1-inch (2.5-cm) piece cinnamon stick

1 2-inch (5-cm) piece carrot, peeled

1 2-inch (5-cm) piece celery

1 medium clove garlic, minced

½ tsp. (2.5 mL) sea salt

2 Tbsp. (30 mL) balsamic vinegar

2 Tbsp. (30 mL) olive oil

2 Tbsp. (30 mL) vegetable oil

pepper to taste

6 5- to 6-oz. (150- to 170-g) skinless halibut fillets

sea salt and freshly ground black pepper

1 Tbsp. (15 mL) vegetable oil

2 medium, ripe tomatoes, seeded and finely diced

1 Tbsp. (15 mL) finely chopped parsley

Wash and drain the lentils, place them in a pot and cover with 4 inches (10 cm) of water. Bring to a boil over high heat, reduce to a simmer and skim off any foam that rises to the top. Add the onion, cinnamon stick, carrot and celery. Simmer until the lentils are tender but not mushy. Drain and discard the vegetables and cinnamon stick.

While waiting for the lentils to cook, mash the garlic to a paste with the salt. Whisk in the balsamic vinegar, then slowly beat in the olive and vegetable oils. Season with pepper. Combine the warm lentils with the vinaigrette and stir well to coat.

Preheat the oven to 350°F (175°C). Sprinkle the halibut fillets with salt and pepper. Heat the 1 Tbsp. (15 mL) oil on medium-high heat in a heavy, ovenproof frying pan. Fry the halibut skin-side up until golden brown. Flip the fillets over and bake in the oven for 10 minutes.

Mix the tomatoes and parsley into the lentils and spoon onto 6 heated plates. Place the halibut on top of the lentils and serve immediately.

Halibut with Pine Nut and Parmesan Crust   serves 4

½ cup (120 mL) pine nuts, coarsely chopped

4 Tbsp. (60 mL) freshly grated Parmesan
  cheese

1 Tbsp. (15 mL) fresh basil, finely chopped

1 clove garlic, minced

1 Tbsp. (15 mL) olive oil

4 6-oz. (170-g) halibut fillets

sea salt

Preheat the oven to 425°F (220°C). Combine the pine nuts, Parmesan cheese, basil, garlic and olive oil. Place the halibut fillets on a baking sheet and season with salt. Pat the pine nut mixture onto the halibut, pressing lightly to make it adhere. Bake in the middle of the oven for 10–15 minutes, until the fish is opaque all the way through.

I know a fish chili seems a little odd, **but it's really tasty and is another cooking class hit.**

White Chili with Halibut serves 6

1 lb. (454 g) navy beans, rinsed and drained

1 Tbsp. (15 mL) olive oil

1 cup (240 mL) diced onions

4 cloves garlic, minced

2 jalapeño peppers, minced

2 tsp. (10 mL) whole cumin seeds

1½ tsp. (7.5 mL) dried oregano

¼ tsp. (1.25 mL) cayenne pepper

5 cups (1200 mL) chicken stock (see page 46)

1 lb. (454 g) boneless, skinless halibut, cut into bite-sized pieces

2 cups (480 mL) grated mild cheese

sea salt and freshly ground black pepper

2 Tbsp. (30 mL) coarsely chopped cilantro

sour cream, optional

salsa, optional

Place the beans in a heavy, large pot. Add enough cold water to cover the beans at least 3 inches, and soak overnight. Drain the beans into a colander. In the same pot, heat the oil over medium heat. Add onions, garlic, peppers, cumin, oregano and cayenne pepper. Add the beans and the chicken stock. Reduce the heat and simmer for two hours, or until the beans are tender. Add the halibut and cook over medium heat until the halibut can be flaked apart with a fork, about 10 minutes. When the fish is done, stir in the cheese until it is melted. Season to taste with salt and pepper. Sprinkle each serving with cilantro and serve with the sour cream and salsa if desired.

This dish was inspired by a customer who asked me if I had ever heard of shrimp with chocolate sauce. The customer had a recipe for it years ago but lost it. I thought of Mexican moles and ancient Spanish dishes that use sweet spices and cocoa in their sauces, did some research and some cooking, and this is what I came up with. A mortar and pestle works best to pound the almonds and garlic to a paste.

Prawns in Cocoa Sauce   serves 3 to 4

3/4 lb. (340 g) large prawns

1 Tbsp.(15 mL) olive oil

1 whole dried chili pepper

1/4 cup (60 mL) finely diced onion

1 cup (240 mL) well-drained, canned plum tomatoes, puréed and sieved to remove their seeds

1/4 cup (60 mL) red wine

1 whole clove

1/2 tsp. (2.5 mL) cocoa

1/4 tsp. (1.25 mL) salt

a large pinch of sugar

a large pinch of cinnamon

10 whole skinless almonds, toasted

1 small clove garlic, peeled

2 tsp. (10 mL) chopped parsley

Peel the prawns, saving the shells. Place the shells in a pot and cover with 1 1/2 cups (360 mL) water. Bring to a boil, and simmer for 20 minutes. Drain the stock, discarding the shells. Reserve 1/2 cup (120 mL) of the liquid.

Heat the olive oil in a large, nonstick frying pan over medium-low heat. Add the chili pepper and fry until it turns dark brown. Add the onion and puréed tomatoes. Cook, stirring frequently, until the tomatoes thicken, about 5 minutes. Discard the chili pepper. Add the red wine, reserved shrimp stock, whole clove, cocoa, salt, sugar and cinnamon. Simmer over low heat for 5 minutes.

With a mortar and pestle, pound the almonds to a paste. Add the garlic clove and pound it to a paste. If you prefer, combine the almonds and garlic in a blender or food processor. Blend until a paste is formed, adding a few spoonfuls of the tomato sauce to help it along. Stir in the chopped parsley.

Add the prawns to the tomato mixture and cook, stirring frequently, until the prawns are cooked through, about 3–4 minutes. Stir in the almond mixture and serve.

Not as impressive as Flaming Prawns!, **page 27,** but every bit as tasty. This can be easily doubled when serving a crowd.

Baked Prawns with Feta Cheese   *serves 4*

2 Tbsp. (30 mL) olive oil

1 tsp. (5 mL) chopped garlic

1 tsp. (5 mL) dried oregano

½ tsp. (2.5 mL) red pepper flakes

1 28-ounce (796-mL) can Italian plum tomatoes with juice, coarsely chopped

sea salt and freshly ground black pepper

1 lb. (454 g) medium peeled and deveined shrimp

4 oz. (113 g) crumbled feta cheese

Preheat oven to 350°F (175°C).

Heat a large skillet over medium-high heat and add olive oil, garlic, oregano and red pepper flakes. Cook briefly, without allowing the garlic to brown. Add the tomatoes, stirring well, and bring to a boil. Cook at a rapid simmer, stirring frequently, until juices are reduced and sauce is slightly thickened, about 5 minutes. Season lightly to taste with salt and black pepper.

Spread half of the sauce in a 9- by 13-inch (23- x 33-cm) baking dish and top with the shrimp. Top with remaining sauce and sprinkle with the crumbled feta. Bake 15–20 minutes, until bubbling hot and shrimp are cooked through.

THE NON-MESSY WAY TO CHOP CANNED PLUM TOMATOES
After opening the can, insert a knife into the can and chop the tomatoes by moving the knife from side to side until the tomatoes are chopped to the size you want. Drain the tomatoes through a sieve if you are not using the juice.

Charring the peppers and tomatoes gives a buttery smooth texture to the final sauce. Leaving the skins on lends a slightly sharp edge that combines beautifully with the sweet prawns. The ultimate resting place for these prawns is on a bed of creamy polenta but pasta, rice or mashed potatoes would make a very agreeable bed as well.

Prawns Smothered in Charred
Sweet Red Pepper and Tomato Sauce   serves 4

1 lb. (454 g) ripe plum tomatoes

2 large sweet red peppers

2 anchovies

1 dried crushed red chili (or to taste)

3 Tbsp. (45 mL) olive oil

½ cup (120 mL) onion, finely chopped

3 cloves garlic, minced

sea salt

1 lb. (454 g) large prawns, peeled

12 fresh basil leaves

Preheat the broiler and adjust the oven rack to approximately 6 inches (15 cm) below the heat source. Place the tomatoes and peppers on a baking sheet and broil them, turning to blacken the skins on all sides. Remove from the broiler and cool.

Keeping the blackened skins on the peppers and tomatoes, cut them in half and remove the seeds. Place in a sieve to drain for ½ hour. Transfer the peppers and tomatoes to a food processor or blender along with the anchovies and chili pepper and purée until smooth. The mixture will be quite thick.

In a medium-sized pot, heat the olive oil over medium heat. Add the onion and garlic and sauté until the onion is translucent. Add the tomato and pepper mixture and simmer over low heat for ½ hour. Taste and season with salt. This mixture may be prepared up to a day in advance.

When you are ready to finish the dish, bring the tomato and pepper sauce to a boil. Add the prawns and stir until they become opaque, 2–3 minutes. Stir in the basil leaves and serve immediately.

I love Romescu sauce! Try it on other fish or with pork or chicken. It also makes a good dip for tortilla chips.

Seared Prawns with Romescu Sauce   serves 4

4 Tbsp. (60 mL) olive oil

½ cup (120 mL) finely chopped onion

4 cloves garlic, minced

1 roasted red pepper, chopped

2 ripe tomatoes, peeled, seeded and chopped

½ tsp. (2.5 mL) dried chili flakes

5 Tbsp. (75 mL) fish stock or clam nectar

2 Tbsp. (30 mL) white wine

10 toasted almonds

1 Tbsp. (15 mL) red wine vinegar

sea salt and freshly ground black pepper

24 large prawns, peeled and deveined

3 Tbsp. (45 mL) extra virgin olive oil

lemon wedges, to serve

Heat 2 Tbsp. (30 mL) of the oil in a medium-sized pot, add the onion and 3 of the garlic cloves and cook until the onion is soft. Add the pepper, tomatoes, chili, fish stock or clam nectar and wine, then cover and simmer for 30 minutes, until thickened.

Transfer to a blender or food processor and grind coarsely. Add the remaining 2 Tbsp. (30 mL) of oil, almonds, vinegar and the last garlic clove and process until evenly combined. Add the tomato and pimiento sauce and process until smooth. Season to taste.

Heat a heavy pan over high heat. Toss the prawns in the 3 Tbsp. (45 mL) olive oil, then spread out in the pan. Sear for about 2–3 minutes on each side, until pink and cooked through. Arrange on a serving platter with the lemon wedges, and the sauce in a small bowl.

Thai basil was one of the first flavors I was introduced to over 25 years ago by Vanipha Southalack at the Rivoli restaurant in Toronto.

Stir-Fried Prawns with Thai Basil   serves 4

3 Tbsp. (45 mL) vegetable oil

3 cloves garlic, minced

24 large prawns, peeled and deveined

6 oz. (170 g) button mushrooms, quartered

3 red Thai chilis, thinly sliced

1 Tbsp. (15 mL) soy sauce

1 Tbsp. (15 mL) ketjap manis (sweet soy sauce)

1 Tbsp. (15 mL) oyster sauce

1 Tbsp. (15 mL) fish sauce

¼ cup (120 mL) Thai basil leaves, packed

1–2 Tbsp. (15–30 mL) chicken stock (see page 46) or water

thickly sliced cucumber and chopped green onion, to garnish

Heat a wok or a large frying pan over high heat until hot. Add the oil and garlic and fry for a few seconds until pale gold.

Add the prawns and stir-fry until they have turned pink. Add the mushrooms and chilies and stir-fry until the mushrooms slightly soften.

Add the soy sauce, ketjap manis, oyster sauce and fish sauce and stir.

Add the basil and the stock and toss for a few seconds until the basil wilts. Transfer to a plate and garnish with the green onion and cucumber.

When I first tasted sablefish, I became an instant convert. Also known as Alaska cod and black cod, it is a richly textured fish with a suave, buttery flavor. It reminded me so much of veal that my friend Steven suggested serving it with the traditional sauce and garnish for osso buco. It worked perfectly! Serve with Saffron Risotto, page 97.

Sablefish Osso Buco   serves 6

4 Tbsp. (60 mL) unsalted butter

1 cup (240 mL) finely chopped onion

2/3 cup (160 mL) finely chopped carrot

2/3 cup (160 mL) finely chopped celery

1 Tbsp. (15 mL) finely chopped parsley

2 medium cloves garlic, minced

2 strips lemon peel, peeled from a lemon with a vegetable peeler

2 bay leaves

1½ cups (360 mL) canned tomatoes, with juice, puréed and sieved to remove the seeds

1 cup (240 mL) white wine

3 cups (720 mL) beef or chicken stock (see page 46)

sea salt and freshly ground black pepper

2 Tbsp. (30 mL) finely chopped parsley

2 tsp. (10 mL) lemon peel, grated

½ tsp. (2.5 mL) garlic, minced

6 sablefish steaks, 1½ inches (4 cm) thick

salt and pepper to taste

2 Tbsp. (30 mL) vegetable oil

½ cup (120 mL) all-purpose flour

To make the sauce, melt the butter over medium heat in a large saucepan. Add the onion, carrot, celery and parsley and sauté until the vegetables are soft but not browned, 8–10 minutes.

Add the garlic, lemon peel, bay leaves, tomatoes, wine and stock. Bring to a boil, then reduce to a simmer. Cook for approximately 1½ hours, stirring occasionally until reduced by two-thirds and thickened. Season with salt and pepper and remove from the heat. (The sauce may be prepared up to 2 days in advance. When cool, cover and refrigerate.)

When you are ready to finish the dish, combine the parsley, lemon peel and garlic in a small bowl and set aside.

Preheat the oven to 350°F (175°C). Salt and pepper the fish. Heat the vegetable oil in a large, heavy frying pan over medium heat. Dip the fish into the flour and shake off the excess. Fry until golden brown on both sides.

Remove from the pan and place in a single layer in a baking dish. Heat the sauce to a boil and pour over the sablefish. Bake for 15 minutes. Sprinkle the parsley, garlic and lemon garnish over the fish and serve immediately.

I love Sablefish. It's one of the most versatile fish to work with and one of the most delicious to eat. Some of it is smoked for consumption here, but the shame is that most of it is exported. I buy it in stores that cater to the Southeast Asian population. The corned beef-style marinade suits the richness and texture of the fish perfectly. Instead of the slaw, try sauerkraut or a fluffy pile of potatoes mashed with horseradish.

"Corned" Sablefish with Warm Red Cabbage and Pear Slaw   serves 4

1½ tsp. (7.5 mL) whole black peppercorns

1½ tsp. (7.5 mL) coriander seeds

1½ tsp. (7.5 mL) yellow mustard seeds

5 whole cloves

3 bay leaves

large pinch cinnamon

2 tsp. (10 mL) paprika

1 Tbsp. (15 mL) Worcestershire sauce

1 tsp. (5 mL) liquid smoke

5 medium cloves garlic, peeled and coarsely chopped

½ stalk celery, chopped

2 tsp. (10 mL) sea salt

1 tsp. (5 mL) sugar

4 8-oz. (225-g) skinless sablefish fillets

1 lb. (454 g) red cabbage, cored and thinly sliced

3 Tbsp. (45 mL) balsamic vinegar

½ tsp. (2.5 mL) sea salt

1 tsp. (5 mL) sugar

1 Tbsp. (15 mL) vegetable oil

2 cloves garlic, minced

½ tsp. (2.5 mL) caraway seeds

¼ cup (60 mL) finely diced shallots

1 firm ripe pear, cored and diced into ¼-inch (.6-cm) cubes

freshly ground black pepper to taste

Coarsely crush the peppercorns, coriander and mustard seeds, cloves and bay leaves in a coffee grinder or mortar and pestle. Place in the workbowl of a food processor or blender with the cinnamon, paprika, Worcestershire sauce, liquid smoke, garlic, celery, salt and sugar. Process to a coarse paste. Coat the fish evenly with the mixture. Cover and refrigerate overnight.

Combine the red cabbage, vinegar, salt and sugar. Mix well and let stand while you prepare the rest of the ingredients. Bring a large pot of water to a boil. Add the marinated cod and turn down to a bare simmer. Cook for 10–15 minutes until the cod flakes easily. It will remain moist-looking on the inside.

While the fish is cooking, heat the vegetable oil in a large frying pan over medium heat. Add the garlic and caraway seeds. Sauté until the garlic starts to turn pale gold. Add the shallots and cook until they start to turn brown. Add the cabbage mixture and cook, stirring frequently, until the cabbage is crisp-tender. Add the pear and cook until heated through. Season with pepper. Place the slaw on heated plates. Remove the fish from the liquid with a slotted spoon and serve on top of the slaw.

*Sablefish pairs wonderfully with bright, intense flavors **like Moroccan charmoula. The recipe makes more charmoula than you need but it keeps well in the fridge and is an excellent marinade for chicken.***

Sablefish with Charmoula, Peppers and Preserved Lemon   serves 6

1½ tsp. (7.5 mL) paprika

¼ tsp. (1.25 mL) cayenne pepper

1 tsp. (5 mL) ground cumin

½ tsp. (2.5 mL) cinnamon

3 cloves of garlic, crushed

¼ cup (60 mL) lemon juice

¼ cup (60 mL) chopped parsley

¼ cup (60 mL) chopped cilantro

½ cup (120 mL) extra virgin olive oil

sea salt and freshly ground black pepper

6 6-oz. (170-g) sablefish fillets or steaks

Pepper Relish with Preserved Lemon

6 red peppers, roasted, seeded and peeled

1 clove garlic, minced

4 Tbsp. (60 mL) extra virgin olive oil

¾ tsp. (3.75 mL) ground cumin

¼ tsp. (1.25 mL) paprika

¼ tsp. (1.25 mL) freshly ground black pepper

1 Moroccan preserved lemon, pulp removed and diced

sea salt

½ cup (120 mL) coarsely chopped parsley

In a food processor or blender, combine the paprika, cayenne, cumin, cinnamon, garlic, lemon juice, parsley, cilantro and olive oil. Pulse to form a coarse paste. Toss ½ cup (120 mL) of the mixture with the fish and let sit for ½ hour.

Preheat the oven to 400°F (200°C). Lay the sablefish out on a baking sheet and bake for 12–15 minutes, until just opaque in the middle. Turn the broiler on to high and lightly brown the top. Serve with the Pepper Relish with Preserved Lemon.

Pepper Relish with Preserved Lemon

You can find preserved lemons at Middle Eastern grocery stores or gourmet food shops. If you're feeling ambitious, you can make your own!

Coarsely chop the peppers. Mix with the garlic, oil, cumin, paprika, pepper and preserved lemon. Season to taste and toss in the parsley. This can be made a day in advance. Cover and refrigerate.

An extremely flavorful and sumptuous meal **in a bowl. One of my favorites.**

Sablefish with Clams and Chorizo Sausage   serves 4

4 1-inch (2.5-cm) slices good, sturdy bread

1 clove garlic, peeled

olive oil

½ lb. (227 g) chorizo sausage, Spanish or
smoked Portuguese-style

1 cup (240 mL) white wine

1 cup (240 mL) drained, canned plum
tomatoes, seeded and finely chopped

1 lb. (454 g) fresh Manila clams

4 4-oz. (113-g) fillets sablefish

olive oil

sea salt and freshly ground black pepper

½ cup (120 mL) orzo, cooked until tender

¼ lb. (113 g) spinach, stems removed

Preheat the oven to 400°F (200°C). Grill or toast the bread
on both sides. Rub the bread on one side with the garlic
clove and drizzle with olive oil. Place one slice in each
of four deep pasta bowls.

Peel the skin from the chorizo sausage and tear it into
½-inch (1.2-cm) pieces. Place in a pot large enough to
hold the clams comfortably. Add the wine and bring to a
boil. Add the tomatoes and clams. Cover with a lid and
steam until the clams just open. Remove from the heat.

Place the fish on an oiled baking sheet. Brush with olive
oil and season with salt and pepper. Bake for 12 minutes,
or until the fish is just done. Remove from the oven and
cover loosely with aluminum foil to keep warm.

Add the orzo and spinach leaves to the clam mixture.
Cover and bring to a boil. Stir once or twice and remove
from the heat. Place the fish on the toasted bread.
Spoon the clam mixture around the fish and serve.

Sablefish has been one of my favorite fish since moving to the West Coast. I was so impressed with it that I couldn't believe it was not widely eaten except in the Asian community. Happily, that is slowly changing. I have come up with many different preparations for it, from an osso buco to curing it like corned beef. This particular preparation is Japanese influenced and the Waldorf salad provides the perfect foil to the rich and succulent texture of the sablefish.

Miso Sablefish with Waldorf Salad serves 4

1/3 cup (80 mL) white miso

1/4 cup (60 mL) sugar

2 Tbsp. (30 mL) sake

3 Tbsp. (45 mL) mirin

4 6-oz. (170-g) sablefish fillets, skin on

2 egg yolks

2 tsp. (10 mL) lemon juice

1/4 tsp. (1.25 mL) salt

1 tsp. (5 mL) Japanese prepared mustard

1/2 cup (120 mL) vegetable oil

3 Tbsp. (45 mL) white miso

1 tsp. (5 mL) grated lemon peel

sea salt

2 cups (480 mL) Fuji, or other flavorful apple, cored and cut into 1/4-inch (.6-cm) dice

1/4 cup (60 mL) celery hearts, cut into 1/4-inch (.6-cm) dice

1/2 cup (120 mL) daikon radish, peeled and cut into 1/4-inch (.6-cm) dice

2 green onions, thinly sliced

2 Tbsp. (30 mL) pine nuts, toasted

2 tsp. (10 mL) black sesame seeds, toasted

In the top of a double boiler combine the miso, sugar, sake and mirin. Cook for 1/2 hour, stirring frequently. Remove from the heat and let cool. Coat the sablefish with the miso mixture. Cover and refrigerate overnight or up to three days.

In a food processor, combine the egg yolks, lemon juice, salt and mustard. With the motor running, pour in the oil in a slow steady stream. When the mayonnaise has emulsified, add the miso and lemon peel. Pulse to combine and season to taste. Cover and refrigerate until needed.

When you are ready to serve the cod, combine the apple, celery, daikon, green onion, pine nuts and sesame seeds. Add the mayonnaise. Mix well and refrigerate.

Position the oven rack approximately 8 inches (20 cm) under the broiler. Preheat the broiler on high. Place the cod skin-side up on a baking tray and broil until browned and crisp around the edges, about 5 minutes. Turn over and broil 5 minutes longer. Serve immediately with the Waldorf salad on the side.

If I had to choose my favorite fish dish, **I would be torn between this and Sablefish Osso Buco, page 124. This is simple, elegant and outrageously delicious. Serve with Horseradish Mashed Potatoes, page 214.**

Pan-Seared Skate with Beef Stock   serves 4

4 6-oz. (170-g) pieces of skate

sea salt and freshly ground black pepper

½ cup (120 mL) all-purpose flour

½ tsp. (2.5 mL) paprika

2 Tbsp. (30 mL) vegetable oil

4 cups (1 L) beef stock

Preheat the oven to 400°F (200°C). Wash the skate and pat dry. Season with salt and pepper. Mix the flour and paprika together on a plate.

Heat the oil over medium heat in a large heavy skillet. Dip both sides of the skate into the flour and shake off the excess. Fry on both sides until golden brown. Transfer to a baking dish and bake for 15 minutes until the flesh turns opaque in the middle.

While the skate is baking, pour off all the oil from the frying pan. Add the beef stock and bring to a boil, scraping up any bits clinging to the frying pan. Reduce the beef stock by half. Season with salt and pepper. Remove from the heat and keep warm.

Place the skate on heated plates. Pour the beef stock over it and serve immediately.

The burnt orange and wasabi glaze **is a charming companion to halibut, prawns and salmon as well.**

Pan-Seared Skate with Burnt Orange and Wasabi Glaze   serves 6

6 5- to 6-oz. (150- to 170-g) pieces of skate

sea salt and freshly ground black pepper

1 Tbsp. (15 mL) vegetable oil

Burnt Orange and Wasabi Glaze

3/4 cup (180 mL) granulated sugar

1/4 cup (60 mL) water

1/2 cup (120 mL) red wine

1/4 tsp. (1.25 mL) sea salt

1 orange, juice and grated rind

1 Tbsp. (15 mL) prepared wasabi, or to taste

2–4 Tbsp. (30–60 mL) unsalted butter

2 green onions, julienned

Preheat the oven to 350°F (175°C). Season the skate with salt and pepper. Heat the oil in a heavy frying pan or two over medium-high heat and cook the skate until it is lightly browned on both sides. Bake in the oven for 10–12 minutes, until opaque throughout. Place on heated plates or a platter. Spoon the sauce over the skate and serve immediately.

Burnt Orange and Wasabi Glaze

To make the glaze, combine the sugar and water in a small, heavy saucepan. Cook over high heat without stirring until the sugar turns a dark mahogany brown. Watch the caramel carefully. You will see the bubbles rise more rapidly and become looser and less viscous.

Remove from the heat, stand back and immediately pour the red wine through a sieve that covers the pot completely. The caramel will splutter furiously. The sieve will protect you from burns.

When the spluttering stops, transfer the caramel to a bowl and add the salt. Cool completely and add the orange juice and rind. (The glaze may be made to this point up to 1 week in advance.) Cover and refrigerate.

Just before serving, bring the glaze to a boil. Whisk in the wasabi. Remove from the heat and whisk in the butter, 1 Tbsp. (15 mL) at a time. Add the green onions.

It's a delicious thing **that local salmon and asparagus share the same season.**

Salmon with Asparagus Sauce   serves 6

1½ lbs. (680 g) medium asparagus spears

2 Tbsp. (30 mL) unsalted butter

1½ cups (360 mL) whipping cream

sea salt and freshly ground black pepper

6 6-oz. (170-g) salmon fillets

2 Tbsp. (30 mL) dry white wine

2 Tbsp. (30 mL) minced chives

Wash the asparagus and snap off the tough, woody ends. Cut off the tips and place in a sieve. Chop the stalks coarsely.

In a large pot of rapidly boiling salted water, dunk the sieve with the asparagus tips. Cook to bright green then remove and cool under cold water. Drain well. Add the stalks to the pot of water and cook until tender. Drain the asparagus thoroughly and, while still hot, run it through a food processor with unsalted butter for 3–4 minutes until smooth, scraping down the sides of the processor frequently. Strain through a sieve, discarding the solids.

In a large pot, bring the cream to a boil. Reduce to a simmer and cook until reduced by almost half. Stir in the asparagus purée and season to taste. Remove from the heat.

Preheat the oven to 350°F (175°C). Season the salmon to taste. Place in a baking pan, sprinkle with the wine and bake until done to your liking, 10–15 minutes.

Gently re-warm the sauce and add the pan juice from the salmon along with the asparagus tips and chives. If the sauce is too thick, add a little water. Serve with the sauce spooned around the salmon.

This is very easy **and always a show-stopper.**

Salmon Baked in Corn Husks with Corn and Zucchini Sauté   serves 4

4 whole ears of corn

4 5- to 6-oz. (150- to 170-g) skinless salmon
   fillets

sea salt and freshly ground black pepper

4 Tbsp. (60 mL) unsalted butter

1 cup (240 mL) diced red onions

1 cup (240 mL) diced zucchini

Carefully peel back the corn husks and snap the cob at the bottom, leaving the husks attached to the stem. Discard the silk and any blemished leaves. Set the husks aside.

Cut 2 cups (480 mL) of kernels from the corn and set aside.

Preheat the oven to 350°F (175°C). Lightly salt and pepper the salmon fillets. Separate the leaves of each corn husk and tuck a salmon fillet into the middle, enclosing it within the husk. Don't try to make it look neat. Tear 4 strips from the discarded leaves and use them to tie the opened end of the husk. Place on a baking sheet and bake for 20 minutes.

While the salmon is baking, melt the butter in a saucepan over medium heat and sauté the red onions until they are translucent. Sauté the zucchini until it just begins to soften. Add the corn and continue to cook until it is heated through.

Place the salmon on heated plates or a platter. Fold back the top of the corn husks and tuck them under the stem. Spoon the corn sauté over the salmon. Serve immediately to a chorus of "oohs" and "aahs." Take a bow.

Simpler, but not quite as authentic as the Miso Sablefish with Waldorf Salad, page 128.

Broiled Salmon with Orange-Miso Glaze   *serves 6*

⅓ cup (80 mL) white miso

2 Tbsp. (30 mL) orange juice

1 Tbsp. (15 mL) mirin

2 tsp. (10 mL) soy sauce

1 tsp. (5 mL) sugar

1 Tbsp. (15 mL) finely grated orange peel

6 6-ounce (170-g) salmon fillets

finely chopped green onions

Whisk the miso, orange juice, mirin, soy sauce, sugar and orange peel together in a small bowl.

Preheat the broiler. Line a baking sheet with aluminum foil. Place the salmon on the foil, skin-side up. Broil about 8 inches (20 cm) from the heat until the skin is brown and crisp. Turn and spread the miso mixture over top. Broil until the glaze begins to blister and brown, about 3 minutes. Cover the fish loosely with foil, turn the oven off and let it sit for 5 minutes. Sprinkle with the onion before serving.

This dish has an out-of-fashion feel to it and, like many out-of-fashion foods, is extremely delicious. Perhaps in 10 years, we will all be feeling a little less than nouveau, remembering the gallons of sun-dried tomatoes and balsamic vinegar that we used indiscriminately. Enjoy with the timeless combination of tiny new potatoes and peas.

Baked Salmon Steaks with Parsley, Vermouth and Cream   serves 4

4 6-oz. (170-g) salmon steaks, 1 inch (2.5 cm) thick

sea salt and freshly ground black pepper

1 cup (240 mL) dry white vermouth

1/4 cup (60 mL) bottled or canned clam nectar

2 Tbsp. (30 mL) shallots, minced

1 clove garlic, minced

1 cup (240 mL) whipping cream

1/4 cup (60 mL) fresh parsley leaves

sea salt and freshly ground black pepper

1 Tbsp. (15 mL) chives or the green tops of green onion, minced

Preheat the oven to 350°F (175°C).

Place the salmon in a baking dish, without overlapping the steaks, and sprinkle with salt and pepper. Place in the oven and bake for 10–15 minutes, until the salmon is just opaque in the middle. Cover and keep warm.

While you are baking the salmon, make the sauce. In a small heavy saucepan, combine the vermouth, clam nectar, shallots and garlic. Bring to a boil and cook until the mixture is reduced to 3/4 cup (180 mL). Add the whipping cream and boil until the mixture is reduced to 1 1/2 cups (360 mL). Place half the mixture in a blender or food processor, add the parsley and purée. Stir into the remaining mixture, then press through a sieve. Return to the pot and boil until the mixture coats a spoon, 2–3 minutes. Season with salt and pepper. Add the pan juices from the salmon along with the chives or green onion.

Place the salmon on heated plates or a platter, pour the sauce around the steaks and serve immediately.

Pomegranate molasses is a rich, sweet and sour syrup **that can be found in Middle Eastern stores and gourmet food shops. It's also good in salad dressings and with lamb.**

Salmon with Pomegranate Glaze and Tahini Salad   serves 4

⅓ cup (80 mL) pomegranate molasses, plus more for garnish

1 clove garlic, minced

1 small red onion, thinly sliced

2 Tbsp. (30 mL) chopped mint leaves

2 tsp. (10 mL) roasted and crushed coriander seeds

1 Tbsp. (15 mL) grated orange zest

4 6-oz. (170-g) salmon fillets

sea salt and freshly ground black pepper

olive oil

pomegranate seeds, optional

Tahini Salad
makes approximately 2 cups (480 mL)

2 garlic cloves, minced

sea salt

¾ cup (180 mL) tahini

1 Tbsp. (15 mL) white vinegar

2 Tbsp. (30 mL) lemon juice

½ tsp. (2.5 mL) ground cumin

½ cup (120 mL) water

½ cup (120 mL) chopped parsley

1 small tomato, seeded and diced

½ cup (120 mL) seeded, diced English cucumber

In a bowl large enough to hold the fish fillets, combine the pomegranate molasses, garlic, onion, mint leaves, coriander and orange zest. Let marinate for 1/2 hour, refrigerated.

Preheat the broiler to high and place the salmon on a foil-lined baking pan. Season salmon with salt and pepper and brush generously with olive oil. Broil for 3–5 minutes. Turn over and cook an additional 5 minutes, or until done. The marinade has sugar in it so it may burn easily. If the fish is browning too quickly, cover loosely with a piece of tin foil.

Drizzle with pomegranate molasses and sprinkle with pomegranate seeds if desired. Serve immediately with the Tahini Salad.

Tahini Salad
Crush garlic to a paste with 1/2 tsp. (2.5 mL) salt. Place tahini in a food processor or blender. With the motor running, slowly add the vinegar, lemon juice, cumin and water. The consistency should be just a little thinner than sour cream. You may need to use more water, depending on your brand of tahini. Pulse in the garlic. Taste and adjust with salt and a little more lemon juice if needed. Transfer to a bowl and stir in the parsley, tomato and cucumber.

The green of the pistachios and herbs looks beautiful on top of the salmon.

Salmon with Pistachio, Basil and Mint Butter serves 6

¼ cup (60 mL) shelled pistachios

¼ cup (60 mL) fresh basil leaves, packed

¼ cup (60 mL) fresh mint leaves, packed

1 clove garlic, minced

½ cup (120 mL) unsalted butter, room temperature

1 Tbsp. (15 mL) lemon juice

6 6-oz. (170-g) salmon fillets

sea salt and freshly ground black pepper

½ cup (120 mL) dry white wine

Pulse pistachios, basil, mint and garlic in a food processor until coarsely chopped. Add the butter and lemon juice and season to taste. Pulse until everything is smoothly mixed. Transfer to a small bowl and refrigerate until cold. The butter can be prepared up to 4 days in advance.

Preheat oven to 400°F (200°C). Butter a 9- by 13-inch (23- x 33-cm) baking dish and lay out the salmon fillets in single layer. Pour the wine over the salmon and season to taste. Bake salmon until almost opaque on top, about 10 minutes. Place 2 Tbsp. (30 mL) of the butter on top of each salmon piece. Continue baking until the salmon is just opaque in the center, about 5 minutes. Transfer to plates and pour the baking juices from the pan over top.

This is fantastic on tuna too. **Don't be afraid of the wasabi. Gentle heating calms its bite.**

Salmon with Soy Wasabi Glaze   serves 6

6 Tbsp. (90 mL) cold unsalted butter

2 Tbsp. (30 mL) fresh lemon juice

3 Tbsp. (45 mL) soy sauce

2 Tbsp. (30 mL) prepared wasabi paste

4 6-oz. (170-g) salmon fillets

vegetable oil

sea salt and freshly ground black pepper

3 green onions, thinly sliced

Combine the butter, lemon juice, soy sauce and wasabi in a small pot.

Preheat the oven to 350°F (175°C). Lightly oil the salmon and season to taste. Place in a baking dish and bake for 10–12 minutes.

While the salmon is cooking, heat the butter mixture over low heat, stirring constantly until smooth and emulsified. Stir in the onions.

Serve the salmon immediately, drenched with the sauce.

When an idea strikes, it is usually a combination of flavors or ingredients. In this case, I had the title "King Salmon Bake" spinning around in my head before I knew what it was. What it turned out to be was a cozy combination of salmon, cheesy spinach and potatoes that became one of the best sellers in the history of the Fish House in Stanley Park. King salmon is the U.S. name for spring salmon.

Salmon Bake with Sour Cream, Bacon and New Red Potatoes   serves 4

1 lb. (454 g) small red potatoes

1 lb. (454 g) spinach, stems removed, washed and drained

1 Tbsp. (15 mL) unsalted butter, melted

1 cup (240 mL) shredded, extra-old white Cheddar cheese or Asiago

1 clove garlic, minced

½ tsp. (2.5 mL) sea salt

sea salt and freshly ground black pepper to taste

1 Tbsp. (15 mL) unsalted butter

4 6-oz. (170-g) skinless, boneless salmon fillets

2 tsp. (10 mL) lemon juice

8 slices good-quality bacon

4 Tbsp. (60 mL) sour cream, heaping

1 Tbsp. (15 mL) minced chives

Preheat the oven to 350°F (175°C).

Cook the potatoes in boiling water until just tender, approximately 20–25 minutes. Drain and cool.

Place the spinach in a large pot, turn the heat to high and cover with a lid. Steam until it wilts, turning it over occasionally. Transfer to a large plate and spread out to cool. When cool, squeeze into small balls with your hands to remove the water. Finely chop and place in a bowl. Add the melted butter, cheese, garlic and salt. Mix well. The potatoes and the spinach mixture may be prepared up to a day in advance. Cover and refrigerate.

Slice the potatoes into ¼-inch (.6-cm) slices and arrange in slightly overlapping rows in an 8- by 11.5-inch (20- by 29-cm) baking dish. Season well with salt and pepper and dot with half the 1 Tbsp. (15 mL) butter. Divide the spinach mixture into 4 equal portions, flatten each into an elongated patty and place one in each quarter of the baking dish over the potatoes. Place a salmon fillet over each patty of spinach, sprinkle with the lemon juice, dot with the remaining butter and season with salt and pepper. Cover snugly with foil and bake for 20–30 minutes, until the salmon is cooked through.

While the salmon is cooking, fry the bacon over medium heat until crisp. Drain on paper towels and crumble when cool. When the salmon is done, lift each portion onto heated individual plates or leave in the baking dish. Top each piece of salmon with a dollop of sour cream. Sprinkle the bacon and chives over the sour cream and serve immediately.

This is also good **with any meaty fish such as marlin or tuna.**

Swordfish with Lemon and Oregano Vinaigrette   serves 4

2 Tbsp. (30 mL) dry white wine

2 Tbsp. (30 mL) extra virgin olive oil

1 clove garlic, minced

grated zest of one lemon

1/2 tsp. (2.5 mL) dried oregano

sea salt and freshly ground black pepper

4 6-oz. (170-g) swordfish fillets

1/2 cup (120 mL) extra virgin olive oil

juice of one lemon

1/2 tsp. (2.5 mL) dried oregano

1 Tbsp. (15 mL) chopped parsley

2 Tbsp. (30 mL) minced shallot

1 small tomato, peeled, seeded and finely chopped

sea salt and freshly ground black pepper to taste

Combine the wine, oil, garlic, lemon zest and oregano. Add salt and pepper to taste. Let the fish sit in this mixture for up to 1/2 hour.

For the vinaigrette, combine the olive oil, lemon juice, oregano, parsley, shallot and tomato. Season to taste.

Heat a heavy cast iron or nonstick pan over high heat. Add the swordfish and sear 2–4 minutes on each side. The time will depend on the thickness of the fish, but in the interest of flavor and texture, it's better to keep it a little on the medium-rare side. Remove from the pan and serve with the vinaigrette.

meat

meat

Imagine two budding chefs,

25 years old, living on Kensington Avenue in Toronto, one of the most interesting urban food markets in North America. The year was 1982 and you could buy live squawking chickens, pigeons and quails from cages, stare at small mountains constructed out of cheese, their cut faces bulging from their collective weight, eat spicy Jamaican patties from the Patty King, buy chunks of pork cut from the ribs, well-cooked and meltingly tender under a crisp exterior, from Rebelo's Portuguese take-out counter and laugh at the giant slab of beef liver (we in fact identified the store as "The Slab of Liver Store") always on display on a massive butcher block, placed just far enough in the depths of the store to be frightening, yet close enough to view.

Steven and I were in the throes of newly found love. Steven was going to the University of Toronto at the time, working as a dishwasher on the weekend and living on cottage cheese and sliced ham. I thought I was a bit more sophisticated as far as food was concerned, having cooked in restaurants for five years, and had progressed as far as Ramen noodles. We thought we were truly in the know and would have small feasts of Brie cheese, pâté and French bread to prove it. It was time, though, for something truly special, something unique, to celebrate our union. Lobster and Champagne was it! We would have a lobster feast on the roof of the house where I lived, gazing into the downtown skyscape of Toronto.

How do you buy a lobster and how do you cook it? Neither of us had cooked or eaten a whole lobster, ever, so it was with great fear and excitement that they were bought and cooked, although knowing myself as I do, I probably bluffed my way through it, imagining that I was shining with confidence. The most painstakingly careful hollandaise in the world was prepared and a bunch of asparagus was gingerly steamed. The Champagne was chilled, and cheese, bread and strawberries laid out. We rushed our dinner up three floors to the roof where pillows, blankets and an electric lamp were set. We toasted each other and toasted the city. I don't remember much about eating except for scooping up the hollandaise with bread, and marvelling at its texture and flavor. What I do remember is that it was one of the sweetest, most romantic and awe-filled nights of my life. We decided to sleep on the roof that night, and several hours into sleep were awakened by drops of rain.

This particular evening has all the elements that make for a permanent celebration. There is anticipation, a bit of anxiety and excitement. There are feelings of discovery, contentment and an experience shared. There is, above all, good food, shared with people we want to be with.

There was a certain Vietnamese restaurant in Toronto that I used to frequent at least once a week for my beef brisket fix. This brisket was mildly sweet and sour with a rich texture. After much contemplation, I figured out that the secret ingredient was… ketchup! Those were my more snobbish days and I could not admit that ketchup was the secret. Now, I gleefully don't care! Serve over fresh rice noodles, with bean sprouts, cilantro and green onions and a squeeze of lime, or with rice or French bread. This is a fabulous winter dish.

Vietnamese-Style Beef Brisket   serves 4 to 6

1–1½ lbs. (454–680 g) beef brisket

1 Tbsp. (15 mL) vegetable oil

1 Tbsp. (15 mL) finely chopped garlic

2½-inch (1.2-cm) slices fresh ginger, lightly crushed

2 stalks lemon grass, trimmed, cut into 3-inch (7.5-cm) pieces and lightly crushed

2 star anise

8 cups (2 L) water or beef stock

1 cup (240 mL) ketchup

½ tsp. (2.5 mL) sea salt

2 medium carrots, peeled and cut into 2-inch (5-cm) pieces

2 medium new potatoes, peeled and cut into quarters

1 Tbsp. (15 mL) fish sauce

1 Tbsp. (15 mL) oyster sauce

Cut the brisket into 1-inch (2.5-cm) pieces. Place in a pot, cover with cold water and bring to a boil. Simmer for 5 minutes and drain. Rinse under cold water and pat dry.

Heat the oil in a large pot over medium heat. Brown the beef in batches and remove to a plate. Add the garlic and ginger to the pot and cook, stirring, until the garlic turns a pale gold. Add the beef, lemon grass, star anise, water or stock, ketchup and salt. Bring to a boil, then reduce to a low, low simmer. Cover with a lid and cook for 2½ hours, until tender, adding water only if the liquid falls below the level of the beef. The stew should be slightly thickened by this point. If not, cook over medium heat, uncovered, until it thickens.

Increase the heat to medium. Add the carrots, potatoes, fish sauce and oyster sauce. Cook, uncovered, for half an hour longer, or until the vegetables are tender. Taste and adjust the seasoning with salt and fish sauce. Like all stews, this is better if allowed to sit overnight.

My co-worker Graham raved about a steak salad with cumin aioli. It was served in a restaurant he used to work in and he often made it at home. His ravings got my wheels turning and out came this interpretation. Serve it with a green salad or Chopped Summer Salad with Mint and Parmesan Dressing, page 56. You can use a sirloin steak in place of the flank steak.

Graham's Grilled Flank Steak with Cumin Aioli   serves 4

3 Tbsp. (45 mL) oyster sauce

2 cloves garlic, minced

½ tsp. (2.5 mL) coarsely ground black pepper

1 flank steak, about 2½ lbs. (1.1 kg)

1 Tbsp. (15 mL) cumin seeds

1 large egg

1 tsp. (5 mL) Dijon mustard

½ tsp. (2.5 mL) sea salt

1 clove garlic, minced

½ cup (120 mL) vegetable oil

½ cup (120 mL) olive oil

4 tsp. (20 mL) lemon juice

Mix the oyster sauce, garlic and black pepper together in a small bowl. Spread on both sides of the steak. Cover and refrigerate.

Dry-roast the cumin seeds in a small frying pan over medium heat until they darken a shade. Remove from the heat. Finely grind half of the cumin seeds in a spice or coffee grinder. In a blender or food processor, combine the egg, mustard, salt, garlic and the finely ground cumin seeds. With the motor on, add half of the oils in a slow steady stream. Add the lemon juice and continue adding the rest of the oil until the aioli is emulsified. If it seems too thick, add a spoonful or two of water. Scrape the aioli into a bowl and stir in the whole cumin seeds.

Preheat the barbecue or broiler to high. Grill or broil the steak 3–4 minutes on each side for medium-rare. Remove the steak from the heat and let it rest for a few minutes. Slice very thinly across the grain and serve with the cumin aioli on the side.

NOTE
If using raw egg makes you uncomfortable, substitute 1 cup (240 mL) prepared mayonnaise for the egg, salt, oil and lemon juice. Stir the ground and whole cumin seeds, mustard and garlic into the mayonnaise.

The Ultimate in Surf and Turf

I have always thought of surf and turf as an odd and frivolous combination of flavors and textures. The seafood never seems to stand up well to the beef. Other combinations that equally baffle me are ribs and spaghetti, steak and lasagna, chicken and tortellini, and so on. But it usually happens that whenever I make fun of something, I end up becoming so intrigued by it that I have to start cooking it—so with this combination, it was the double whammy of surf and turf and steak and spaghetti. In this case, the heady clam pasta can really hold its own against the steak.

I like ribeye steaks to be at least 12 ounces (340 g) each. Now, you can split it two or three ways if you want, but it has to be thick, thick, thick. I use the same marinade that I use for My Birthday Ribs, page 4, to which I add several spoonfuls of mayonnaise, right out of the jar (now you can laugh at my food preferences). I grill the steaks on high so they get nice and crusty. This is where the mayonnaise helps. The White Clam Linguine, page 94, is made and served alongside the steaks on piping hot plates. Surf and Turf Heaven!

You can make the steak in your usual way, with the cut you prefer, or use my method above.

I am picky about oxtails on one point — they have to be cut through the joint, not sawed into segments. You are probably not as dogmatic as I am about certain things pertaining to food and you should be relieved about that. I use whole oxtails that I buy at a Chinese butcher shop, and a heavy knife. I locate the joints and cut right through them. If you feel adventurous enough to try this, use 2 oxtails for the recipe. If not, buy 5 lbs. (2.25 kg) of cut oxtails. Serve with the Winter Vegetable Casserole, page 208.

Oxtails Braised in Red Wine   serves 6 to 8

¼ cup (60 mL) olive oil

1 cup (240 mL) finely diced onion

½ cup (120 mL) finely diced carrot

½ cup (120 mL) finely diced celery

1 Tbsp. (15 mL) minced garlic

2 Tbsp. (30 mL) finely chopped parsley

5 lbs. (2.25 kg) oxtails

1 large sprig rosemary or thyme

3 cups (720 mL) dry red wine

2 cups (480 mL) beef or chicken stock (see page 46)

⅔ cup (160 mL) well-drained, seeded and finely chopped canned Italian plum tomatoes

salt and pepper to taste

Preheat the oven to 300°F (150°C).

In a large heavy pot with a tight-fitting lid that will hold the oxtails comfortably, heat the olive oil over medium heat. Add the onion, carrot, celery, garlic and parsley. Sauté until the vegetables are lightly browned. Add the oxtails, rosemary or thyme, red wine, stock and tomatoes. If the liquid does not cover the oxtails, make it up with more stock or water. Bring to a boil and cover tightly. Place in the oven and bake for 4 hours, until the oxtails are very tender but not falling apart. Check occasionally to make sure the liquid has not evaporated. Add water if the level falls below the oxtails.

Transfer the oxtails to a serving dish. Cover and place in the oven to keep warm. Skim the fat from the liquid and boil over high heat until the liquid thickens slightly, 5–8 minutes. Season with salt and pepper and pour over the oxtails. If you are making the dish in advance, transfer the oxtails to a storage container and pour the sauce over them. Cool, cover and refrigerate for up to three days. Gently reheat, adding a bit of water, until heated through.

Chuck roasts are cheap and extremely flavorful cuts of meat. The onion provides almost all the liquid needed to cook the roast, with a little help from some red wine. Ask your butcher to net the roast to make it easier to handle. This serves a crowd and makes great leftovers.

Pot Roast Smothered in Onion   serves 8

2 medium carrots, sliced

2 leeks, white part only, cleaned and sliced
(see page 162)

1 stalk celery, sliced

1/2 medium white onion, sliced

6 allspice berries

1/4 tsp. (1.25 mL) black peppercorns

12 cloves garlic, peeled and cut in half

5 small sprigs rosemary

3 cups (720 mL) dry red wine

1 chuck roast, approximately 8 lbs. (3.5 kg)

4 Tbsp. (60 mL) vegetable oil

6 lbs. (2.7 kg) onion, thinly sliced into half
moons

2 tsp. (10 mL) salt

The day before you are going to serve the pot roast, combine the carrots, leeks, celery, onion, allspice, peppercorns, garlic, rosemary and red wine in a noncorrodible pot. Bring to a boil, turn down the heat and simmer over low heat for 5 minutes. Remove from the heat and cool completely.

Place the chuck roast in a high-sided container that will hold it snugly (I like to use a pot). Pour the red wine mixture over the beef, lifting it to ensure that some of the wine gets underneath. Cover and refrigerate overnight or up to 3 days, turning the roast over every day.

Preheat the oven to 300°F (150°C). Heat 1 Tbsp. (15 mL) of the vegetable oil in a very large frying pan over medium heat. Remove the beef from the marinade and brown it on all sides. Remove to a plate. Add the remaining 3 Tbsp. (45 mL) oil to the pan along with the onion and the 2 tsp. (10 mL) salt. Sauté the onion, stirring frequently, until it softens slightly. A bit of browning is fine. Place the beef in a large, high-sided pot that will fit it snugly. You want the onion to completely surround the beef. If you use a large roasting pan, the onion juices will evaporate quickly, rather that create the cooking medium for the beef. Pour the red wine through a sieve over the beef and onion. Cover with aluminum foil and a tight-fitting lid. Place in the oven and bake for 4 hours. Check the roast by inserting a small knife through the top of the roast. There should be little resistance. If the roast seems a bit tough, cover again and cook for another hour.

2 cups (480 mL) sour cream

2 Tbsp. (30 mL) freshly grated horseradish or
  4 Tbsp. (60 mL) prepared horseradish

salt and pepper to taste

2 small sprigs rosemary

4 whole cloves

1 Tbsp. (15 mL) balsamic or red wine vinegar

salt and pepper to taste

Stir the sour cream and horseradish together. Season with salt and pepper.

Remove the pot from the oven and carefully remove the beef. Cover and keep warm. Strain the onion through a sieve, saving the rich stock. Remove the fat from the stock. Place the onion, stock, rosemary, and cloves in a large pot or frying pan and cook over medium heat, stirring frequently, until the mixture thickens and turns a rich brown, about 20 minutes. Remove the rosemary sprigs and cloves. Stir in the vinegar and season with salt and pepper. Remove the net and any bones from the roast. Slice or cut the beef into chunks and place on a heated platter. Pour the onion sauce over the beef. Serve with any additional onion sauce and the sour cream and horseradish on the side.

This is a very grand Shepherd's Pie. It started with just a layer of creamed corn and mashed potatoes on top, then grew to mashed white and sweet potatoes, then turned into bacon and buttermilk mashed potatoes. It makes a big pie too; think of those fabulous leftovers. You can use ground lamb instead of beef.

Shepherd's Pie   serves 8

For the ground beef layer:

1 Tbsp. (15 mL) unsalted butter

1 cup (240 mL) onion, finely diced

1/2 cup (120 mL) celery, finely diced

1/2 cup (120 mL) carrot, finely diced

2 cloves garlic

2 lbs. (900 g) lean ground beef

1 tsp. (5 mL) sea salt

1/4 tsp. (1.25 mL) freshly ground black pepper

2 Tbsp. (30 mL) all-purpose flour

1 cup (240 mL) water or stock

For the creamed corn layer:

2 Tbsp. (30 mL) unsalted butter

3 Tbsp. (45 mL) all-purpose flour

2 1/2 cups (600 mL) milk

2 1/2 cups (600 mL) fresh or frozen corn,
    thawed and drained

1/2 tsp. (2.5 mL) sea salt

To make the beef layer, melt the butter in a large pot over medium heat. Add the onion, celery, carrot and garlic and sauté until lightly browned. Add the ground beef and turn the heat to high. Cook, crumbling the beef with the back of a spoon, until it loses its raw color. Add the salt and pepper. Place the flour in a small bowl and slowly stir in the water or stock to form a lump-free mixture. Remove the beef from the heat and slowly stir in the flour mixture. Return to the heat and bring to a boil. Turn down to a simmer and cook for 20 minutes. Spread the beef mixture evenly into a 9- by 13-inch (23- by 33-cm) baking dish.

For the creamed corn layer, melt the butter in a large nonstick pot over medium heat. Stir in the flour with a whisk and cook for a few moments. Raise the heat to high and slowly dribble in the milk, whisking constantly until the mixture thickens and comes to a boil. Add the corn and salt and bring to a boil. Turn down to a simmer and cook for about 20 minutes, stirring frequently to prevent sticking. The mixture should thicken to a pancake batter consistency and become distinctly corny tasting. It may take a bit longer if you are using fresh corn. Add the salt. Spread the creamed corn over the beef mixture.

For the mashed potato layer:

3 lbs. (1.4 kg) russet potatoes peeled and cut into chunks

4 oz. (113 g) bacon, diced

4 Tbsp. (60 mL) unsalted butter

1 cup (240 mL) buttermilk

2 green onions, thinly sliced

sea salt and freshly ground black pepper to taste

For the mashed potatoes, place the potato chunks in a large pot and cover with cold water. Salt liberally and bring to a boil. Cook until the potatoes are very tender when pierced with a fork, about 15–20 minutes. While the potatoes are cooking, cook the bacon in a small frying pan over medium-low heat until it is crisp and browned. Drain off the fat through a strainer and place the bacon on paper towels. Crumble when cool. Drain the potatoes and return to the pot. Mash the potatoes until smooth. Add the butter and stir until the butter is incorporated. Stir in the buttermilk, bacon and green onions and beat until smooth. Add salt and pepper. Spread the mashed potatoes over the creamed corn.

Preheat the oven to 350°F (175°C). Place the pie on the middle rack of the oven and bake for 45 minutes to 1 hour, until bubbly. Let sit for 15 minutes before serving.

Everybody and everybody's mother has a meatloaf recipe that is the best meatloaf (or sometimes the worst) in the entire world. Well, the one I make is, of course, the best in the entire world. So there!

My Meatloaf   serves 6 to 8

1 cup (240 mL) milk

2½ cups (600 mL) ½-inch (1.2-cm) cubes of good white bread, crust removed

1½ lbs. (680 g) lean ground beef

1½ lbs. (680 g) ground pork

¾ cup (180 mL) onion, finely diced

4 Tbsp. (60 mL) fresh parsley, finely chopped

½ tsp. (2.5 mL) sea salt

½ tsp. (2.5 mL) freshly ground black pepper

1 cup (240 mL) freshly grated Parmesan cheese

6 oz. (170 g) prosciutto, finely diced

3 eggs

Preheat the oven to 350°F (175°C). Heat the milk in a small saucepan until it is quite hot. Add the bread cubes, stir a few times and remove from the heat to cool. In a large bowl, combine the beef, pork, onion, parsley, salt, pepper and Parmesan cheese.

Place the prosciutto in the work bowl of a food processor and pulse until finely chopped. Add the cooled bread mixture and the eggs and pulse until the mixture is homogeneous. If you don't have a food processor, mix with a whisk until well combined. Add to the meat.

Mix with your hands until everything is well combined. Pack into a 10- by 5-inch (25- by 13-cm) loaf pan. Bake for 1½ hours. Let rest for 10 minutes before serving.

I never realized that you could roast veal shanks (silly me!), thinking they would be tough. Why else would they always be braised? Dinner at Hubert's proved my assumption wrong when he roasted whole shanks to a state of ultimate succulence. That plus lots and lots of delicious marrow, good company and his mother's incredible blueberry schnapps made a memorable evening. The shanks are equally good without the sauce. Start this dish a day in advance.

Hubert's Whole Roasted Veal Shanks   serves 6

1 cup (240 mL) carrots, cut into ½-inch (1.2-cm) dice

1 cup (240 mL) celery, cut into ½-inch (1.2-cm) dice

½ cup (120 mL) onion, cut into ½-inch (1.2-cm) dice

1 leek, white and light green part only, thinly sliced (see page 162)

6 large sprigs fresh thyme, coarsely chopped

1 Tbsp. (15 mL) fresh parsley, finely chopped

2 milk-fed veal shanks, 2½ lbs. (1.1 kg) each

1 tsp. (5 mL) sea salt

2 Tbsp. (30 mL) vegetable oil

1 cup (240 mL) white wine, heated

3 cups (720 mL) chicken stock (see page 46)

1 Tbsp. (15 mL) butter, softened

1 Tbsp. (15 mL) all-purpose flour

Combine the vegetables and herbs in a 9- by 13-inch (23- by 33-cm) glass baking dish. Sprinkle the veal shanks with the salt and place them in the pan, packing half the vegetables on top. Cover and refrigerate overnight.

Preheat the oven to 350°F (175°C). Heat the oil over medium heat in a large frying pan. Brown the shanks on all sides and replace on top of the vegetables in the baking dish. Roast for 1 hour. Reduce the heat to 300°F (150°C) and roast for 1½ hours longer. Let the meat rest for 15 minutes. With the aid of a kitchen towel, tongs and a knife, remove the meat from the bones in one piece. Slice thinly across the grain and place on a heated platter. Serve the bones too, for those who like marrow.

To make a sauce for the shanks, pour the heated white wine into the roasting pan after you have removed the shanks, and scrape to loosen any brown bits stuck to the pan. Transfer to a pot and add the chicken stock. Bring to a boil and simmer for 10 minutes. Remove any fat that has collected on the top. Mix butter with the flour until smooth. Whisk into the sauce and cook for a few minutes longer. Strain through a sieve and season with salt and pepper. Serve on the side.

I wasn't a big fan of venison until I tried it with this sauce. **With a pile of garlicky mashed potatoes... heaven. You can substitute lamb for the venison if you wish.**

Venison with Sun-Dried Sour Cherry and Blue Cheese Butter   serves 4

¼ cup (60 mL) red wine

¼ cup (60 mL) sun-dried sour cherries

¼ lb. (113 g) unsalted butter, softened

2 Tbsp. (30 mL) honey

¼ cup (60 mL) blue cheese, crumbled

1 Tbsp. (15 mL) vegetable oil

8 3-oz. (90-g) venison medallions

sea salt and freshly ground black pepper

To make the butter, place the red wine and cherries in a small pot and bring to a boil. Cover and remove from the heat. Cool. With a mixer or whisk whip the butter until light. Mix in the honey, blue cheese and cool cherry mixture. Place in a container, cover and refrigerate overnight. (The butter can be made up to a week in advance.) Bring to room temperature before using.

Season the venison medallions.

Heat the oil in a skillet large enough to hold the venison in a single layer. Over high heat, sear the meat on both sides until medium rare, about 1½ minutes total cooking time.

Place the venison on heated plates or a large platter and top with the butter. Serve immediately.

This rabbit goes perfectly **with the Mashed Sweet Potatoes with Blue Cheese, page 221.**

Seared Rabbit with Mustard and Fennel   serves 6

3 rabbits, 2 – 2½ lbs. (about 1 kg)

3 Tbsp. (45 mL) Dijon mustard

¾ tsp. (3.75 mL) sea salt

1½ tsp. (7.5 mL) coarsely crushed fennel seeds

2 Tbsp. (30 mL) finely minced shallots

½ tsp. (2.5 mL) freshly ground black pepper

2 Tbsp. (30 mL) vegetable oil

½ cup (120 mL) white wine

Remove the leg and thigh portions from the rabbits in one piece and debone the thigh. Set aside. Debone the loin. You may want to get an accommodating butcher to do this for you; if you're doing it yourself, imagine the rabbit is an elongated chicken and the loin is the breast.

Place the legs and loins in a bowl and add the mustard, salt, fennel, shallots and pepper. Mix well, cover and refrigerate overnight.

Preheat the oven to 350°F (175°C). Heat the vegetable oil in a large, heavy frying pan over medium-high heat. Add the legs and sear on both sides until brown. Remove the legs to a baking sheet. Add the loins to the frying pan and sear until brown on all sides. Remove to a plate. Deglaze the pan with the white wine, scraping up the browned bits, and pour over the rabbit legs. (The rabbit may be prepared up to this point 2 hours in advance.) Bake the legs for 15 minutes, then add the loins and bake for 5 minutes more. Serve on heated plates with the pan juices.

Finding a bunch of tender, glowing carrots was the inspiration for this recipe. The prosciutto and olives temper their sweetness and the wine adds the needed sour edge. A beautiful combination of flavors.

Flat Roasted Chicken with Sweet Carrots, Prosciutto and Olives   serves 4

1 chicken, 3½– 4 lbs. (1.6–1.8 kg)

sea salt and freshly ground black pepper

½ cup (120 mL) prosciutto, diced into ¼-inch (.6-cm) cubes

⅓ cup (80 mL) shallots, minced

2 cups (480 mL) carrots, peeled and cut into ½-inch (1.2-cm) cubes

2 cloves garlic, minced

½ cup (120 mL) whole green olives, unpitted

½ cup (120 mL) white wine

sea salt and freshly ground black pepper

Preheat the oven to 350°F (175°C).

With a sharp heavy knife, split the chicken down the backbone and open it up. Turn it breast side up and flatten with the palm of your hand. Cut a slit in the skin at the bottom of the breast and slip the "ankles" of the chicken through the slit. Sprinkle liberally with salt and pepper. Transfer the chicken, breast side down, to a lightly oiled roasting pan. Bake for 45 minutes. While the chicken is baking, prepare and combine the prosciutto, shallots, carrots, garlic and olives.

Remove the chicken from the oven and transfer to a plate. Remove any accumulated fat from the roasting pan. Scatter the carrot mixture evenly in the roasting pan and add the white wine. Place the chicken in the pan skin side up. Bake for 45 minutes longer.

Remove the chicken from the pan. Either carve the chicken or transfer it whole to a heated platter. Pour the carrot mixture over the chicken and serve.

I used to love going into Rebelo's, a Portuguese store in Kensington Market. They had a large take-out counter of prepared meat, sausages and fish. One of the highlights was tuna cooked with Portuguese red pepper paste. Being a fan of all things spicy, I started cooking chicken slathered with the paste. I first saw this unusual way of cutting chicken at a barbecue stand in Mexico. It seemed a little strange until I thought about it. The thighs, which are the thickest part of the chicken, are closest to the heat, while the breast is slightly curved away from the heat. The thickness of the chicken is more even, so all the parts cook at the same time. This works extremely well when barbecuing on a grill.

Portuguese-Style Chicken with Olive Oil Mashed Potatoes   serves 3 to 4

1 chicken, preferably free-range, 2–2½ lbs. (.9–1.1 kg)

½ cup (120 mL) Portuguese hot red pepper paste (look for Vinga or Melo's brand)

2 cloves garlic, minced

2 Tbsp. (30 mL) extra virgin olive oil

1 recipe Olive Oil Mashed Potatoes (see page 215)

Split the chicken through the breast (that's right, the breast). Flip it skin side up and hit it with the heel of your hand to flatten it. Combine the red pepper paste, garlic and oil. Slather over the inside and outside of the chicken. If you have the time, refrigerate the chicken for a few hours or up to overnight. If you don't have time, don't worry — the chicken will still be delicious.

Preheat the oven to 375°F (190°C). Place the chicken skin-side up in a pan and cook for 1½ hours. Let the chicken rest for 10 minutes. Transfer to a cutting board and cut the chicken in half, along the back. Cut into leg, thigh, wing and breast sections. Pour the pan juices over the chicken and serve immediately with the potatoes.

This dish is well worth the price of a steamer and has the sort of innocent, pure flavors that make me wish it would never stop. Serve it with steamed rice and Wok-Seared Bean Sprouts, page 191.

Chicken Steamed with Ginger and Sherry   serves 4

2 green onions

6 ¼-inch (.6-cm) slices fresh ginger

2 tsp. (10 mL) sea salt

¼ cup (60 mL) medium dry sherry or Chinese cooking wine

1 chicken, approximately 2½ lbs. (1.1 kg)

1 4-inch (10-cm) piece peeled ginger, sliced

2 green onions, chopped

¼ tsp. (1.25 mL) sea salt

2 Tbsp. (30 mL) vegetable oil

STEAMERS AND STEAMING

Large, lightweight aluminum steamers can be purchased in Asian grocery stores and well-stocked cookware shops. They usually have two steamer baskets that fit snugly over the pot with a tight-fitting lid. A whole meal or all the vegetables for, say, Christmas dinner can be cooked in separate bowls with a minimum of fuss and bother. Steaming is a very fast and gentle method of cooking. Most people are familiar with the great taste of steamed vegetables but may not be aware that the same technique produces equally delicious fish and meat. If fat is a concern to you, marinating and steaming fish and meat is a way to delicious, healthful cooking.

With the flat of a knife, lightly smash the green onions and sliced ginger. Place in a bowl large enough to hold the chicken and comfortably fit in the steamer. Add the 2 tsp. (10 mL) salt and sherry or wine and mix well. Place the chicken in the bowl, rolling it around in the marinade, and place a few spoonfuls inside the chicken. Let stand for half an hour. Bring 4 inches (10 cm) of water to a boil in the bottom of the steamer. Place the chicken in the steamer basket, cover with the lid and place on top of the boiling water. Steam for 40 minutes without removing the lid. Turn off the heat and let stand for 15 minutes.

While the chicken is steaming, prepare the ginger sauce. Place the second amount of ginger, chopped green onions, ¼ tsp. (1.25 mL) salt and oil in a blender or food processor. Pulse until the ingredients are finely chopped but still have some texture. Don't purée it. Scrape into a bowl.

Remove the chicken from the steamer. Either carve the chicken or chop it as I do into sections, using a heavy knife or cleaver. Place on a heated platter and pour some of the steaming juices over it. If you don't care about a fancy presentation, just put it back in the bowl you steamed it in. Serve immediately with the ginger sauce on the side. Strain and save the delicious steaming juices. I like to heat them with cooked orzo and a bit of Parmesan cheese for a quick soupy pasta. If there is any chicken left over, I dice it and add it too.

You can bake the chicken **in heavy-duty aluminum foil instead of parchment paper.**

Whole Spiced Chicken Baked in Parchment Paper   serves 4 to 6

1 whole chicken, about 3 lbs. (1.4 kg)

For the marinade:

1 1-inch (2.5-cm) piece of fresh ginger,
    peeled and chopped

2 cloves garlic, peeled and chopped

6 Tbsp. (90 mL) yogurt

½ tsp. (2.5 mL) turmeric

1 tsp. (5 mL) sea salt

¼ tsp. (1.25 mL) cayenne pepper

For the spice paste:

1 medium onion, chopped

4 cloves garlic, peeled and chopped

1 walnut-sized piece of ginger, peeled
   and chopped

2 tsp. (10 mL) ground cumin seeds

2 tsp. (10 mL) ground coriander seeds

½ tsp. (2.5 mL) turmeric

1 Tbsp. (15 mL) paprika

¼ tsp. (1.25 mL) cayenne pepper

1 tsp. (5 mL) sea salt

½ tsp. (2.5 mL) freshly ground black pepper

½ tsp. (2.5 mL) garam masala (see page 205)

4 Tbsp. (60 mL) vegetable oil

2 Tbsp. (30 mL) lemon juice

Remove the skin and fat from the chicken. Place all the marinade ingredients in the work bowl of a food processor or blender and process until a fine paste is formed. Rub the chicken inside and out with the paste. Cover and refrigerate for 2 hours.

While the chicken is marinating, make the spice paste. Combine the onion, garlic and ginger in the work bowl of a blender or food processor. Purée until a fine paste is formed. Add all the remaining ingredients except the oil and lemon juice and blend until combined.

Heat the oil in a nonstick pan over medium-high heat. Add the spice paste and fry, stirring frequently, until the paste is dry and light brown. Remove from the heat and add the lemon juice. Let cool.

Preheat the oven to 350°F (175°C). Lay out two pieces of parchment paper that are large enough to enclose the chicken comfortably. Place one on top of the other. Rub the chicken inside and out with the spice paste. Place the chicken on the parchment paper. Bring the ends of the parchment paper over the chicken and fold down to form a tight seal. Fold the remaining ends tightly.

Place in the oven and bake for 2 hours. An instant-read thermometer is extremely useful to check if the chicken is done. Push the thermometer through the parchment into the thickest part of the thigh. It should read 180°F (85°C). Remove from the oven and let the chicken sit for 10 minutes. You may serve the chicken at the table, opening up the parchment to enjoy the first delicious rush of fragrance, or cut it up in the kitchen. Serve with the juices.

This recipe, inspired by former coworker Marnie, has a cosy, old-fashioned taste and appearance. If you have a cast iron pan, use it for cooking and serving the chicken.

Casseroled Chicken with Bacon, Cream and Thyme serves 4

4 boneless 6-oz. (170-g) chicken breasts, with skin

8 slices bacon

8 small sprigs fresh thyme

1 Tbsp. (15 mL) vegetable oil

1 clove garlic, minced

½ cup (120 mL) chicken stock (see page 46) or water

1 cup (240 mL) heavy or whipping cream

sea salt and freshly ground black pepper to taste

Wrap two pieces of bacon around each piece of chicken to form an X in the middle of each breast. Tuck a piece of thyme behind each X.

Preheat the oven to 350°F (180°C). Heat the vegetable oil over medium heat in a large, heavy frying pan that can go into the oven. Add the chicken breasts, bacon side down, and cook until the bacon is browned. Turn the chicken over and cook on the other side until browned. Remove the chicken to a plate and discard the fat. Add the garlic, chicken stock or water, and cream. Season with salt and pepper. Bring to a boil and return the chicken to the pan. Place in the oven and bake for 20 minutes. If the cream seems too thin at the end of cooking, return the pan to the stove and boil over high heat until the cream is lightly thickened. Serve immediately.

This dish is based on bouillabaisse, the Provençal fish stew flavored with tomatoes, saffron and fennel, and enriched with aioli, a garlic mayonnaise. These flavors go equally well with chicken, and it's much less intimidating than making a bouillabaisse.

Chicken Stew in the Style of Fish Soup   serves 4 to 6

2 Tbsp. (30 mL) olive oil

2 lbs. (900 g) bone-in chicken breasts, cut in quarters

2 lbs. (900 g) bone-in chicken thighs

sea salt and freshly ground black pepper

1 cup (240 mL) onion, finely diced

3 large leeks, white and light green part only, thinly sliced (see page 162)

2/3 cup (160 mL) fresh fennel bulb, finely diced

4 cloves garlic, minced

3 cups (720 mL) well-drained, canned plum tomatoes, finely chopped

3 cups (720 mL) chicken stock (see page 46)

2 cups (480 mL) dry white wine

large pinch of saffron threads

2 bay leaves

1 tsp. (5 mL) fennel seeds

1/2 tsp. (2.5 mL) crushed dried chilies

2 small sprigs fresh thyme

1 strip fresh orange rind

sea salt and freshly ground black pepper to taste

1 lb. (454 g) small red potatoes, quartered

2 Tbsp. (30 mL) fresh parsley, finely chopped

6 thick slices good-quality toasted baguette

1 recipe Aioli (see page 163)

In a large frying pan, heat 1 Tbsp. (15 mL) of the olive oil over medium heat. Remove the skin from the chicken if you prefer and season the chicken with salt and pepper. Cook in batches until golden brown on both sides. Transfer to a plate.

In a large heavy pot, heat the remaining olive oil over medium heat. Add the onion, leeks, fennel and garlic and cook, stirring occasionally, until the vegetables become soft but not brown, 4–5 minutes. Add the tomatoes and cook, stirring frequently, until most of the liquid has evaporated. Add the chicken stock, wine, saffron, bay leaves, fennel, chilies, thyme, orange rind and the chicken pieces with any liquid on the plate. Season lightly with salt and pepper. Cover and simmer over low heat for 35–40 minutes, until the chicken is tender and cooked through. Transfer the chicken to a plate and remove any fat accumulated on top of the liquid. Boil over high heat for 5 minutes. Return the chicken to the pot and remove from the heat.

While the chicken is cooking, cook the potatoes. Place the potatoes in a pot and cover with cold salted water by a few inches (8 cm). Bring to a boil and cook until the potatoes are tender, 10–15 minutes. Drain and reserve.

When you are ready to serve the chicken, add the potatoes to the pot and bring to a vigorous simmer. Stir in the chopped parsley. Place a piece of toasted bread in each of 6 heated bowls. Ladle the stew into the bowls and serve with the aioli on the side.

A Bit About Leeks

Recipes using leeks often include the admonition "white part only." But if you study a leek, you will notice that about one inch (2.5 cm) of it is white and the rest is light green. Do these people want us to go out and buy ten pounds (4.5 kg) of leeks for a cup (240 mL) of sliced leeks? I hope not. When I use leeks, I look for the ones that have the greatest ratio of light green and white to the coarse green leaves. Growing leeks is a tedious operation. They are grown in trenches and soil is packed over them as they grow to keep them light in color. (This is why leeks have to be washed well. All that soil gets into the crevices.) Depending upon the skill and patience of the grower, you can get a leek that has a nice, long, edible white and light green part or a short, mean-spirited stub. I try to avoid the stubs, but sometimes this is all that is available. Anyway, use the white and light green parts of the leek and you will be just fine. (I once worked with someone who actually made a soup out of the green leaves. It was dreadful.)

To clean leeks, cut off the green tops and remove the outer covering. Thinly slice the leeks and place them in a large bowl of cold water. Swish the leeks around with your hand to dislodge any grit. Let stand for a few minutes and remove the leeks with a slotted spoon to a sieve to drain. If you need bigger pieces of leek, split them in half longthwise instead of slicing them. Riffle the leaves under cold running water until they are free of grit, then drain.

Traditional aioli doesn't have lemon juice in it, **but I like the flavor.**

Aioli   makes 1 1/3 cups (320 mL)

1/2 tsp. (2.5 mL) sea salt

3 cloves garlic, minced

3 large egg yolks

1 cup (240 mL) olive oil

4 tsp. (20 mL) lemon juice

In a small bowl, mash the salt and garlic to a paste with the back of a spoon. Place the egg yolks in a food processor or blender. Add the garlic paste and turn the motor on. Slowly dribble the olive oil into the egg yolks. If the mixture seems too thick at any point, add a dribble of water. When all of the oil has been incorporated and the mixture is emulsified, add the lemon juice. To make by hand, whisk the egg yolks and mashed garlic together in a medium-sized bowl. Whisking constantly, add the oil, drop by drop, until all of the oil is incorporated and the mixture is emulsified. Whisk in the lemon juice. Cover and refrigerate for up to 3 days.

NOTE
If using raw eggs makes you uncomfortable, stir the garlic and 2 tsp. (10 mL) lemon juice into 1 1/4 cups (300 mL) prepared mayonnaise.

Serve this with a cucumber, tomato and onion salad sprinkled with fresh mint or cilantro, and extra yogurt on the side. The chicken may be grilled or pan-roasted if you prefer.

Chicken Breasts with Far Eastern Spices   serves 4 to 6

6 6-oz. (170-g) boneless, skinless chicken breast halves

¼ cup (60 mL) freshly squeezed lemon juice

½ tsp. (2.5 mL) sea salt

4 Tbsp. (60 mL) yogurt

4 tsp. (20 mL) ground coriander

2 tsp. (10 mL) ground cumin

1 tsp. (5 mL) turmeric

1 tsp. (5 mL) bright red paprika

½ tsp. (2.5 mL) ground ginger

pinch cayenne pepper

4 cloves garlic, minced

¼ cup (60 mL) green onion, thinly sliced

1 Tbsp. (15 mL) vegetable oil

Combine the chicken breasts, lemon juice and salt in a bowl and mix well. Let stand for 30 minutes. Mix the yogurt, coriander, cumin, turmeric, paprika, ginger, cayenne pepper, garlic, green onion and oil together. Pour over the chicken and stir well to coat. Cover and refrigerate 2 hours or up to overnight.

Preheat the broiler to high. Place the chicken on a baking pan and broil 4 inches (10 cm) away from the heat for 4–6 minutes, until lightly browned. Turn the chicken over and broil for 2–3 minutes, until the chicken is cooked through.

Serve this chicken with sautéed or grilled peppers **and Lemon Orzo and Warm Spinach "Salad", page 71.**

Garlicky Chicken with Feta and Oregano   serves 4

½ cup (120 mL) yogurt

1 green onion, thinly sliced

1 tsp. (5 mL) fresh parsley, finely chopped

4 cloves garlic, minced

½ tsp. (2.5 mL) dried oregano

⅓ tsp. (1.7 mL) sea salt

¼ tsp. (1.25 mL) freshly ground black pepper

4 6-oz. (170-g) boneless, skinless chicken
  breast halves

½ cup (120 mL) crumbled feta cheese

Combine the yogurt, green onion, parsley, garlic, oregano, salt and pepper in a medium-sized bowl. Add the chicken breasts and mix well to coat with the marinade. Refrigerate, covered, for at least 30 minutes or up to 1 day.

Preheat the broiler to high. Place the chicken on a baking pan and broil 4 inches (10 cm) away from the heat for 4 – 6 minutes; until lightly browned. Turn the chicken over and sprinkle with the feta cheese. Broil for 2 – 3 minutes, until the chicken is cooked through and the cheese is speckled with brown. Serve on heated plates.

OREGANO
The most fragrant dried oregano I've found is in Greek and Italian food stores. It comes in a long cellophane package, with the leaves still attached to the stalk. For easier storage, strip the leaves from the stalks and store in a smaller container.

This is a "knock 'em dead" recipe. **Its popularity is due to it being a) extremely tasty, b) easy to make, and c) a lot of fun to eat.**

Pepper and Cilantro Marinated Chicken (a.k.a. Thai Barbecue Chicken)   serves 6

1 bunch fresh cilantro, washed and dried

1 tsp. (5 mL) freshly ground black pepper

3 Tbsp. (45 mL) fish sauce or soya sauce

2 cloves garlic, minced

6 boneless chicken breasts, skin left on

1 head leaf lettuce, washed and dried

1/2 English cucumber, sliced

1 bunch mint, washed and dried

1 recipe Sweet and Sour Dipping Sauce
(see page 167)

STORING CILANTRO
To store cilantro, cut the bottom stems from the bunch. Wash the leaves in cold water and shake them dry. Lay out a continuous sheet of 5 – 6 paper towels or a tea towel and spread the cilantro out on it in a nearly single layer. Roll it up like a jelly roll and lightly dampen the outside of the towel. Store in a plastic bag in the fridge. If you have a large bunch of cilantro, divide it in half and make two rolls. Your cilantro will stay fresh and green for at least 2 weeks.

Divide the cilantro in half and set half aside. Place the remaining cilantro, pepper, fish sauce and garlic in a food processor or blender and pulse until the cilantro is finely chopped. Alternatively, finely chop the cilantro and combine with the pepper, fish sauce and garlic. Pour over the chicken and marinate for at least 2 hours or overnight.

When you are ready to cook the chicken, preheat the broiler or barbecue. Cook the chicken until the skin is crispy and the meat is cooked all the way through, 4 – 5 minutes per side. Arrange the lettuce, cucumber, mint and the half-bunch of cilantro attractively on a platter. Place the dipping sauce in 6 individual bowls. Cut the chicken into 1-inch (2.5-cm) pieces and serve with the vegetable platter and dipping sauce.

To eat the chicken, take a piece of lettuce and tear it in half. Place a slice of cucumber, a bit of mint, cilantro and piece of chicken on the lettuce. Roll the lettuce up, dip it into the sauce and enjoy.

This is the sauce for spring rolls **and Pepper and Cilantro Marinated Chicken, page 166.**
It's so good, you'll find other ways of using it.

Sweet and Sour Dipping Sauce   makes 3 cups (720 mL)

1½ cups (360 mL) granulated sugar

2 cups (480 mL) water

4 cloves garlic, peeled and sliced

½ red bell pepper, green stem only removed

3 Tbsp. (45 mL) fish sauce

5 Tbsp. (75 mL) lemon juice

1 tsp. (5 mL) sea salt

1 Tbsp. (15 mL) hot chili paste or to taste

Place the sugar and water in a saucepan and bring to a boil. Boil for 10 minutes, remove from the heat and cool.

Place ½ cup (120 mL) of the sugar syrup and the remaining ingredients in the work bowl of a food processor or blender and blend until the pepper and garlic are puréed. The seeds will remain whole. Add the remaining sugar syrup and pulse briefly to combine. This sauce keeps almost forever, covered and refrigerated.

Thinking Beyond Turkey

I know that turkey is one of the symbols of holiday celebrations (I can hear my mother's voice of the past here, "Why do you always have to be different?"), but let's face it: turkey can be a complete pain. You have to be ready when the turkey is ready, it takes up all your oven space, you have to make gravy, the breast is usually dry, it has to be carved, it rarely stays hot. I am not anti-turkey, I just prefer to have it at a less hectic time of year. For celebrations here are a few of the things I prefer.

Oxtails Braised in Red Wine, page 147, were my staple for years. The oxtails can be made a few days in advance and reheated gently before serving, leaving you free to concentrate on side dishes and dessert. It is easy to double or triple the recipe for a large crowd.

Roast Leg of Pork with Crackling, page 179, is always a treat. It's easier to carve and stays hot for a long time. Then, there is that delicious crackling.

I've always cooked stuffing separately and am partial to the Oyster Stuffing, page 104.

I like vegetable casseroles too because they're easy. They can be made in advance and reheated. Winter Vegetable Casserole, page 208, Sweet Potatoes with Candied Ginger, page 222, and Sweet Potato and Apple Purée with Bourbon, page 220, are a few examples.

For desserts, Aunt Toni's Steamed Cranberry Pudding with Eggnog Sauce, page 272, Christmas Pie, page 280, Pumpkin Cheesecake, page 240, Candied Cranberry Cheesecake, page 241, and Steamed Pumpkin Pudding with Cool Maple Sauce, page 273, are all excellent finales.

This is one of my favorite methods of roasting turkey. It emerges from the oven well seasoned and succulent.

Roast Turkey with Pancetta, Rosemary and Garlic   serves 8

1 15-lb. (7-kg) turkey

½ lb. (227 g) pancetta

½ cup (120 mL) fresh rosemary leaves

4 whole heads garlic

6 cloves garlic, minced

½ tsp. (2.5 mL) sea salt

1 tsp. (5 mL) coarsely ground black pepper

olive oil

2 cups (480 mL) dry red wine

½ cup (120 mL) shallots, finely chopped

Preheat the oven to 350°F (175°C). Rinse the turkey and pat dry. Finely chop half the pancetta and cut the other half into large chunks. Stuff the large chunks of pancetta, half the rosemary leaves and the whole heads of garlic into the cavity of the turkey. Transfer the finely chopped pancetta to the workbowl of a food processor with the remaining rosemary, minced garlic, salt and pepper. Pulse until everything is finely chopped.

Loosen the skin of the turkey over the breast and around the legs. Slide the pancetta mixture over the breast and legs, under the skin, patting it out evenly. Transfer to a roasting pan and rub the turkey with olive oil. Tie the legs loosely. Roast for 3–3½ hours (see How Do I Know When It's Done?, page 171), basting the turkey with ½ cup (120 mL) of the red wine every 30 minutes. After the second basting, scatter the shallots in the bottom of the roasting pan.

Remove the turkey from the roasting pan. Degrease the juices with a fat separator or skim with a spoon. Strain through a sieve into a pot; keep warm over low heat and adjust the seasoning.

Remove the whole garlic from the cavity and separate the cloves. Remove and discard the pancetta and rosemary, or save to use in soup. Carve the turkey into slices and garnish with the cloves of garlic, which are meant to be eaten. Serve with the pan juices on the side.

Using steam instead of direct heat to gently braise the duck produces extremely tender, flavor-infused meat. The parsley, orange, garlic and prosciutto garnish works in harmony with the deep rich flavors of the braising liquid. I served this with spaetzle and was completely ecstatic with the results. See Steamers and Steaming, page 158.

Red Wine Steamed Duck Legs
with Orange, Rosemary and Prosciutto   serves 4

1¼-inch (.6-cm) slice prosciutto

2 medium shallots, peeled

4 medium cloves garlic, peeled

12 whole black peppercorns

2 allspice berries

½ tsp. (2.5 mL) whole coriander seeds

2 small sprigs fresh rosemary

4 duck legs, ½ lb. (227 g) each, or 1 large duck, 6–7 lbs. (2.8–3.2 kg), backbone removed, quartered and rib bones removed from the breast, trimmed of all fat

3 cups (720 mL) dry red wine

1 Tbsp. (15 mL) unsalted butter, softened

1 Tbsp. (15 mL) all-purpose flour

sea salt and freshly ground black pepper to taste

1 tsp. (5 mL) olive oil

3 Tbsp. (45 mL) finely diced prosciutto

2 Tbsp. (30 mL) finely chopped parsley

1 tsp. (5 mL) garlic, finely chopped

zest of ½ orange, finely chopped

½ tsp. (2.5 mL) finely chopped fresh rosemary leaves

Choose a 1½-quart (1.5-L) pot or casserole dish with a lid that will hold the duck snugly and fit comfortably in the steamer. Place the slice of prosciutto, shallots, garlic, peppercorns, allspice, coriander and rosemary in the bottom of the dish. Add the duck in a single layer and pour in the red wine. If the wine does not quite cover the duck, add water to cover by ½ inch (1.2 cm). Cover the pot tightly with a double thickness of aluminum foil and then cover with a lid.

Fill the steamer pot almost full with water and bring to a boil. Place the pot or casserole in the steaming basket and cover with the lid. Steam for 2 hours, replenishing with boiling water if the level becomes too low. Remove the duck pieces to a plate and cover. Skim all the fat from the top of the liquid and strain the liquid through a sieve. Reduce over high heat to half. Mix the softened butter and flour together to form a smooth paste. Whisk into the boiling sauce by teaspoonfuls until it is lightly thickened. You may not need to use all the flour paste. Season with salt and pepper and set aside.

In a small, nonstick frying pan, heat the olive oil over medium-low heat. Add the diced prosciutto and cook until it is brown and crisp, about 10 minutes. Remove the prosciutto with a slotted spoon to drain on a paper towel. Mix the parsley, garlic, orange zest, rosemary and prosciutto together. You may prepare the recipe to this point 1 or 2 hours in advance.

Preheat the broiler. Place the duck on a baking sheet and broil 4 inches (10 cm) from the heat until the skin is brown and crispy, about 5–6 minutes. While the duck is broiling, reheat the sauce. Place the duck on heated plates and pour the sauce over it. Sprinkle the parsley mixture over the duck and serve immediately.

HOW DO I KNOW WHEN IT'S DONE?

One of the questions I'm asked frequently is, "How do I know when it's done?" My answer is to buy yourself an instant-read thermometer and use the recommendations below for meats and fish. Having an instant-read thermometer takes all the anxiety and guesswork out of cooking meat.

To use it, insert the thermometer into the thickest part of the meat so the point is in the middle, and give it a few seconds to adjust.

105°F–110°F (40°C–43°C) Rare.

115°F–125°F (46°C–52°C) Medium-rare. I prefer 115°F.

130°F–140°F (54°C–60°C) Medium.

Over 150°F (65°C) Well done!

Roasts, big steaks and large birds should sit for at least 10–15 minutes before slicing. As the meat rests, it continues to cook, so keep this in mind when checking the temperature. It is recommended that poultry be cooked to 180°F (85°C). I personally find chicken and turkey cooked to this temperature to be overcooked and extremely dry, but I can't tell you to do as I do in this instance.

A simple summer dish. **Placing a brick on each bird ensures even and speedy cooking.**

Herbed Cornish Hens Grilled Under a Brick serves 4

4 Cornish hens

2 cloves garlic, minced

1 tsp. (5 mL) sea salt

1 tsp. (5 mL) freshly ground black pepper

2 tsp. (10 mL) fresh thyme leaves

2 tsp. (10 mL) fresh rosemary leaves

1 tsp. (5 mL) fresh lavender leaves

4 Tbsp. (60 mL) lemon juice

4 Tbsp. (60 mL) olive oil

Split each Cornish hen down the breast bone. Open up the hens, turn them skin-side up and flatten with the palm of your hand. Mix the remaining ingredients together and rub over the hens. Marinate for at least 2 hours or overnight.

Preheat the barbecue to medium low. Place the hens on the barbecue skin-side up and place a tin foil-covered brick on top of each hen. Cook for 10–15 minutes until well browned. Turn the hens over and replace the brick. Cook for 10–15 minutes longer until the skin is crispy and the thigh juices run clear when pricked with a knife.

Graham's Grilled Flank Steak with Cumin Aioli   page 145

Herb and Parmesan Roasted Dungeness Crab   page 109

Braised Lamb Shanks with Creamy Polenta   page 176

The lamb is also delicious cooked on the barbecue. **If you want to barbecue it, place the lamb on a grill preheated to high and sear it for 5–8 minutes on each side. Turn the heat to low and cook for 10–15 minutes on each side for medium-rare. Brush frequently with the marinade while the lamb is cooking. Remove from the barbecue and let rest 10 minutes before carving across the grain.**

Leg of Lamb with Ginger and Sweet and Hot Spices   serves 6

1 butterflied leg of lamb, 3–4 lbs. (1.4–1.8 kg)

1 medium-sized onion, chopped

1 piece of fresh ginger, 3 inches (7.5 cm) long, peeled and chopped

6 cloves garlic, chopped

⅓ cup (80 mL) lemon juice

1 Tbsp. (15 mL) ground coriander seeds

1 tsp. (5 mL) ground cumin

1 tsp. (5 mL) garam masala (see page 205)

1 tsp. (5 mL) turmeric

¼ tsp. (1.25 mL) ground nutmeg

¼ tsp. (1.25 mL) ground cinnamon

¼ tsp. (1.25 mL) ground cloves

½ cup (120 mL) vegetable oil

2 tsp. (10 mL) sea salt

½ tsp. (2.5 mL) ground black pepper

½ tsp. (2.5 mL) cayenne pepper

Trim the fat from the lamb leg. Prick the leg with the point of a small knife about 20 times on both sides.

Blend the chopped onion, ginger, garlic and lemon juice to a fine purée in the work bowl of a blender or food processor. Place in a container large enough to hold the lamb leg and add all the remaining ingredients except the lamb. Mix well.

Place the lamb in the container with the spice mixture and rub it thoroughly into both sides of the leg. Cover and refrigerate overnight.

Preheat the oven to 400°F (200°C). Place the lamb on a baking sheet and bake for 45 minutes for medium-rare (see How Do I Know When It's Done?, page 171). Heat the broiler and broil the lamb on both sides until crusty and brown. Let the lamb rest 10 minutes before carving across the grain.

Skordalia, or cold potato sauce, is a perfect summer accompaniment to grilled lamb. To round out the meal, all you need is a platter of sliced ripe tomatoes, cucumbers, onions and fennel and a loaf of good bread to slice thickly and grill on the barbecue after the lamb is done.

Grilled Lamb Leg with Skordalia   serves 6

1 Tbsp. (15 mL) fresh thyme leaves

1 tsp. (5 mL) sea salt

1 tsp. (5 mL) cracked black pepper

2 Tbsp. (30 mL) olive oil

1 butterflied lamb leg, 2½–3 lbs. (1.1–1.4 kg)

1 recipe Skordalia (see page 19)

Combine the thyme, salt, pepper and olive oil and spread over the lamb leg. (The lamb may be prepared up to 48 hours in advance. Cover and refrigerate.) Grill on a preheated, medium-low barbecue, about 15–20 minutes per side for medium rare. Remove from the grill and let rest for 10 minutes. Slice and arrange on a platter. Serve the Skordalia on the side.

This is an impressive centerpiece for a Greek dinner. Start the meal with Tzatziki, page 18, then finish with the Orange and Semolina Cake, page 236.

Roasted Lamb Rack with Oregano and Lemony Artichoke Sauce   serves 4

2 Frenched lamb racks, 16 – 18 oz. (454–510 g) each

olive oil for frying

2 cloves minced garlic

½ tsp. (2.5 mL) sea salt

1 tsp. (5 mL) dried oregano

freshly ground black pepper

2 Tbsp. (30 mL) extra virgin olive oil

Lemony Artichoke Sauce

1 cup (240 mL) chicken stock (see page 46)

6 egg yolks

⅓ cup (80 mL) lemon juice, strained

sea salt and freshly ground black pepper

1 Tbsp. (15 mL) chopped parsley

4 artichoke hearts, cut into 6 wedges each

Preheat oven to 425°F (220°C).

In a frying pan over high heat, sear the lamb in a scant amount of oil until browned. Remove from the pan and cool. Crush the garlic to a paste with the salt. Combine with the oregano, pepper and oil and spread over the lamb. Place fat-side up in a roasting pan and roast for 15–20 minutes until 130°F (54°C) when tested with an instant-read thermometer for medium. See How Do I Know When It's Done?, page 171.

Remove from the oven and let rest for 10 minutes before slicing.

Lemony Artichoke Sauce

If you don't have the inclination to prepare your own fresh artichoke hearts, using canned ones is fine.

In a smallish pot, bring the chicken stock to a boil.

Whisk the yolks until pale and frothy. Slowly whisk in the lemon juice. Add one third of the hot stock in a steady stream, constantly whisking. Add remaining broth. Return the mixture to the pot and heat gently. Whisk while heating, until mixture thickens enough to coat the back of a spoon. Do not boil. Season to taste and stir in the parsley and artichoke hearts.

The popularity of lamb shanks has peaked and waned. **No matter! If you don't have the patience for making polenta, serve them with a small pasta shape such as orzo, or with mashed potatoes or a good bread.**

Braised Lamb Shanks with Creamy Polenta   serves 4 to 6

6 lamb shanks

2 cups (480 mL) red wine

1 28-oz. (796-mL) can whole plum tomatoes,
drained, puréed and sieved to remove
the seeds

8 cups (2 L) chicken stock (see page 46)
or water

3 Tbsp. (45 mL) vegetable oil

4 medium cloves garlic, minced

1½ cups (360 mL) onion, finely diced

¾ cup (180 mL) celery, finely diced

¾ cup (180 mL) carrots, finely diced

1 Tbsp. (15 mL) parsley, finely chopped

1 bay leaf

1 tsp. (5 mL) sea salt

3 Tbsp. (45 mL) parsley, finely chopped

1 tsp. (5 mL) garlic, minced

finely grated peel of one lemon

Preheat the oven to 300°F (150°C). Trim any visible fat from the lamb shanks. Rinse, pat dry and place them in an ovenproof pot large enough to hold them in a single layer. Add the red wine, tomatoes and the stock or water (use enough to cover the shanks by 2 inches / 5 cm). Bring to a boil.

While waiting for the lamb shanks to boil, heat the vegetable oil in a frying pan over medium heat. Sauté the garlic, onion, celery, carrots and 1 Tbsp. (15 mL) parsley until the vegetables are lightly browned. Set aside.

When the lamb shanks come to a boil, turn the heat down to a simmer and skim off any foam that rises to the top. Add the sautéed vegetables, bay leaf and salt. Cover and place in the oven. Bake for 2½ hours, checking occasionally to make sure the liquid is covering the lamb shanks. If not, use water to top up the liquid.

Combine the 3 Tbsp. (45 mL) parsley, garlic and lemon peel. Cover and refrigerate.

10 cups (2.5 L) water

2 tsp. (10 mL) sea salt

2 cups (480 mL) cornmeal

6 Tbsp. (90 mL) butter

2 cups (480 mL) grated Parmesan cheese

When the lamb shanks have cooked for 1 1/2 hours, start the polenta. Bring the water and salt to a boil in a large, wide, heavy-bottomed pot. Stirring constantly, add the cornmeal in a slow steady stream. Turn the heat to medium low and cook at a lively simmer for 1 hour, stirring occasionally. Remove from the heat and cover.

Remove the lamb shanks from the oven. Take the meat out of the liquid and cover. Strain the liquid through a sieve and reserve. Force the vegetables through the sieve or purée them in a food processor until smooth. Add the puréed vegetables to the liquid and boil over high heat until it starts to thicken.

Return the shanks to the pot. (The shanks may be cooked to this point up to 2 days in advance. Cool, cover and refrigerate.) Simmer the shanks for 1/2 hour. If you are reheating the shanks after being refrigerated, slowly bring to a simmer then simmer for 1/2 hour.

While the shanks are simmering, finish the polenta. Slowly reheat the cornmeal mixture, stirring occasionally. Add the butter and Parmesan cheese and stir until the butter is melted. Serve the shanks with the polenta and pass the parsley, garlic and lemon garnish.

Fantastic with sausages, roast chicken and pork. You can substitute 3 lbs. (1.35 kg) of marionberries or blackberries for the cherries if you wish. This is served with rack of lamb to rave reviews.

Sour and Sweet Cherry Ketchup   makes 3 cups (720 mL)

1½ lbs. (680 g) sour cherries, pitted

1½ lbs. (680 g) sweet cherries, pitted

3/4 cup (180 mL) diced onions

2 cups (480 mL) water

1/2 cup (120 mL) dark brown sugar, packed

1/2 cup (120 mL) light corn syrup

1/2 cup (120 mL) cider vinegar

3/4 tsp. (3.75 mL) ground cinnamon

1 tsp. (5 mL) sea salt

3/4 tsp. (3.75 mL) ground ginger

1/4 tsp. (1.25 mL) ground allspice

1/4 tsp. (1.25 mL) ground cloves

1/4 tsp. (1.25 mL) ground black pepper

Place the cherries, onions and water in a large saucepan and bring to a boil. Turn the heat down to a simmer and cook for 10 minutes, until the onions are translucent.

Remove from the heat and purée in a food processor or blender until smooth. Return to the saucepan and add the remaining ingredients. Bring to a boil and cook, stirring frequently, until thick, about 30–40 minutes.

Place several small saucers in the refrigerator before you start the ketchup. To check for doneness, place a small amount of ketchup on a saucer and return it to the fridge until chilled. Draw your finger through the ketchup. If the track remains, the ketchup is done. Remove the pot from the heat when testing the ketchup to prevent overcooking.

Strain the ketchup through a sieve into a bowl. Cool and transfer to a sterilized jar. Covered and refrigerated, it keeps indefinitely.

There is nothing quite so beauteous as this. **And the aroma! Distract yourself by catching up on the ironing.**

Roast Leg of
Pork with Crackling
serves more than 8, but you can make hot pork sandwiches with the leftovers

1 small whole pork leg with skin, about
10 lbs. (4.5 kg)

1/4 cup (60 mL) sea salt

1/4 cup (60 mL) fresh sage leaves, coarsely
chopped

8 cloves garlic, minced

2 Tbsp. (30 mL) coarsely crushed black pepper

1 Tbsp. (15 mL) coarsely crushed fennel seeds

1/2 cup (120 mL) vegetable oil

2 cups (480 mL) dry white wine

The day before serving, trim any extra fat from the leg of pork. Turn the pork with the shank end away from you and imagine the roast as a leaf with a middle rib and the smaller ribs branching away from the middle. Using a very sharp knife, score the pork on each side of the midrib, following the imaginary smaller ribs, starting at the middle and continuing down along both sides of the roast without the cuts meeting in the center. Make the cuts 1 inch (2.5 cm) apart and about 1/2 inch (1.2 cm) deep. Combine the remaining ingredients except for the wine, and rub all over the pork and into the incisions. Cover and refrigerate overnight.

Five to six hours before serving, preheat the oven to 325°F (165°C). Brush the marinade lightly off the meat and transfer the roast to a large roasting pan. Roast for 4 1/2 hours or 25 minutes per pound (454 g). After 1 hour, pour the wine into the pan and baste the roast with pan juices every 1/2 hour. Check for doneness by inserting an instant-read thermometer into the thickest part of the leg. It should read 165–170°F (74–78°C).

Remove the roast from the pan and let it rest for 10 minutes. Remove the fat with a spoon or a fat separator. Transfer the juices to a pot and keep warm over low heat. Check the flavor of the pan juices, adding water if they seem too strong. Remove the crackling and trim off and discard any fat. Cut a V-shaped notch of meat out of the roast just above the shank end, and slice through the meat, freeing the slices by making a horizontal cut under the slices, along the top of the bone. Cut the crackling into strips and arrange with the meat on a heated platter. Serve the pan juices separately.

My love of charcuterie inspired me to experiment with dry-curing meats. These pork chops take on a hint of sausage flavor that is quite appealing. Try them with Sweet and Sour Cherry Ketchup, page 178 (and mashed potatoes, of course).

Pepper and Garlic Cured Pork Chops   serves 6

1½ tsp. (7.5 mL) black peppercorns

1 Tbsp. (15 mL) coriander seeds

1½ tsp. (7.5 mL) sea salt

1½ tsp. (7.5 mL) sugar

6 cloves garlic, peeled and thinly sliced

6 1-inch-thick (2.5-cm) rack pork chops or center-cut pork chops

1 Tbsp. (15 mL) vegetable oil

Coarsely crush the black peppercorns and coriander seeds and combine with the salt and sugar.

In a dish large enough to hold the pork chops in a single layer, sprinkle half the salt mixture and half the garlic. Place the chops in the dish and sprinkle with the remaining salt mixture and garlic, pressing it in with your fingers. Cover tightly and refrigerate for 1–3 days.

When you are ready to cook the chops, scrape the marinade from them. Preheat the oven to 350°F (175°C). Heat the vegetable oil in a heavy skillet over medium-high heat. Brown the chops well on both sides and place them in a single layer in a baking pan. Bake for 8–10 minutes. Serve immediately.

Rich and sumptuous, this doesn't need much more except simply steamed vegetables like cauliflower, green beans and spinach.

Pork Tenderloin with Gorgonzola Butter   serves 6

4 pork tenderloins, approximately 2 lbs. (900 g) in total

salt and pepper to taste

oil for frying pan

1/2 cup (120 mL) dry white wine

3/4 cup (180 mL) whipping cream

1/4 lb. (113 g) gorgonzola cheese at room temperature

1/2 cup (120 mL) unsalted butter, at room temperature

freshly ground black pepper to taste

1 Tbsp. (15 mL) minced chives

Preheat the oven to 350°F (175°C). Season the pork with salt and pepper.

Merely wipe a heavy cast iron frying pan with vegetable oil and heat over high heat. Add the pork and brown on all sides. Remove from the pan to a baking sheet and bake for 10–15 minutes until cooked through but still a bit pink.

In a small saucepan, reduce the wine over moderate heat to 1 Tbsp. (15 mL). Add the cream and reduce by half.

Remove from the heat and whisk the gorgonzola and butter into the sauce, whisking constantly until incorporated. Season to taste and add the chives.

To serve: Slice the tenderloin into 1-inch (2.5-cm) slices and place on heated plates. Surround with the sauce and serve immediately.

I like to double the meatballs in this recipe. They make fantastic sandwiches, pizzas and pastas. If you've eaten all the meatballs and have some cabbage left over, it can be thinned out to make a very good soup with the addition of some cooked pinto beans, small pasta shapes, or both!

Braised Savoy Cabbage with Meatballs serves 4 to 6

1 1-inch-thick (2.5-cm) slice of good white bread, crust removed

⅓ cup (80 mL) milk

½ lb. (227 g) ground beef

½ lb. (227 g) ground pork

2 oz. (57 g) pancetta, finely chopped

1 large egg

1 Tbsp. (15 mL) fresh parsley, chopped

3 Tbsp. (45 mL) freshly grated Parmesan cheese

2 Tbsp. (30 mL) onion, finely chopped

freshly ground black pepper

1 cup (240 mL) fine, dry breadcrumbs

2 Tbsp. (30 mL) olive oil

2 cloves garlic, minced

1½ lbs. (680 g) Savoy cabbage, cored and thinly sliced

sea salt and freshly ground black pepper

1 cup (240 mL) canned plum tomatoes, well-drained and coarsely chopped

Put the bread and milk in a small saucepan and turn the heat to low. When the bread has soaked up the milk, mash it to a paste and remove from the heat. Cool completely.

Combine the beef, pork, pancetta, egg, parsley, Parmesan, onion, pepper and the bread paste. Mix thoroughly. Alternatively, place the pancetta, egg, parsley, Parmesan, onion, pepper and bread paste in the work bowl of a food processor and pulse until everything is well combined, then add to the pork and beef and mix well.

Shape into meatballs about 1½ inches (3.8 cm) across. Roll in the breadcrumbs. Place on a baking sheet and brush the tops lightly with vegetable oil. Broil, turning the meatballs until they are lightly browned on all sides.

Heat the olive oil over medium heat in a wide pot or frying pan. Sauté the garlic until golden. Add the cabbage and stir for a moment. Turn the heat down to low and cover the pan. Cook the cabbage, stirring occasionally, until it is very soft and reduced by ⅓ of its original mass, about 1 hour. If the cabbage seems in danger of burning at any point, add a bit of water.

Season with salt and pepper. Turn the heat to medium and, with the pan uncovered, cook the cabbage until it is colored a light nut brown. Add the chopped tomatoes and cook for 10 minutes, stirring occasionally. Tuck the meatballs under the cabbage. Turn the heat to low. Cover and cook for 15–20 minutes.

A few simple ingredients can make a great dish. **If you don't have the time or patience for polenta, the sauce can be served over pasta. Porcini mushrooms, also known as cèpes, can be found in Italian delis and well-stocked supermarkets.**

Sausages with Polenta and Porcini Mushrooms   serves 4

1 oz. (28 g) dried porcini mushrooms

1 cup (240 mL) boiling water

1½ lbs. (680 g) sweet Italian sausage

1 Tbsp. (15 mL) olive oil

½ cup (120 mL) onion, finely diced

½ cup (120 mL) red wine

1 28-oz. (796-mL) can plum tomatoes, drained and finely chopped

sea salt and freshly ground black pepper

10 cups (2.5 L) water

2 tsp. (10 mL) sea salt

2 cups (480 mL) cornmeal

6 Tbsp. (90 mL) unsalted butter

1 cup (240 mL) freshly grated Parmesan cheese

Soak the porcini mushrooms in the boiling water until soft. Remove the mushrooms from the water and strain the soaking liquid through a coffee filter to remove the sand. Reserve the liquid. Examine the stem ends for sandy deposits and trim.

Cut the sausage into 1-inch (2.5-cm) pieces. Heat the olive oil in a frying pan over medium heat. Add the sausages and sauté until brown. Remove the sausages and add the onion. Sauté until the onion is translucent. Return the sausage to the pan and add the red wine. Simmer until the wine is reduced by half. Add the porcini liquid and reduce by half. Add the tomatoes and porcini. Simmer until thickened, about 20 minutes. Season with salt and pepper and remove from the heat.

In a large, heavy-bottomed pot, bring the water to a boil. Add the salt, then stir in the cornmeal in a slow steady stream. Turn the heat to medium-low and cook at a lively simmer for 1 hour, stirring frequently. Stir in the butter and Parmesan cheese. Spread the polenta on a platter or into individual bowls. Reheat the sauce and spoon over the polenta.

I would love to say that this tourtière has been passed down to me from my great-great-grandmother, and eaten by my family on countless Christmas Eves, but I can't. Instead, it is the culmination of years of my own tourtière making. I like it best as a leftover, right out of the fridge. It's the kind of food that is good to have while you are looking in the fridge, deciding what to eat.

Tourtière (for Nora)   serves 6

2½ lbs. (1.1 kg) ground pork

1½ cups (360 mL) onion, finely diced

3 cups (720 mL) water

1 tsp. (5 mL) sea salt

¼ tsp. (1.25 mL) freshly ground black pepper

1 tsp. (5 mL) ground dried ginger

large pinch cinnamon

½ tsp. (2.5 mL) ground nutmeg

¼ tsp. (1.25 mL) ground allspice

⅛ tsp. (.5 mL) ground cloves

½ tsp. (2.5 mL) dried thyme

½–1 cup (120–240 mL) fine dry breadcrumbs

3 cups (720 mL) all-purpose flour

½ tsp. (2.5 mL) sea salt

9 oz. (255 g) lard

7 Tbsp. (105 mL) cold water

In a large nonstick or heavy pot, cook the pork and onion over medium heat, crumbling the pork with the back of a spoon, until it is cooked through. Transfer to a sieve to drain off the fat and return to the pot. Add the water, salt, pepper, ginger, cinnamon, nutmeg, allspice, cloves and thyme. Simmer over low heat, stirring occasionally, until the pork is tender, about 1 hour. The mixture should not be dry. Add a bit more water if you think it necessary while the pork is simmering.

Remove from the heat and stir in ½ cup (120 mL) of the breadcrumbs. Check the consistency. The pork mixture should be soft and flowing, with all of the liquid absorbed by the breadcrumbs. Use up to 1 cup (240 mL) of bread-crumbs if you think it necessary. Check the seasoning and adjust it, as the breadcrumbs will make the filling less zesty.

While the filling is cooking, make the crust. Combine the flour and salt in a large bowl. Cut the lard into ½-inch (1.2-cm) cubes and toss with the flour. Gently work the lard into the flour with your fingertips or a pastry blender until it forms pea-sized pieces. Pour in the chilled water and mix with your fingertips until it forms a loosely struc-tured ball. There may be a few bits and pieces left in the bottom of the bowl — don't try to incorporate them. Wrap the dough in plastic wrap and keep in a cool place until you are ready to roll it out. The tourtière filling and the pastry may be made 2 days in advance. Wrap well and refrigerate.

1 egg yolk

2 tsp. (10 mL) water

Preheat the oven to 425°F (220°C). Remove the pastry and tourtière filling from the refrigerator and let them sit at room temperature for ½ hour to take the chill off if you have made them in advance. Divide the dough into two balls, one slightly larger than the other, and flatten out on a well-floured surface. Roll out the larger piece with a floured rolling pin to ¼-inch (.6-cm) thickness. Roll the pastry around the pin as if you are rolling up a jelly roll and unroll over a 9-inch (23-cm) deep pie pan. Without stretching it, gently smooth and pat the dough into the pan.

Place the filling in the pan and smooth the top. Brush the rim lightly with water. Roll out the smaller piece of dough in the same manner as you rolled out the bottom and place over the top. Trim the edge to ½ inch (1.2 cm) and crimp in any way that pleases you. You can cut leaves out of the remaining dough and use them to decorate the top of the tourtière, gluing them on by lightly brushing the underside with water. Cut a V or a decorative pattern in the top to let the steam escape. Beat the egg yolk with the water and brush the top of the pie. Place on a tray (to catch any drips) and bake for 15 minutes. Reduce the heat to 375°F (190°C) and bake for 45–60 minutes, until the tourtière is a deep golden brown. Remove from the oven and let stand for 15 minutes before cutting.

Cauliflower is nothing but cabbage
with a college education.

MARK TWAIN

Fennel is nothing but celery
with a college education.

KAREN BARNABY

vegetables

vegetables

Simple and good. One of my favorite ways of cooking asparagus. This is just fine served at room temperature, but save the final flourish till just before serving.

Seared Asparagus with Aged Balsamic Vinegar   serves 4

1 lb. (454 g) fresh, medium-sized asparagus

sea salt and freshly ground black pepper

extra virgin olive oil

good-quality aged balsamic vinegar

Choose a large, heavy skillet: cast iron is ideal. Heat the pan over high heat until searingly hot. Add the asparagus in a single layer with the tips pointing in the same direction. As the asparagus turns bright green and gets a little charred in spots, rotate the spears to cook them on all sides. Continue with the remaining asparagus, heating the pan to searing between each batch. When all the spears are cooked, sprinkle with the salt, pepper, olive oil and balsamic vinegar.

These beans can be served hot or cold as a salad. If you want to be cheeky, divide the recipe in half and use yellow tomatoes, purple basil and green beans for one half; and yellow beans, red tomatoes and green basil for the other half. Serve them side by side. Ooo la la!

Smothered Green Beans with Tomatoes and Basil   serves 4 to 6

1 lb. (454 g) ripe plum tomatoes, or a 28-oz. (796-mL) can plum tomatoes, well drained and coarsely chopped

4 Tbsp. (60 mL) olive oil

4 medium cloves garlic, minced

1½ lbs. (680 g) green beans, topped and tailed

sea salt and freshly ground black pepper

1 cup (240 mL) fresh basil leaves

Peel and seed the tomatoes if you are using fresh ones, and cut them into 1-inch (2.5-cm) pieces.

In a large pot, heat the olive oil over medium heat and sauté the garlic until it turns pale gold. Add the tomatoes and cook for a few minutes until the tomatoes soften. Stir in the green beans and season lightly with salt and pepper. Cover with a lid and cook, stirring occasionally, until the beans are tender but firm. If the tomatoes are still watery, turn up the heat and cook until the liquid evaporates. Stir in the basil just before serving.

Technique is the most important ingredient here. The pan has to be smokingly hot before adding the oil and bean sprouts, to give them a desirable smoky edge. Perfect with Chicken Steamed with Ginger and Sherry, page 158.

Wok-Seared Bean Sprouts   serves 2 to 3

1 Tbsp. (15 mL) vegetable oil

1 lb. (454 g) bean sprouts

½ tsp. (2.5 mL) sea salt

pinch sugar

1 Tbsp. (15 mL) Chinese cooking wine or
   dry sherry

4 tsp. (20 mL) light soy sauce

Heat a heavy wok or cast iron frying pan over high heat until smoking. Add the oil, then the bean sprouts. Let them sit for a minute, until a thin dark line forms on the sprouts that are in contact with the pan. Flip the sprouts over and sear them for another minute. Sprinkle with the salt and sugar and stir-fry for a minute. Splash on the wine or sherry, stir and fry, and when it has almost evaporated, add the soy sauce. Stir and fry until the sprouts are tender-crisp. Transfer to a heated plate and serve immediately.

This is great in the dead of winter. **Serve it with any meat, but it goes especially well with sausages.**

Scalloped Savoy Cabbage   serves 6 to 8 generously

1 2-lb. (900-g) savoy cabbage

2 cups (480 mL) thinly sliced onions

4 cups (1 L) whipping cream

1 cup (240 mL) 18% or light cream

1½ tsp. (7.5 mL) sea salt

freshly ground black pepper to taste

Remove and discard the outer leaves of the cabbage and cut it into quarters. Core and thinly slice the cabbage. Place in a bowl and toss with the onions. Transfer to a deep 9- by 13-inch (23- by 33-cm) baking dish.

Preheat the oven to 350°F (175°C). Bring the creams, salt and pepper to a boil. Pour over the cabbage and cover tightly with tin foil or with a lid. Place on a baking pan that has also been covered with tin foil (to protect from drips). Place in the oven and bake for 45 minutes. Remove the lid and bake for 30 minutes longer. Remove from the oven and let the dish sit for 10 minutes before serving.

Corn with Guacamole

If you like corn chips with guacamole, you can bring the whole idea closer to its roots and have corn with guacamole. I love slathering the cool guacamole on the hot corn, studying the green swipe flecked with red on the gold background, and then chowing down on the crunchy cob.

I am a fanatic about making guacamole. Lime juice, not lemon, must be used, no food processor is used to blend it, and no garlic, cumin or shocking seasonings should distract your tongue from its smooth, creamy greenness. Since I'm on a bandwagon, I'll take the opportunity to moan over the omnipresence of Peaches and Cream corn. Where has all the good, yellow, corny-flavored corn gone?

To make guacamole, peel and pit 3 ripe Haas avocados. Place them in a bowl and coarsely mash them with a fork. Chunks of avocado are just fine — it shouldn't be completely smooth. Stir in 3/8 tsp. (2 mL) sea salt and 2 Tbsp. (30 mL) lime juice. Stir in a seeded and finely diced tomato, 1 Tbsp. (15 mL) coarsely chopped cilantro, 2 Tbsp. (30 mL) finely chopped white onion and a finely chopped fresh hot chili pepper. Add pepper to taste. Cover and refrigerate. Serve it within half an hour.

Corn, cream and eggs, pure and simple. **You can use the fancy presentation described here or just serve it plain. I have an attachment to simple corn dishes — pancakes, fritters, spoon bread served with a drizzle of maple syrup. Serve it for brunch with bacon or sausages. Dee-licious!**

Fresh Corn Pudding   serves 4 to 6

6 large ears fresh corn

1 cup (240 mL) whipping cream or milk

3 large eggs at room temperature, separated

2 Tbsp. (30 mL) unsalted butter, melted

1 Tbsp. (15 mL) sugar

3/4 tsp. (3.75 mL) sea salt

pinch cayenne pepper

Husk the corn and remove all the silk. Reserve 20 of the nice inner husks. Stack them up, and place a baking sheet over them. Place a weight on top of the baking sheet and let stand for 1/2 hour. You are flattening the cornhusks to line the baking dish. If you want to keep it simple, the dish will be fine without this step.

Preheat the oven to 350°F (175°C). Butter an 8-inch-square (20-cm) glass baking dish. Position one of the husks with the pointed end a few inches (8 cm) above the rim of the dish and the blunt end toward the center. Press the husk along the side of the dish and across the bottom. Continue along the side of the dish, slightly overlapping the cornhusks. Do the same on the opposite side. You may not need all the husks. Remember, this step may be omitted if you prefer.

Slice the corn kernels from each cob into a bowl. Scrape along each cob to extract any juices. Whisk in the cream or milk, egg yolks, butter, sugar, salt and cayenne. In a separate bowl, beat the egg whites until stiff but not dry. Fold into the corn mixture. Pour the batter into the prepared pan. Place the baking dish in a larger pan and pour enough hot water into the outer pan so that it comes halfway up the side of the baking dish. Bake for 25–30 minutes, until barely set in the middle. Serve either hot or warm.

The celery in this eggplant dish lightens the flavor. **Serve it hot, warm or at room temperature with simply prepared meats, fish and fowl. The eggplant may be grilled if you prefer.**

Eggplant Braised with Tomatoes, Pancetta and Balsamic Vinegar serves 4 to 6

1 lb. (454 g) eggplant, peeled and cut into 1-inch (2.5-cm) slices

extra virgin olive oil for brushing

2 Tbsp. (30 mL) extra virgin olive oil

3 cloves garlic, minced

2 oz. (57 g) pancetta, finely diced

½ cup (120 mL) finely diced celery

6 fresh sage leaves

4 Tbsp. (60 mL) balsamic vinegar

1 28-oz. (796-mL) can plum tomatoes, well drained and coarsely chopped

2 Tbsp. (30 mL) tomato paste (see page 84)

salt and pepper to taste

2 Tbsp. (30 mL) coarsely chopped parsley

1 clove garlic, minced

Preheat the broiler to high. Lightly brush both sides of the eggplant with olive oil and place in a single layer on a baking sheet. Broil, turning once until golden brown and tender. Cool.

Heat the 2 Tbsp. (30 mL) olive oil over medium heat in a large pan. Add the 3 cloves garlic, pancetta, celery and sage to the pan. Sauté until the celery becomes translucent. Add the vinegar. When it has almost evaporated, add the tomatoes and tomato paste. Bring to a simmer and season with salt and pepper. Cook over low heat for a few minutes until the sauce thickens slightly.

Cut the eggplant into 1-inch (2.5-cm) cubes. Add to the sauce and simmer for a few minutes to heat it through. Add the parsley and garlic, mix well and serve.

A delicious accompaniment **to simple roast chicken and pork.**

Parsnip and Pear Purée   serves 4 to 6

1¼–1½ lbs. (570–680 g) parsnips

1 medium red-skinned potato, peeled and cut into 1-inch (2.5-cm) pieces

2 ripe Bartlett pears, peeled, cored and cut into 1-inch (2.5-cm) pieces

1 whole clove

sea salt and freshly ground black pepper

2 Tbsp. (30 mL) unsalted butter

1 tsp. (5 mL) good-quality balsamic vinegar

Peel the parsnips, cut them into quarters and remove the woody cores. Cut the parsnips into 1-inch (2.5-cm) pieces. Cook the potatoes and parsnips in water to cover until they are tender. Drain.

While the potatoes and parsnips are cooking, simmer the pears and the clove in water until the pears are just tender but not mushy. Drain the pears and discard the clove.

Purée the vegetables and pears in the work bowl of a food processor or a food mill. Transfer to a saucepan and reheat gently. Season with salt and pepper. Stir in the butter and balsamic vinegar just before serving.

Rutabagas are those large golden and purple roots that are often called turnips. Turnips are smaller, white-bottomed and purple-topped. Quarter the rutabagas with a cleaver or large heavy knife before peeling them. This makes them much easier to handle. The balsamic vinegar balances the sweetness of the vegetable.

Rutabaga Purée with Balsamic Vinegar   serves 8

4 lbs. (1.8 kg) rutabagas, peeled and cut into 1-inch (2.5-cm) cubes

6 Tbsp. (90 mL) unsalted butter

2 Tbsp. (30 mL) sour cream or crème fraîche (see page 291)

sea salt and freshly ground black pepper

2 Tbsp. (30 mL) balsamic vinegar

Place the rutabagas in a pot and cover with cold water. Cook at a moderate boil until tender, 45 minutes to 1 hour. Drain well.

Purée the rutabagas in a food processor in 2 batches until completely smooth, or mash by hand. Return to the pot and stir in 1/2 the butter, the sour cream or crème fraîche and salt and pepper to taste. Stir over low heat until hot. Transfer to a large gratin or baking dish and bake in a 400°F (200°C) oven for 20–30 minutes. You can make the purée up to 2 days ahead, cover and refrigerate. If you do, bring the purée to room temperature and reheat, covered, for 35–45 minutes.

To finish the purée, melt the remaining butter and balsamic vinegar together over low heat. Drizzle over the purée and serve immediately.

My mother used to make a creamy and cheesy salmon casserole that used a lot of frozen spinach. It was the inspiration for Salmon Bake with Sour Cream, Bacon and New Red Potatoes, page 138. That creamy, cheesy spinach was also the inspiration for this quickly assembled dish with an updated Italian touch.

Broiled Spinach with Four Cheeses   serves 4

½ cup (120 mL) grated Asiago cheese

½ cup (120 mL) ricotta cheese

¼ cup (60 mL) crumbled Gorgonzola or blue cheese

2 Tbsp. (30 mL) freshly grated Parmesan cheese

2 Tbsp. (30 mL) chopped fresh basil

1 large egg yolk

2 Tbsp. (30 mL) extra virgin olive oil

2 cloves garlic, minced

2 10-oz. (285-g) packages fresh spinach, coarsely chopped

Preheat the broiler to medium. Lightly butter a baking dish 11 by 7 by 2 inches (28 by 18 by 5 cm).

Mix the cheeses, basil and egg yolk in a large bowl. Heat the oil in a large pot over medium high heat, then add the garlic. Stir and cook for a minute until fragrant. Pour garlic and oil into the prepared baking dish. Add the spinach to the pot and sauté until wilted. Transfer the spinach to a strainer; drain well. Place the spinach over the garlic in the baking dish. Toss to coat it with the oil and spread it out evenly. Sprinkle with the cheese mixture. Broil until the cheese is golden on top and the spinach is heated through.

This is excellent served with lamb. Garam masala is an East Indian blend of sweet spices, such as cinnamon, nutmeg and cardamom. It is usually added at the last minute to cooked foods for an extra boost of flavor. The recipe for Punjabi-Style Garam Masala is on page 205.

Creamed Spinach with Garam Masala   serves 8

4 lbs. (1.8 kg) fresh spinach, stemmed, washed and dried

1 Tbsp. (15 mL) unsalted butter

4 cloves garlic, minced

4 Tbsp. (60 mL) shallots, finely chopped

1 cup (240 mL) whipping cream

½ tsp. (2.5 mL) sea salt

1 cup (240 mL) cream cheese, cut into cubes

1 tsp. (5 mL) fennel seeds

½ tsp. (2.5 mL) garam masala (see page 205)

pinch cayenne pepper

Coarsely chop the spinach and set aside. Melt the butter over medium heat in a large, heavy, preferably nonstick pot. Add the garlic and shallots and sauté until the shallots are translucent. Add the whipping cream and salt and bring to a simmer. Stir in the spinach by handfuls, adding more as it cooks down. Turn to low and cook, stirring frequently, until the spinach is extremely soft and the cream is almost absorbed, about 20 minutes. Add the cream cheese and stir until melted. Heat a small frying pan over high heat. Add the fennel seeds and roast, shaking the pan, until the seeds turn one shade darker. Add to the spinach along with the garam masala and cayenne. Mix well.

Make this in the summer when you can find small sui choy. Most of the flavor of this dish comes from grilling as much of the surface area as possible. Sui choi is also known as Napa cabbage or Chinese cabbage.

Grilled Sui Choy with Mustard and Caraway   serves 6

2 lbs. (900 g) sui choy

½ cup (120 mL) Dijon mustard

¼ cup (60 mL) water

2 Tbsp. (30 mL) vegetable oil

1 tsp. (5 mL) caraway seeds

freshly ground black pepper to taste

Preheat the barbecue to medium high. Remove the outer leaves of the sui choy and cut them into quarters.

Mix the remaining ingredients in a large bowl. Add the sui choy and toss well to coat with the Dijon mixture. Place the cabbage on the grill and cook until deeply marked on all sides. Transfer to a platter and serve.

This simple wintry dish will complement **almost any simple meat or fish dish. You can substitute green Swiss chard, mustard greens or rapini for the red Swiss chard, if you like.**

Red Swiss Chard with Bacon, Garlic and White Wine   serves 4

1 lb. (454 g) red Swiss chard, coarse stems removed, washed and drained

1 tsp. (5 mL) vegetable oil

2 slices bacon, finely chopped

2 cloves garlic, thinly sliced

⅓ cup (80 mL) white wine

⅛ tsp. (.5 mL) sea salt

freshly ground black pepper to taste

Coarsely chop the Swiss chard and reserve.

Heat the vegetable oil in a large pot over medium heat. Sauté the bacon and garlic until the bacon is crisp and the garlic is lightly browned. Add the Swiss chard, white wine and salt. Cover and cook over low heat until tender, approximately 10 – 12 minutes. Season with pepper just before serving.

Stir-Fried Swiss Chard with Garlic, Anchovies and Raisins   serves 4

1 Tbsp. (15 mL) golden raisins

2 tsp. (10 mL) balsamic vinegar

2 tsp. (10 mL) water

1 Tbsp. (15 mL) olive oil

3 medium cloves garlic, minced

3 anchovies, finely chopped

1 dried hot red pepper, finely chopped

2 medium bunches Swiss chard, washed and dried, leaves coarsely chopped and stems thinly sliced

sea salt and freshly ground black pepper to taste

In a small frying pan, combine the raisins, balsamic vinegar and water. Bring to a boil and remove from the heat. Cover and let stand while preparing the rest of the ingredients.

Heat a wok or heavy frying pan over high heat. Add the oil and garlic and stir-fry for 10 seconds. Add the anchovies and hot pepper and stir well. Add the Swiss chard and stir-fry over high heat until it wilts. Turn the heat to medium and continue stir-frying until the chard is tender. Add the raisins and balsamic vinegar and season with salt and pepper.

These look so good **when cooked it is hard to resist eating them out of the pan! Great hot, cold or at room temperature.**

Roasted Summer Tomatoes with Parsley, Garlic and Olive Oil   serves 6 to 8

2 lbs. (900 g) perfectly ripe tomatoes, about 8

½ tsp. (2.5 mL) sea salt

4 Tbsp. (60 mL) olive oil

4 cloves garlic, minced

2 Tbsp. (30 mL) fresh parsley, finely chopped

1 tsp. (5 mL) freshly ground black pepper

Preheat the oven to 400°F (200°C). Wash and cut the tomatoes in half crosswise. Place them, cut side up, in a 9- by 13-inch (23- by 33-cm) baking dish. They will fit snugly. Sprinkle with the salt and drizzle with 2 Tbsp. (30 mL) of the olive oil. Place on the middle rack of the oven and bake for 45 minutes. Mix together the remaining olive oil, garlic, parsley and black pepper. Remove the tomatoes from the oven and spread with the mixture. Return to the oven and bake 45 minutes longer.

Cherry tomatoes used to scare me. I ate a rotten one as a child and found the way it popped in my mouth utterly vile. Now, I can barely wait for cherry tomato season. There are so many wonderfully sweet varieties available now, especially from organic growers, that I just eat them plain. This is a quick dish that I make with my new-found love. Using different varieties of cherry tomatoes is especially attractive.

Cherry Tomatoes in Brown Butter Sauce   serves 4

3 Tbsp. (45 mL) unsalted butter

3 cups (720 mL) cherry tomatoes, stems removed

1/4 cup (60 mL) chopped fresh parsley

1/4 cup (60 mL) fresh basil leaves

1 Tbsp. (15 mL) lemon juice

sea salt and freshly ground black pepper to taste

Melt the butter over medium heat, stirring constantly until brown. Add the tomatoes and cook about 3 minutes, or until the skins pop, stirring constantly. Add the parsley, basil and lemon juice. Season with the salt and pepper and serve immediately.

Mashed Potatoes and Carrots   page 213

Oatmeal Raisin Cake with Broiled Coconut Cashew Icing   page 235

Instant Ecstasy Chocolate Cookies page 249

Aunt Toni's Steamed Cranberry Pudding with Eggnog Sauce   page 272

I love using French lentils. They hold their shape when cooked and have a bright, earthy flavor. Originally from Le Puy, France, a lot of them are now grown in Saskatchewan. Some specialty stores carry them, but they are not necessary to make the recipe. This is a no-fuss method of cooking beans and lentils. Check them every hour if you want firm, shapely beans, otherwise cook them overnight. Simple to prepare, packed with flavor, these lentils are spicy, so adjust the cayenne to your taste.

Punjabi-Style French Lentils   serves 4

1⅓ cups (320 mL) French lentils

1 Tbsp. (15 mL) grated fresh ginger

1 Tbsp. (15 mL) minced garlic

2 medium tomatoes, finely chopped

1½ tsp. (7.5 mL) cayenne

sea salt

1½ tsp. (7.5 mL) Punjabi-Style Garam Masala (recipe follows)

4 Tbsp. (60 mL) unsalted butter

1 tomato, finely chopped

2 Tbsp. (30 mL) coarsely chopped cilantro

2 Tbsp. (30 mL) finely chopped red onion

1 Tbsp. (15 mL) freshly squeezed lime juice

sea salt

Punjabi-Style Garam Masala
makes ¾ cup (180 mL)

3 Tbsp. (45 mL) coriander seeds

3 Tbsp. (45 mL) cumin seeds

2½ Tbsp. (37.5 mL) black peppercorns

2½ Tbsp. (37.5 mL) black cardamom seeds (seeds removed from pods)

1½ tsp. (7.5 mL) green cardamom seeds (seeds removed from pods)

1 2-inch (5-cm) stick cinnamon

5 whole cloves

⅙ of a whole nutmeg

Preheat the oven to 250°F (120°C). Pick over the lentils for stones and wash them. Place them in a large pot with 8 cups (2 L) water. Bring to a boil and skim off any foam that rises to the top. Cover with a tight-fitting lid and place in the oven. Check the lentils after 1 hour, or 2 hours for regular lentils. They should be tender.

Remove from the oven and mash half the lentils to a paste. Stir in the ginger, garlic, 2 chopped tomatoes, cayenne, salt and garam masala. Cover, return to the oven and cook for 30 minutes longer. Stir in the butter until melted.

Before serving, combine the tomato, cilantro, onion, lime juice and salt. Serve on the side with lentils.

Punjabi-Style Garam Masala
It is gratifying and rewarding to make your own spice blends. You will rarely find the same sparkle and flavor in a store-bought blend—especially if it has been sitting on the shelf for a while.

Heat a small frying pan over medium heat, add the coriander and cumin and dry-roast, stirring frequently, until the seeds turn one shade darker. Pour into a bowl to cool. Combine with the remaining spices and grind to a powder in a coffee grinder. Store, tightly covered, in a cool dark place.

These beans are more savory and spicy than the traditional, molasses-sweetened version. Chinese pork belly is a sweet cured bacon sold in pieces in Oriental grocery stores. Chinese sausage or regular bacon can be used instead.

Hoisin Baked Beans serves 6 to 8

3 cups (720 mL) dried navy beans

1 cup (240 mL) finely diced onions

4 cups (1 L) water

2/3 cup (160 mL) ketchup

1/2 cup (120 mL) soy sauce

1 Tbsp. (15 mL) Dijon mustard

3 Tbsp. (45 mL) hoisin sauce

1 tsp. (5 mL) chili paste

2 1/4-inch (.6-cm) slices ginger

6 cloves garlic, cut in half

1/4 lb. (113 g) cured Chinese pork belly or
    salt pork, diced (optional)

Place the beans in a large pot and cover with 6 inches (15 cm) of water. Bring to a boil, then turn down to a simmer, skimming off the foam that rises to the top. Cook until the beans are tender. Drain.

Preheat the oven to 250°F (120°C). Combine the beans and remaining ingredients in a tall, narrow casserole dish with a tight-fitting lid. Cover and bake for 6 hours.

*This summery vegetable dish **may be served either hot, or cold as a salad.***

Spaghetti Squash with Roasted Garlic and Sun-Dried Tomatoes   serves 4 to 6

1 small spaghetti squash, about 2 lbs. (900 g)

½ cup (120 mL) water

1½ Tbsp. (20 mL) cider vinegar

½ tsp. (2.5 mL) sea salt

¼ tsp. (1.25 mL) ground black pepper

3 sun-dried tomatoes, rehydrated or oil-packed

10 cloves roasted garlic (see below)

½ cup (120 mL) olive oil

2 medium, ripe tomatoes, seeded and diced into ¼-inch (.6-cm) pieces

½ cup (120 mL) chopped parsley

¼ cup (60 mL) basil leaves, torn into small pieces

Stove-Top Roasted Garlic
makes 1½-pint (250-mL) jar

4 heads garlic

vegetable or olive oil

Preheat the oven to 350°F (175°C). Cut the squash in half and place cut side down in a baking dish. Pour the water around the squash and cover tightly with tin foil or a lid. Bake for about 1 hour, until tender.

While the squash is baking, prepare the rest of the ingredients. To make the dressing, purée the vinegar, salt, pepper, sun-dried tomatoes and garlic in the work bowl of a food processor or blender. With the motor on, add the olive oil in a slow steady stream. Transfer to a bowl.

When the squash is done, scrape it from the shell into a bowl. Toss with the dressing. If you are serving the squash hot, combine with the remaining ingredients and serve immediately. If you are serving it cold, let it cool to room temperature then toss with the tomatoes, parsley and basil.

Stove-Top Roasted Garlic
Choose impeccably fresh, firm heads of garlic with no green sprouts. Separate the heads into cloves and peel them. Place the peeled cloves in a small heavy pot or frying pan and cover with oil. Place on the stove over medium-low heat.

As soon as bubbles form around the garlic, turn the heat to low and cook cloves until golden brown and completely soft. This will take anywhere from 20–40 minutes. Remove from the heat and cool. Covered and stored in the refrigerator, the garlic keeps for 1 month.

This is a good thing to eat **for dinner with a green salad or steamed spinach.**

Winter Vegetable Casserole serves 6 to 8

butter for baking dish

1½ lbs.(680 g) russet potatoes, peeled and cut into 1-inch (2.5-cm) chunks

1½ lbs. (680 g) rutabaga, peeled and cut into 1-inch (2.5-cm) chunks

1 small Savoy cabbage, cut into 4 wedges, cored and cut into ½-inch (1.2-cm) slices

½ lb. (227 g) peeled carrots, thinly sliced

1 lb. (454 g) cream cheese, preferably natural, cut into small pieces

½ cup (120 mL) freshly grated Parmesan cheese

sea salt and freshly ground black pepper

2 Tbsp. (30 mL) unsalted butter

Butter a 9- by 13-inch (23- by 33-cm) baking dish and preheat the oven to 350°F (175°C).

Place the vegetables in a large pot, cover with cold water and bring to a boil. Salt liberally. Cook until the potatoes are tender, 10–15 minutes. Drain well and return to the pot. Mash the vegetables, being concerned only that the potatoes are well mashed.

Stir in the cream cheese and Parmesan cheese and season with salt and pepper. Transfer the vegetables to the buttered baking dish and dot the top with butter. Bake for 45 minutes, until the top is lightly browned. You may prepare and refrigerate the casserole a day in advance. Remove from the fridge and bake for 1 to 1¼ hours until hot all the way through.

Celeriac are knobbly, hairy root vegetables that appear for sale in the fall. They have a distinct celery flavor and are delicious mixed with potatoes as a purée or in a gratin. The traditional French celeriac remoulade is made from julienned celeriac tossed with a mustardy vinaigrette.

Potato and Celery Root Gratin   serves 8

1½ lbs. (680 g) celery root, washed

1½ lbs. (680 g) russet potatoes

¾ cup (180 mL) whipping cream

1 Tbsp. (15 mL) Dijon mustard

1 tsp. (5 mL) sea salt

freshly ground black pepper

1 clove garlic, minced

¼ tsp. (1.25 mL) nutmeg

1 cup (240 mL) grated Swiss or Gruyère cheese

Preheat the oven to 375°F (190°C). Butter a 2-qt. (2-L) gratin dish. Peel the celery root, cut in quarters and remove the core if spongy. Thinly slice crosswise. Bring a large pot of water to a boil and add the celery root. Cook until barely tender, about 5 minutes. Remove with a slotted spoon to a colander to drain. Keep the water boiling.

Peel the potatoes, cut into ¼-inch (.6-cm) slices and transfer to the boiling water. Cook until they are barely tender, about 5 minutes. Transfer with a slotted spoon to the same colander. Reserve 1¼ cups (300 mL) of the cooking liquid.

Gently toss the celeriac and potatoes together. Spread out evenly in the baking dish. Bring the reserved cooking water, cream, mustard, salt, pepper, garlic and nutmeg to a simmer and pour over the vegetables. Bake until the sauce is bubbly and the vegetables tender, about 45 minutes. Sprinkle with the grated cheese and bake for 15 minutes longer.

This stands well on its own **with an interesting salad, or as an accompaniment to grilled steaks, or cut in small pieces on a buffet. Serve warm or at room temperature.**

Potato and Goat Cheese Cake with Rosemary   serves 6

1½ lbs. (680 g) small red potatoes

4 Tbsp. (60 mL) unsalted butter, at room temperature

¼ lb. (113 g) soft goat cheese, crumbled

½ cup (120 mL) sour cream

2 large eggs

½ tsp. (2.5 mL) sea salt

½ tsp. (2.5 mL) freshly ground black pepper

2 tsp. (10 mL) fresh parsley, finely chopped

1 tsp. (5 mL) fresh rosemary, finely chopped

Put the potatoes in a large pot, cover with cold water by 2 inches (5 cm), bring to a boil and cook until the potatoes are barely tender. They should be very firm and barely cooked in the center. Drain and cool.

Oil a 9-inch (23-cm) square baking dish and line with parchment paper or well-buttered, heavy-duty aluminum foil, allowing the ends to hang over the side for easy removal later. Preheat the oven to 375°F (190°C).

In a large bowl, cream the butter and goat cheese together. Beat in the sour cream, eggs, salt, pepper, parsley and rosemary. Slice the cooled potatoes into ¼-inch (.6-cm) slices. Gently stir the potatoes into the goat cheese mixture. Transfer to the baking pan and gently smooth the top. Bake for 35–45 minutes, until the potatoes are tender when pierced with a knife. Place on a rack to cool. Lift the potato cake out of the pan and cut into pieces, discarding the foil or parchment paper.

A friend of mine was enthusiastic about these potatoes but commented that they were not burnt enough — the way he enjoyed them growing up. Sometimes sentimentality surpasses cultivated adult taste buds and he went home with a pan of potatoes to burn at his leisure If you share his sentiment, by all means cook them until burnt!

Decadent Scalloped Potatoes *serves 6 to 8 generously*

3 lbs. (1.4 kg) medium red-skinned potatoes, peeled

1 medium clove garlic, minced

1¼ tsp. (6.2 mL) sea salt

½ tsp. (2.5 mL) freshly ground black pepper

1 cup (240 mL) freshly grated Parmesan cheese

3 cups (720 mL) whipping cream

1 cup (240 mL) 18% or light cream

Preheat the oven to 350°F (175°C). Thinly slice the potatoes as if making potato chips. Mash the garlic to a paste with some of the salt. Add to the potatoes with the rest of the salt, pepper and Parmesan cheese. Toss the potatoes well and place in a deep 9- by 13-inch (23- by 33-cm) baking dish.

Combine the creams in a saucepan and bring to a boil. Pour over the potatoes and cover tightly with tin foil. Place the baking dish on a pan that you have also covered with foil (to protect from drips). Bake covered for 1 hour. Remove the foil from the top of the potatoes and bake for ½ hour longer until golden brown.

Rapini, also known as broccoli rabe, appears in winter and early spring. As with most winter greens, cooking until tender brings out the sweet mellow flavor. This dish can be cooked without the chorizo if you prefer. It is sublime tossed with a crumbling of goat cheese before it leaves the pot.

A "Mess" of Potatoes, Rapini and Chorizo Sausage   serves 4 to 6

1 raw, unsmoked chorizo sausage

1½ lbs. (680 g) rapini

1 Tbsp. (15 mL) olive oil

1 lb. (454 g) red-skinned potatoes, unpeeled, sliced ¼ inch (.6 cm) thick

2 cups (480 mL) water, lightly salted

sea salt and freshly ground black pepper to taste

lemon wedges

Remove the sausage from its casing and set aside. Pluck the leaves, tender stems and florets from the rapini and discard the tough stalks. Wash and drain the leaves and florets.

Heat the olive oil in a saucepan over medium heat and sauté the chorizo until it loses its raw color. Add the potatoes and salted water. Bring to a boil and cook until tender, about 20–30 minutes. The liquid will reduce as the potatoes cook, but if they look like they are in danger of drying out, add another ½ cup (120 mL) of water.

When the potatoes are tender, add the rapini. There should be about ½ cup (120 mL) of liquid left in the pot. Add water if needed. Cover and cook for about 10 minutes over medium heat, stirring occasionally, until the rapini is tender. Season with salt and pepper. Serve with the lemon wedges.

My grandmother made this for me, **plain and simple, with a bit of butter melting in a small crater in the middle. I was quite content to eat it all by itself for dinner.**

Mashed Potatoes and Carrots serves 4 to 6

1½ lbs. (680 g) russet potatoes, peeled and cut into 1-inch (2.5-cm) cubes

½ lb. (227 g) small carrots, peeled and thinly sliced

2 tsp. (10 mL) sea salt

4 Tbsp. (60 mL) unsalted butter

½ cup (120 mL) hot milk

sea salt and freshly ground black pepper

Place the vegetables in a large pot. Cover them with cold water, add the salt and bring to a boil. Cook until the potatoes are completely tender, 15–20 minutes. Drain well and return to the pot. Mash until the potatoes are completely smooth; the carrots will remain in small pieces. Add the butter and beat until incorporated, then stir in the milk. Season to taste.

KEEPING MASHED POTATOES HOT

You can keep mashed potatoes hot by using a double boiler. Transfer the hot mashed potatoes to a non-metal bowl and place over a pot of simmering, not boiling, water and cover with a clean, dry cloth. The potatoes will keep hot for up to 2 hours.

One of the ultimate treatments **for the humble bowl of mash!**

Horseradish Mashed Potatoes   makes about 4 cups (1 L)

2 lbs. (900 g) russet or Yukon gold potatoes, peeled and cut into 1-inch (2.5-cm) cubes

2 tsp. (10 mL) sea salt

4 Tbsp. (60 mL) unsalted butter

½ cup (120 mL) hot milk

1 Tbsp. (15 mL) prepared horseradish

sea salt and freshly ground black pepper

Place the potatoes in a large pot with enough cold water to cover them by 4 inches (10 cm). Bring to a boil and add the salt. Cook until the potatoes are completely tender, about 20 minutes. Drain immediately and return them to the pot.

Mash the potatoes until smooth, or press through a ricer. Stir in the butter. When the butter is completely incorporated, stir in the hot milk and horseradish. Season with salt and pepper.

Serve immediately or keep warm over hot water in a double boiler, uncovered but covered with a clean, dry cloth, until ready to serve.

Olive Oil Mashed Potatoes   serves 4

1½ lbs. (680 g) russet potatoes

sea salt

⅓ cup (80 mL) extra virgin olive oil

½–¾ cup (120–180 mL) homogenized milk, heated

2 Tbsp. (30 mL) unsalted butter

sea salt to taste

Peel the potatoes and cut them into 1½-inch (3.7-cm) pieces. Place in a deep pot and cover with cold water. Add enough salt to make the water taste like sea water and bring to a boil. Cook until the potatoes are tender, approximately 20 minutes.

Drain the potatoes well. If you have a ricer, press the potatoes through the ricer back into the pot. If not, return them to the pot and mash by hand until smooth. With a wooden spoon, slowly beat in the olive oil. Add the warmed milk a little at a time, until the potatoes are light and fluffy. You may not need all the milk. Stir in the butter and adjust the seasoning with salt if needed.

I stumbled upon the wheat berry and mashed potato combo while eating a spoonful of wheat berries and checking the mashed potatoes at work a few years ago; I was captivated by the contrasting textures of the chewy wheat and the smooth potatoes. Since then, they have graced rare duck breast and venison with sour cherry and blue cheese butter. Plain old mashed potatoes and wheat berries are great together, but they become even more of an event when combined with grainy mustard and cheddar. This dish goes well with plainly prepared meats, or have it with a mound of spinach sautéed with prosciutto.

Yukon Gold Potatoes Mashed with Wheat Berries, Mustard and Cheddar Cheese   serves 6

½ cup (120 mL) soft wheat berries, washed and drained

1½ lbs. (680 g) Yukon Gold potatoes, peeled and cut into 1-inch (2.5-cm) cubes

2 Tbsp. (30 mL) unsalted butter

¼ cup (60 mL) warm milk

2 Tbsp. (30 mL) grainy mustard

1 cup (240 mL) grated, sharp white Cheddar cheese

sea salt to taste

Place the wheat berries in a medium saucepan and cover with ample cold water. Bring to a boil, turn down to a simmer and cover. Cook for 1–1½ hours until the wheat berries just start to open, replenishing the water if necessary. Drain, return to the pot and cover. The wheat berries may be prepared several hours ahead up to this point or refrigerated, covered, overnight.

Place the potatoes in a large pot and cover with ample cold water. Bring to a boil and cook for about 15 minutes, or until tender.

Reserve ½ cup (120 mL) of the cooking water and drain the potatoes. Return them to the pot and mash until smooth. Stir in the butter, milk and enough of the cooking water to make the potatoes smooth and creamy. If the wheat berries are cold, warm them in a pot over medium heat with a scant amount of water. Drain them and add to the potatoes. Stir in the mustard and cheese. Check for salt and adjust the seasoning. Serve immediately.

These are also good **at room temperature as a potato salad.**

Balsamic Roast Potatoes with Feta and Mint   serves 4 to 6

1 tsp. (5 mL) Dijon mustard

½ tsp. (2.5 mL) sea salt

1 clove garlic, minced

4 Tbsp. (60 mL) balsamic vinegar

½ cup (120 mL) extra virgin olive oil

4 large russet potatoes

½ tsp. (2.5 mL) salt

1 Tbsp. (30 mL) extra virgin olive oil

½ cup (120 mL) crumbled feta cheese

½ cup (120 mL) coarsely chopped mint

freshly ground black pepper

To make the vinaigrette, whisk the Dijon, salt, garlic and balsamic vinegar together. Slowly beat in the olive oil.

Preheat the oven to 450°F (225°C). Scrub the potatoes, pat them dry and cut them into 6 wedges each lengthwise. Toss with the ½ tsp. (2.5 mL) salt and 1 Tbsp. (30 mL) olive oil. Spread them out into a single layer, one of the cut sides down, on a baking sheet. Bake for 15 minutes. Turn over and bake for 15 minutes longer until browned and cooked through. Remove from the oven and toss with the vinaigrette, feta, mint and pepper.

Home fries, move over! This is one of the most delicious potatoes in the pan-fried category you will ever come across. The lengthy cooking tones down the black pepper, but it still makes its presence known.

Crispy Potatoes with Garlic, Ginger and Black Pepper   serves 4

1½ lbs. (680 g) small new potatoes

1 3-inch (7.5-cm) piece fresh ginger, peeled

4 cloves garlic

4 Tbsp. (60 mL) water

¾ tsp. (3.75 mL) sea salt

1½ tsp. (7.5 mL) coarsely ground black pepper

2 Tbsp. (30 mL) vegetable oil

2 Tbsp. (30 mL) coarsely chopped cilantro

2 green onions, thinly sliced

lime wedges

Scrub the potatoes and place them in a pot. Cover with cold water and cook over high heat until the potatoes are just barely tender, about 15 minutes. Drain and cool completely.

Coarsely chop the ginger and garlic. Place in a blender or food processor with the water and salt. Blend until a fine paste is formed. Add the pepper and pulse briefly to combine.

Cut the potatoes into 1-inch (2.5-cm) cubes.

Heat the oil over medium-high heat in a large, heavy, non-stick frying pan or well-seasoned cast iron pan. Add the ginger paste and cook, stirring frequently, for about 2 minutes, until the paste separates from the oil. Add the potatoes and cook, turning frequently, until the potatoes are a crusty brown, 7–10 minutes. Regulate the heat to allow the potatoes to become tender and browned without burning. Stir in the cilantro and green onions. Serve garnished with lime wedges.

The lemon balances **the sweetness of the potatoes.**

Lemon Roasted Sweet Potatoes   serves 4

4 medium unpeeled sweet potatoes, cut in half lengthwise, then into 1-inch (2.5-cm) pieces

1 lemon, thinly sliced and seeded

3 small sprigs fresh rosemary, torn into 1-inch (2.5-cm) pieces

½ tsp. (2.5 mL) sea salt

2 Tbsp. (30 mL) olive oil

2 Tbsp. (30 mL) freshly grated Parmesan cheese

Preheat the oven to 400°F (200°C). Combine and toss the potatoes, lemon, rosemary, salt and olive oil. Lay out in a single layer on a baking sheet. Bake for 40–45 minutes, until the potatoes are tender, turning once halfway through. Remove from the oven and toss with the Parmesan cheese.

This recipe illustrates that the whole is tastier than the sum of its parts. **The bourbon gives a great "edge" to the potatoes. This goes especially well with pork. Another cooking class favorite.**

Sweet Potato and Apple Purée with Bourbon   serves 8

5 lbs. (2.25 kg) sweet potatoes or yams

4 Granny Smith apples, cored

2 Tbsp. (30 mL) unsalted butter

¼ cup (60 mL) sour cream

¼ cup (60 mL) brown sugar

¼ cup (60 mL) bourbon

sea salt and freshly ground black pepper

Preheat the oven to 400°F (200°C). Prick the sweet potatoes with a fork and place them on a baking sheet. Place the apples in the middle of the potatoes. Roast for about an hour, until the potatoes and apples are completely tender. Check the apples after ¼ hour and remove them if they are tender. Remove from the oven and cool for 15 minutes.

Cut the potatoes and apples in half and scoop out all the flesh. Either purée the potatoes and apples in a food processor or with a hand mixer, or mash them by hand, depending upon the texture you like. Place in a heavy pot. Stir in the butter until melted, then add the sour cream, brown sugar and bourbon. Season with salt and pepper. The dish can be made a day in advance. Cover and refrigerate. Warm over low heat until heated through.

*I like to demonstrate this recipe in cooking classes **as it wins instant converts. Remember this one the next time you serve turkey.***

Mashed Sweet Potatoes with Blue Cheese   serves 4 to 6

3 large sweet potatoes, or yams, about
  2 lbs. (900 g), peeled and cut into
  1-inch (2.5-cm) cubes

4 Tbsp. (60 mL) unsalted butter

sea salt and freshly ground black pepper

1 cup (240 mL) crumbled blue cheese

Cook the sweet potatoes in boiling water until tender, about 25 minutes. Drain.

Mash by hand if you like a chunky texture or purée in a food processor. Add the butter. Season with salt and pepper and stir in the blue cheese. (The potatoes may be prepared a day in advance and reheated over low heat on top of the stove or in a microwave oven. Stir in the blue cheese just before serving.)

The candied ginger used in this recipe is the dry crystallized one, dusted with granulated sugar. I have a real fondness for it and like to nibble it with chocolate after dinner. Its sharpness is a great match for the silky sweet potatoes.

Sweet Potatoes with Candied Ginger   serves 6 to 8

½ cup (120 mL) candied ginger

3 lbs. (1.4 kg) sweet potatoes, peeled and cubed

4 Tbsp. (60 mL) unsalted butter

½ cup (120 mL) sour cream

sea salt and freshly ground black pepper

Either by hand or with a food processor, chop the ginger until it's almost puréed. Reserve.

Place the sweet potatoes in a large pot and cover with cold water. Bring to a boil and cook until the potatoes are tender, about 15 minutes. Drain and mash the potatoes by hand or purée in a food processor until smooth. Stir in the butter until melted, then the sour cream and ginger. Season with salt and pepper. The potatoes may be prepared up to 2 days in advance. Reheat over low heat, stirring frequently, until piping hot.

cakes

I'm not one to enter contests and competitions, **but the Ambrosia Apple Recipe Contest in 2002 appealed to me. Inspired by the Pillsbury Tunnel of Fudge Cake, I set to work and, miracle of miracles, I actually won the contest!**

Tunnel of Ambrosia Cake   serves 12 to 16

½ lb. (227 g) cream cheese, at room temperature

½ cup (120 mL) dark brown sugar

½ cup (120 mL) bourbon

1 tsp. (5 mL) pure vanilla extract

1 large egg

1½ lbs. (680 g) peeled, cored Ambrosia apples, cut into ½-inch (1.2-cm) dice

1 cup (240 mL) sweetened flaked coconut

1 cup (240 mL) coarsely chopped pecans

3 cups (720 mL) all-purpose flour

2 tsp. (10 mL) baking soda

½ tsp. (2.5 mL) sea salt

1 Tbsp. (15 mL) dried ground ginger

2 tsp. (10 mL) ground cinnamon

1 tsp. (5 mL) freshly grated nutmeg

½ tsp. (2.5 mL) ground cardamom

½ cup (120 mL) unsalted butter, at room temperature

½ cup (120 mL) white sugar

¾ cup (180 mL) dark brown sugar

2 Tbsp. (30 mL) molasses

2 tsp. (10 mL) pure vanilla extract

2 large eggs

1 cup (240 mL) buttermilk

You can use any firm and tasty apple for this cake if Ambrosia Apples are unavailable.

Preheat the oven to 350°F (175°C). Spray a 10-inch (25-cm) tube pan generously with nonstick spray.

Combine the cream cheese and brown sugar and beat with an electric mixer until well combined. Beat in the bourbon, vanilla and the egg until smooth. Stir in the apple, coconut and pecans. Set aside. Sift the flour, baking soda, salt and spices together.

Cream the butter. Add the white and brown sugar and beat until light and fluffy. Add the molasses, vanilla and then the eggs, one at a time, beating well after each. Add the flour mixture in three additions, alternating with the buttermilk. Spread ⅓ of the batter into the pan. Spoon the apple mixture evenly over the batter. Spread the remaining batter on top of the apples. Bake for 1 hour. Let cool in the pan on a rack for ½ hour before turning out of the pan. Let cool completely before slicing.

TUNNEL OF FUDGE CAKE
I have to credit Ella Rita Helfrich of Houston, Texas, who took second place for the Tunnel of Fudge Cake for the Pillsbury Bake-Off contest in 1966. She was 49 at the time.

The winner that year was Mari Petrelli of Ely, Nevada for her Golden Gate Snack Bread which had a baked-in filling of process cheese spread and onion soup mix.

It's odd that we never hear of the snack bread and that the Tunnel of Fudge Cake is very familiar to those of a certain age. In fact, it's almost synonymous with the bake-off contest.

The pan the cake was baked in was a bundt pan. After the contest, the sales for these pans soared.

Choose a fragrant honey for the sauce **of this simple cake. It makes all the difference. Without the sauce it's an everyday cake, great with butter.**

Apple Cake with Warm Honey Sauce   serves 12

3 cups (720 mL) all-purpose flour

1½ tsp. (7.5 mL) baking soda

1 tsp. (5 mL) cinnamon

¼ tsp. (1.25 mL) sea salt

¼ tsp. (1.25 mL) grated nutmeg

¾ cup (180 mL) vegetable oil

¼ cup (60 mL) unsalted butter, melted

1 cup (240 mL) granulated sugar

1 cup (240 mL) dark brown sugar, packed

3 large eggs

2 tsp. (10 mL) pure vanilla extract

3 large apples, peeled, cored and thinly sliced

1 cup (240 mL) honey

½ cup (120 mL) unsalted butter

½ cup (120 mL) whipping cream

pinch sea salt

Preheat the oven to 350°F (175°C). Butter and flour a 9- by 13-inch (23- by 33-cm) baking pan.

Combine the flour, baking soda, cinnamon, salt and nutmeg in a large bowl. Stir well with a whisk. In another large bowl, beat the oil, butter, sugars, eggs and vanilla together with a whisk until light. Beat in the flour mixture until smooth, then fold in the apples. Pour into the prepared pan and smooth the top. Bake for 45–50 minutes, until a cake tester comes out clean. Remove to a rack to cool in the pan.

To make the honey sauce, combine the honey, butter, cream and salt in a heavy pot. Bring to a boil, stirring occasionally, and boil for 1 minute. Serve warm over the cake.

STICKY TIP
When measuring honey, molasses, corn syrup or any sticky liquid, oil your measuring utensils or use a non-stick spray. The ingredient you are measuring will literally fall right out.

This is a combination of two childhood memories—a moist, dense banana and sour cream cake that my mother made in a small tube pan, and the yogurt sprinkled with brown sugar my grandmother fed me. This cake is moist and marvelous on its own or can be dressed up with the Cappucino Cream. To grate chocolate, either use the grating attachment of a food processor or put a plastic bag over your hand to hold the chocolate and grate it on a box grater or microwave.

Banana Chocolate Chiffon Cake with Cappucino Cream   serves 12

1 cup (240 mL) egg whites, from approximately 8 large eggs

½ tsp. (2.5 mL) cream of tartar

2¼ cups (540 mL) sifted cake flour

1¼ cups (300 mL) sugar

1 Tbsp. (15 mL) baking powder

1 cup (240 mL) grated bittersweet chocolate

½ tsp. (2.5 mL) sea salt

5 large egg yolks

1 cup (240 mL) very ripe mashed bananas

½ cup (120 mL) vegetable oil

6 Tbsp. (90 mL) water

1 tsp. (5 mL) pure vanilla extract

Preheat the oven to 325°F (165°C). Have an ungreased 10-inch (25-cm) tube pan with a removable bottom at hand. Do not use a nonstick pan.

In a large bowl, combine the egg whites and cream of tartar. With an electric mixer, beat on high speed to stiff-but-moist peaks.

Stir the flour, sugar, baking powder, chocolate and salt together. Make a well in the dry ingredients and add the egg yolks, bananas, oil, water and vanilla. With an electric mixer, beat the ingredients in the center of the well, gradually drawing in the dry ingredients. Beat just until smooth. Pour ⅓ of the batter over the egg whites and fold it in quickly but thoroughly. Repeat twice with the remaining batter.

Pour the batter into the pan and bake on the middle rack of the oven for 55 minutes. Increase the temperature to 350°F (175°C) and bake for 10–15 minutes longer, until a cake tester inserted into the center comes out clean. Immediately remove from the oven and turn upside down. Most tube pans have "feet" that will support the pan while upside down. If yours does not, hang the pan upside down from the center tube over the neck of a bottle. Let cool completely.

Cappucino Cream
makes 1³/4 cups (420 mL)

1½ cups (360 mL) sour cream

1½ tsp. (7.5 mL) instant espresso or coffee

½ cup (120 mL) brown sugar

Turn the pan right side up and run a long, thin-bladed knife around the inside and outside of the cake. Invert onto a plate and remove the outside of the pan. Run the knife between the top of the pan and the cake and remove the top of the pan. Serve with the Cappucino Cream if you like.

Cappucino Cream
Mix the sour cream and espresso or coffee together until the powder dissolves. Just before serving, sprinkle the brown sugar on top of the sour cream mixture and fold it in, leaving large streaks of brown sugar through the mixture for a contrast of flavor and texture.

While Black Bottom Cake is not new, it should be remembered. I have updated it by adding brandy and sour cherries, which combine marvelously with the chocolate and cream cheese. It is very easy to make and will keep for 5 days in the refrigerator if well wrapped.

Black Bottom Brandy and Sour Cherry Cake   makes 1 10-inch (25-cm) tube pan

½ cup (120 mL) brandy

1 cup (240 mL) dried sour cherries

8 oz. (227 g) cream cheese

½ cup (120 mL) sugar

1 large egg

1 tsp. (5 mL) pure vanilla extract

12 oz (340 g) bittersweet chocolate, chopped into ½-inch (1.2-cm) chunks

3 cups (720 mL) all-purpose flour

½ cup (120 mL) cocoa powder

2 tsp. (10 mL) baking soda

½ tsp. (2.5 mL) sea salt

2 cups (480 mL) sugar

⅔ cup (160 mL) vegetable oil

2 large eggs

1 cup (240 mL) water

1 cup (240 mL) milk

1 Tbsp. (15 mL) white vinegar

1 tsp. (5 mL) pure vanilla extract

In a small pot, gently warm the brandy. Add the cherries. Simmer for a minute, then remove from the heat. Let cool completely.

With a hand mixer or by hand, cream the cream cheese. Gradually add the ½ cup (120 mL) sugar. Beat in the egg and vanilla, scraping down the sides of the bowl. Stir in the brandy-soaked cherries, any brandy left in the pot and the chocolate chunks. Set aside.

Preheat the oven to 350°F (175°C).

In a large bowl, sift the flour, cocoa, baking soda, salt and sugar together. In a separate bowl, either by hand or with an electric mixer, beat the oil, eggs, water, milk, vinegar and vanilla until well mixed. Combine with the dry ingredients and beat until smooth, scraping down the sides of the bowl.

Pour half the batter into a well-buttered and floured 10-inch (25-cm) tube pan. Spoon the cream cheese mixture evenly over the batter. Pour the remaining batter over the cream cheese and smooth the top.

Bake on the middle shelf for 1¼–1½ hours, or until a cake tester comes out clean. Let cool on a rack for 10 minutes. Run a spatula around the outside of the pan to loosen it, then turn out of the pan onto the rack. Let cool completely before cutting.

This is called lava cake because the delicious, oozy chocolate center runs out onto the plate when you cut into the cake. People go wild over this and it's one of the most popular desserts at the Fish House in Stanley Park, where it was born.

Chocolate Lava Cake   serves 6

butter at room temperature for buttering the pans

cocoa powder for dusting the pans

6½ oz. (185 g) good-quality bittersweet chocolate, chopped into ½-inch (1.2-cm) pieces

3 Tbsp. (45 mL) unsalted butter

pinch sea salt

4 large egg yolks

¼ cup (60 mL) granulated sugar

2 large egg whites

1 recipe Coffee Crème Anglaise (see page 232)

Assemble six 4- by 2-inch (10- by 5-cm) nonstick tart pans, preferably smooth-sided with removable bottoms, or six 4-inch (10-cm) disposable aluminum pie pans. Thoroughly butter the insides of the pans and dust with cocoa. Tap out the excess.

Combine the chocolate, unsalted butter and pinch of salt in a large, heatproof bowl. Place over a pot of simmering water and stir occasionally until the chocolate is almost completely melted. Remove from the heat and stir until the chocolate is smooth. Cool to room temperature.

Combine the egg yolks with all but 1 Tbsp. (15 mL) of the sugar and beat with an electric mixer or by hand at high speed for about 2 minutes, until the mixture thickens and becomes lighter in color. Fold the cooled chocolate mixture into the egg yolks until smoothly combined.

With clean beaters, whip the egg whites with the remaining 1 Tbsp. (15 mL) of sugar until soft peaks form. Stir ⅓ of the egg whites into the chocolate mixture. Fold the remaining egg whites into the chocolate mixture.

Spoon the batter into the prepared tart tins. If you are not baking the Lava Cakes immediately, cover with plastic wrap and refrigerate for up to 8 hours.

Preheat the oven to 425°F (220°C). Place the cakes well apart on a baking sheet and bake for 8 minutes, or 9 minutes if the cakes have been refrigerated. The centers will be jiggly. Remove from the oven and carefully loosen the tarts with a small knife. Flip the cakes over onto individual plates and remove the pans.

Serve with Coffee Crème Anglaise poured around the Lava Cakes, and unsweetened whipped cream if you wish.

The inspiration for this cake came from two sources—sampling chocolate-covered cherries from a well-known West Coast coffee purveyor and wondering what to do with some delicious dried sour cherries. They both had intense flavors, just begging to be captured in a cake. You may use any chocolate-covered cherry that strikes your fancy as long as it is not gooey. I gave this away as Christmas cake and the crowd went wild. If you can resist temptation, the cake keeps for 4 weeks, wrapped and refrigerated.

Sour Dried Cherry and Chocolate Pound Cake
makes 1 10-inch (25-cm) tube pan, about 20 slices

3/4 lb. (340 g) dried sour cherries

1 cup (240 mL) bourbon

2 cups (480 mL) all-purpose flour

1 tsp. (5 mL) baking powder

1/2 tsp. (2.5 mL) sea salt

1 cup (240 mL) unsalted butter

2 cups (480 mL) granulated sugar

6 large eggs, separated

1/2 lb. (227 g) chocolate-covered cherries, cut in half

1/4 lb. (113 g) finely chopped bittersweet chocolate

1 lb. (454 g) walnut halves

A day before baking the cake, combine the sour cherries and bourbon in a small saucepan. Bring to a simmer and remove from the heat. Transfer to a bowl, cool and cover. (The cherries may be prepared up to 5 days in advance. Keep tightly covered.)

Preheat the oven to 275°F (135°C). Generously butter a 10- by 4-inch (25- by 10-cm) tube pan (a nonstick pan works best for this). Line the bottom with parchment paper and butter the paper. Dust the pan with flour and shake out the excess.

Sift the flour, baking powder and 1/4 tsp. (1.25 mL) of the salt together. In a large bowl, cream the butter with an electric mixer until light. Gradually incorporate 13/4 cups (420 mL) of the sugar, beating for 5 minutes until creamy. Beat in the egg yolks. On low speed beat in a third of the flour mixture, then half the cherries and bourbon, then another third of the flour mixture, the rest of the cherries and bourbon, and the remaining flour. Beat only until the ingredients are incorporated after each addition, as over-beating will make the cake tough. Stir in the chocolate-covered cherries, chocolate and walnuts.

Using clean beaters, beat the egg whites with the reserved ¼ tsp. (1.25 mL) salt until the whites form a soft shape. Gradually add the reserved ¼ cup (60 mL) sugar and beat to soft peaks.

Stir a quarter of the egg whites into the batter, then fold in the rest. Turn the batter into the prepared pan and smooth the top. Bake on the middle shelf for 2½ hours, until a cake tester comes out clean. Remove from the oven and cool on a rack for 30 minutes.

Carefully run a knife around the sides of the pan and turn the cake out onto a rack. Remove the parchment paper and cool completely. Wrap the cake in plastic wrap and age it for at least a day before serving.

This is good with any kind of chocolate dessert. It's important to use a large pot and let the cream come to a full boil that rises to the top of the pot or it won't thicken properly.

Coffee Crème Anglaise   makes 2½ cups (600 mL)

5 large egg yolks

½ cup (120 mL) granulated sugar

1 cup (240 mL) half-and-half cream

1 cup (240 mL) whipping cream

1 tsp. (5 mL) instant coffee

1 Tbsp. (15 mL) espresso coffee beans,
coarsely ground

In a large bowl, beat the egg yolks and sugar together until well combined.

Place the creams in a large, heavy saucepan and bring to a full frothy boil. Remove from the heat and slowly pour ¼ of the cream into the yolk mixture, stirring constantly, then stir in the remaining cream. Pour through a sieve into a clean bowl. Stir in the instant coffee until dissolved, then the coarsely ground espresso beans. Place in the fridge and stir every 10 minutes until the mixture is cold. Cover with plastic wrap. Keeps for 4 days, refrigerated.

TWO USES FOR DISPOSABLE CHOPSTICKS
When I melt chocolate in a microwave, I put a disposable chopstick in the bowl and leave it there while the chocolate is microwaving. When I remove the chocolate to check its progress, I use the chopstick to stir it. This eliminates messy, chocolate-coated spoons and plates that they rest on.

If a recipe specifies that the liquid has to be reduced to a certain amount, pour the amount of water that the liquid will be reduced to into the pot or pan that you will be using and insert a disposable chopstick. Mark the water level on the chopstick by notching it with a knife. When you are reducing the liquid and think you are close to the mark, place the chopstick into the liquid to measure it against the mark. Continue reducing and checking until the liquid is at the mark.

Besides being mouth-warming, **this super-moist ginger cake has a heart-warming flavor. Eat it warm with butter while looking out the window on a rainy day.**

Fresh Ginger and Buttermilk Cake   makes 1 10-inch (25-cm) cake, serves 8 to 10

3/4 cup (180 mL) unsalted butter, softened

1/2 cup (120 mL) brown sugar

2 eggs

1 cup (240 mL) molasses

3 Tbsp. (45 mL) finely grated fresh ginger

3 Tbsp. (45 mL) finely chopped crystallized ginger

1 cup (240 mL) all-purpose flour

1 cup (240 mL) whole-wheat pastry flour

2 tsp. (10 mL) baking soda

1/4 tsp. (1.25 mL) sea salt

1 tsp. (5 mL) ground dried ginger

1 cup (240 mL) buttermilk or yogurt

Preheat the oven to 350°F (175°C). Butter and flour a 10-inch (25-cm) springform pan.

Cream the butter and sugar until light and fluffy. Beat in the eggs one at a time, then the molasses, fresh ginger and crystallized ginger. The mixture will look curdled. Sift the flours, baking soda, salt and dried ginger together. Fold the dry ingredients and the buttermilk alternately into the butter mixture, a third at a time.

Pour the batter into the prepared pan. Bake in the center of the preheated oven for about 50 minutes, or until a cake tester comes out clean. Cool on a rack for 10 minutes before turning it out of the pan. Allow to cool completely before cutting. The cake will fall a bit in the center and this is how it should be.

You can serve this cake as is, or with a bowl of rhubarb compote on the side to dunk your piece of cake into. Or, go all out and serve it with crème fraîche, page 291, and rhubarb compote, page 283.

A very easy cake that can be made entirely by hand. Serve warm with whipping cream if you don't have the inclination to make lemon curd.

Lemon Crumb Cake with Lemon Curd   makes 1 8-inch (20-cm) square cake

2 cups (480 mL) all-purpose flour

1 cup (240 mL) granulated sugar

½ cup (120 mL) well-packed light brown sugar

2 Tbsp. (30 mL) lemon zest, finely chopped

¼ tsp. (1.25 mL) ground nutmeg

½ cup (120 mL) vegetable oil

4 Tbsp. (60 mL) freshly squeezed lemon juice

1 cup (240 mL) sour cream

1 large egg

1 tsp. (5 mL) pure vanilla extract

1 tsp. (5 mL) baking soda

1 tsp. (5 mL) baking powder

1 recipe Lemon Curd

Lemon Curd
makes about 2 cups (480 mL)

4 large eggs

1 cup (240 mL) granulated sugar

⅔ cup (160 mL) lemon juice (about 4 lemons)

zest of 2 lemons, finely chopped

8 Tbsp. (120 mL) unsalted butter, cut into small pieces

Preheat the oven to 325°F (165°C). Lightly butter and flour an 8-inch (20-cm) square glass baking dish.

Whisk the flour, sugar, brown sugar, lemon zest and nutmeg together. Whisk in the oil and lemon juice until it forms a lumpy mixture. Reserve 1 cup (240 mL) for the topping.

Combine the sour cream, egg, vanilla, baking soda and baking powder. Whisk into the flour mixture or beat in with an electric mixer until smooth. Spread the batter into the prepared pan and sprinkle the crumb mixture evenly over the top. Bake for 35–40 minutes until a cake tester comes out clean. Serve with a dollop of Lemon Curd.

Lemon Curd
This is great to have on hand to spread on toast. You can thin it out with a bit of cream or water for a quick lemon sauce. It is foolproof and can be easily doubled, tripled or quadrupled.

Whip the eggs and sugar together until doubled in volume and light in color. Stir in the lemon juice and zest. Transfer to the top of a double boiler and cook over simmering water until very thick, about 20–30 minutes, stirring occasionally with a whisk. Remove from the heat and add the butter, stirring until melted. Cool and refrigerate. Will keep one month refrigerated.

I started making this cake 25 years ago, before food became a form of entertainment or cause for paranoia and was eaten just because it tasted good. This cake still tastes good.

Oatmeal Raisin Cake with Broiled Coconut Cashew Icing
makes 1 9-inch (23-cm) cake

½ cup (120 mL) all-purpose flour

1 tsp. (5 mL) baking soda

1 tsp. (5 mL) ground cinnamon

½ tsp. (2.5 mL) ground allspice

¼ tsp. (1.25 mL) sea salt

2 cups (480 mL) large-flake rolled oats

⅔ cup (160 mL) unsalted butter, at room temperature

½ cup (120 mL) golden raisins

1¼ cups (300 mL) boiling water

1 cup (240 mL) light brown sugar

2 eggs

1 cup (240 mL) brown sugar

½ cup (120 mL) butter

½ cup (120 mL) whipping cream

1 cup (240 mL) roasted cashew pieces

1½ cups (360 mL) unsweetened large-flake coconut

Preheat the oven to 325°F (165°C). Butter and flour a 9-inch (23-cm) springform pan.

Sift together the flour, baking soda, cinnamon, allspice and salt. Combine the oats, ⅔ cup (160 mL) butter and raisins and pour the boiling water over the mixture. Allow to cool completely, stirring occasionally. Beat in the 1 cup (240 mL) light brown sugar and eggs, then the flour mixture. Pour the batter into the prepared pan and bake for 35–40 minutes, until a cake tester comes out clean. Place on a rack to cool.

To make the icing, combine the 1 cup (240 mL) brown sugar, ½ cup (120 mL) butter and whipping cream in a heavy pot. Bring to a boil and cook, stirring occasionally, for 3 minutes. Remove from the heat and stir in the cashews and coconut. Allow to cool slightly, then spread it over the top of the cake. Heat the broiler to high. Place the cake about 4 inches (10 cm) below the heat and broil until the icing is brown and bubbly. Place on a rack and allow the cake to cool completely before removing it from the pan.

Orange and Semolina Cake with
Orange Flower Water Whipped Cream   serves 10 to 12

3/4 cup (180 mL) sugar

2 oranges, finely zested and juiced

1½ cups (360 mL) water

¼ tsp. (1.25 mL) almond extract

½ cup (120 mL) all-purpose flour

½ tsp. (2.5 mL) baking powder

1⅓ cups (320 mL) semolina

4 eggs, separated

½ cup (120 mL) granulated sugar

½ cup (120 mL) olive oil

2 oranges, finely zested

½ tsp. (2.5 mL) almond extract

½ cup (120 mL) orange juice

½ cup (120 mL) sliced almonds

Orange Flower Water Whipped Cream
makes 3 cups (720 mL)

1½ cups (360 mL) whipping cream

1 Tbsp. (15 mL) granulated sugar

1–1½ tsp. (5–7.5 mL) orange flower water

Make the syrup by combining the sugar, orange zest and juice and water in a saucepan. Bring to a boil, simmer for 5 minutes, then add the almond extract. Cool.

Preheat the oven to 350°F (175°C).

Using parchment paper, line a 10-inch (25-cm) round cake pan that is at least 3 inches deep. Sift together the flour and baking powder, then stir in the semolina. Beat the egg yolks, sugar, olive oil, zest, and almond extract together until pale and creamy. Beat in the flour mixture, then beat in the orange juice.

Beat the egg whites until stiff peaks form and fold into the batter. Pour into the pan and sprinkle with the almonds. Bake for about 45 minutes, until golden brown. Remove from the oven and, while still hot, cut into wedges. Slowly pour the cooled syrup over the cake and cool to room temperature before serving with the whipped cream.

Orange Flower Water Whipped Cream
Combine the ingredients and whip until soft peaks form. Chill until ready to serve.

Rhubarb Coconut Cake makes 1 9-inch (23-cm) cake

2 cups (480 mL) rhubarb chopped into
⅟₂-inch (1.2-cm) pieces

1½ cups (360 mL) granulated sugar

½ cup (120 mL) brown sugar

¼ cup (60 mL) butter

½ cup (120 mL) shredded, sweetened
coconut

1 tsp. (5 mL) ground cinnamon

2 cups (480 mL) all-purpose flour

1 tsp. (5 mL) baking soda

½ cup (120 mL) butter

1 egg

1 cup (240 mL) buttermilk

Preheat the oven to 350°F (175°C). Butter a 9-inch (23-cm) springform or square cake pan.

Sprinkle the rhubarb with 2 Tbsp. (30 mL) of the granulated sugar and set aside while you prepare the rest of the cake. In a separate bowl, mix the brown sugar, ¼ cup (60 mL) butter, coconut and cinnamon by hand until chunky but well incorporated. Set aside.

Whisk together the flour and baking soda. Combine the remaining white sugar and the ½ cup (120 mL) butter. Beat with an electric mixer on medium-high speed for 3–5 minutes, or beat by hand until light and fluffy. Add the egg and buttermilk and mix on slow speed, scraping down the sides of the bowl. Add the flour mixture and mix on slow speed just until incorporated. Fold in the rhubarb along with any juice in the bowl, mixing it in with a rubber spatula. Pour the batter into the prepared pan and sprinkle with the brown sugar-coconut topping.

Bake for 30–40 minutes, or until a toothpick inserted in the center comes out clean. Cool on a rack before cutting.

Broil day-old slices of this cake **and serve warm with coffee ice cream.**

Buttered Rum and Raisin Cake   makes 1 8-inch (20-cm) cake

¼ cup (60 mL) dark rum

½ cup (120 mL) golden raisins

½ cup (120 mL) granulated sugar

1 Tbsp. (15 mL) water

¼ cup (60 mL) water

3 Tbsp. (45 mL) unsalted butter, softened

2 Tbsp. (30 mL) dark rum

1 cup (240 mL) all-purpose flour

1¼ tsp. (6.25 mL) baking powder

¼ tsp. (1.25 mL) nutmeg

¼ tsp. (1.25 mL) sea salt

½ cup plus 2 Tbsp. (150 mL) unsalted butter

¾ cup (180 mL) light brown sugar, firmly packed

3 large eggs

1 tsp. (5 mL) pure vanilla extract

½ cup (120 mL) walnuts, coarsely chopped

In a small pot, bring the rum to a boil. Add the raisins, remove from the heat and cover. Let stand for 1 hour.

To make the sauce, combine the granulated sugar and the 1 Tbsp. (15 mL) water in a small pot. Bring to a boil and cook over high heat until the sugar caramelizes and is almost smoking. Remove from the heat and place a sieve over the top of the pot. Stand back from the pot and add the ¼ cup (60 mL) water. The caramel will splutter. When it stops spluttering, remove the sieve and stir in the 3 Tbsp. (45 mL) unsalted butter until melted. Stir in the 2 Tbsp. (30 mL) rum. Set aside.

Preheat the oven to 350°F (175°C). Butter and flour an 8-inch (20-cm) deep round cake pan. Whisk the flour, baking powder, nutmeg and salt together in a bowl. With an electric mixer, beat the butter until light and fluffy. Gradually add the brown sugar and beat for 1 minute. Beat in the eggs one at a time, then the vanilla. On low speed, blend in the flour mixture, then the rum-soaked raisins and the walnuts. Scrape the batter into the cake pan and smooth the top. Bake for 35 – 45 minutes, or until a tester comes out clean. Remove from the oven and cool on a rack for 5 minutes. Run a knife around the edge of the pan and lift the cake. Place back in the pan. With a skewer, poke about 15 holes through the cake. Slowly spoon the caramel sauce over the top. Let stand until cool before removing from the pan.

Thank you Stu! Glorious, and gloriously easy to make. Advise your guests to attack the cheesecake from the middle, not from the sides. Go seasonal and use fresh berries instead of the plum compote if you prefer.

Stu's Mascarpone "Cheesecake" with Plum Compote   serves 8

1/2 lb. (227 g) cream cheese at room temperature

1/2 cup (120 mL) granulated sugar

1 tsp. (5 mL) pure vanilla extract

12 oz. (340 g) mascarpone cheese, at room temperature

2 cups (480 mL) whipping cream, chilled

6 sheets phyllo pastry

3/4 cup (180 mL) melted butter

6 Tbsp. (75 mL) brown sugar

1 recipe Plum Compote

Plum Compote
makes 2 cups (475 mL)

12 plums, peeled, pitted and quartered

1/4 cup (60 mL) water

1/3 cup (80 mL) granulated sugar

1/2 cinnamon stick

pinch turmeric

Preheat the oven to 400°F (200°F).

Lay a sheet of phyllo out on your work surface and brush with butter. Sprinkle evenly with 1 1/2 Tbsp. (20 mL) sugar. Place a second sheet over the first and press firmly over the entire surface. Brush with butter and sprinkle evenly with another 1 1/2 Tbsp. (20 mL) sugar. Cover with a third sheet of phyllo and press firmly again. Brush generously with butter. Cut the sheet in thirds lengthwise and in quarters widthwise to make 12 even squares. Carefully transfer to a baking sheet lined with parchment paper. Repeat the above procedure with the remaining phyllo, butter and sugar.

Bake one tray at a time for 4 – 4 1/2 minutes until very lightly browned. Transfer to a wire rack to cool. The squares may be made a day in advance and kept in a tightly covered container.

Just before serving, assemble the cheesecakes. Place a square of phyllo in the middle of a plate. Place a large dollop of the mascarpone mixture in the middle of the square. Top with a phyllo square and another large dollop of the mascarpone mixture. Cover with the third square. Spoon the plum compote over the top and serve immediately.

Plum Compote
Place all the ingredients in a heavy pot and cook over high heat until the plums begin to fall apart. Remove from the heat and transfer to a bowl to cool. The plums may be made 3 days in advance. Cover and refrigerate.

Better than pumpkin pie. **Serve it for Thanksgiving this year.**

Pumpkin Cheesecake   makes 1 8-inch (20-cm) cheesecake

1¼ cups (300 mL) graham wafer crumbs

½ tsp. (2.5 mL) dried ground ginger

¼ tsp. (1.25 mL) ground cinnamon

¼ cup (60 mL) unsalted butter, melted

1 Tbsp. (15 mL) molasses

1¾ lbs. (800 g) cream cheese

½ 25-oz. (750-mL) can pumpkin purée

¾ cup (180 mL) brown sugar, packed

4 large eggs

½ tsp. (2.5 mL) dried ground ginger

¼ tsp. (1.25 mL) ground allspice

¾ tsp. (3.75 mL) ground cinnamon

¼ tsp. (1.25 mL) freshly grated nutmeg

2 Tbsp. (30 mL) molasses

To make the crust, combine the graham wafer crumbs, ginger and cinnamon and mix well. Combine the melted butter and molasses and stir well. Mix thoroughly with the dry ingredients. Press into the bottom of an 8-inch (20-cm) springform pan.

In a food processor, combine the remaining ingredients. Blend, scraping down the sides of the bowl occasionally until smooth. Pour into the prepared pan. Bake at 350°F (175°C) for 30–45 minutes until the cake is barely jiggly in the center. Remove from the oven and cool to room temperature. Refrigerate overnight before serving.

My mother used to make a sort of cheesecake from a package of Dream Whip, cream cheese and a can of cherry pie filling spread on top. The sweet-and-sour tang and creaminess of this cheesecake takes me back.

Candied Cranberry Cheesecake   makes 1 8-inch (20-cm) cheesecake

3 cups (720 mL) granulated sugar

3 cups (720 mL) water

3/4 lb. (340 g) fresh or frozen cranberries

1 1/2 cups (360 mL) graham wafer crumbs

1/2 tsp. (2.5 mL) ground cinnamon

1/2 cup (120 mL) unsalted butter, melted

2 lbs. (900 g) cream cheese

1 cup (240 mL) granulated sugar

4 large eggs

1 1/2 cups (360 mL) sour cream

2 Tbsp. (30 mL) granulated sugar

1 tsp. (5 mL) pure vanilla extract

One day before you plan to make the cheesecake, combine the 3 cups (720 mL) sugar and 3 cups (720 mL) water in a saucepan and bring to a boil. Turn down to a simmer and add the cranberries. Cook just until they pop. Remove from the heat. Cool, cover and refrigerate overnight. (The cranberries may be prepared up to one month in advance.)

One hour before making the cheesecake, drain the cranberries in a sieve over a bowl to catch the syrup. Reserve the syrup.

Preheat the oven to 350°F (175°C). Lightly butter an 8-inch (20-cm) springform pan. Combine the graham wafer crumbs, cinnamon and melted butter. Mix thoroughly and press into the bottom of the pan. Set aside.

Cream the cream cheese, then beat in the 1 cup (240 mL) sugar. Add the eggs, one at a time, beating only until each egg is incorporated. By hand, fold in the cranberries. Pour into the prepared pan and bake for 30–45 minutes. The center of the cake should still jiggle a bit. While the cake is baking, mix the sour cream, 2 Tbsp. (30 mL) sugar and vanilla together. Spread the sour cream mixture over the top when the cake is done and return to the oven for 5 minutes. Cool the cheesecake completely and refrigerate overnight.

Serve the cheesecake with a pool of the reserved cranberry syrup.

How can such a simple dessert be so glorious? **Oh richly browned, sweet and sour splendor!**

Rhubarb Cobbler   serves 8

3 cups (720 mL) rhubarb, chopped into
  1-inch (2.5-cm) pieces

3/4 cup (180 mL) brown sugar

4 Tbsp. (60 mL) butter, melted

2 eggs, lightly beaten

1/2 cup (120 mL) milk

1 1/2 cups (360 mL) flour

2 tsp. (10 mL) baking powder

1 tsp. (5 mL) pure vanilla extract

1 cup (240 mL) sugar

Preheat the oven to 350°F (175°C). Generously butter a 9- by 13-inch (23- by 33-cm) baking dish.

In a medium-sized bowl, combine the rhubarb and brown sugar and set aside. In a large bowl, combine the remaining ingredients. Beat only until smooth.

Pour the batter into the buttered baking dish, then evenly spread the rhubarb mixture over the batter. Bake for 40 minutes. Serve warm, in a puddle of cream or with really good vanilla ice cream.

cookies

My colleague Trevor developed this recipe for a dessert wine competition. All of the kitchen got involved in the process, making suggestions and tasting. Alas, his recipe did not win, but it was a winner as far as we were concerned.

Trevor's Apricot, Ginger and Black Pepper Biscotti   makes about 45 biscotti

3 cups (720 mL) all-purpose flour

1 cup (240 mL) granulated sugar

1 tsp. (5 mL) sea salt

1½ tsp. (7.5 mL) coarsely ground black pepper

2½ tsp. (12.5 mL) baking powder

1 Tbsp. (15 mL) fresh ginger, grated

¾ cup (180 mL) unsalted butter, chilled and cut into ½-inch (1-cm) cubes

1 cup (240 mL) whole almonds, roasted and coarsely chopped

2 eggs

2 Tbsp. (30 mL) sweet dessert wine

¾ cup (180 mL) dried apricots, finely chopped

Place the flour, sugar, salt, pepper, baking powder and ginger in the work bowl of a food processor. Pulse a few times to combine the ingredients.

Scatter the butter over the top of the flour mixture and pulse until a fine meal forms. Add the almonds and pulse a few more times to chop them coarsely.

Beat the eggs and wine together. Add the apricots and the flour-butter mixture. Mix only until combined.

Preheat the oven to 350°F (180°C). Line a baking sheet with parchment paper. Divide the dough in two and shape into logs that are 3 inches (7.5 cm) across. Refrigerate for ½ hour.

Bake for 20 – 30 minutes, until golden brown. Remove from the oven and cool completely. Slice on a deep diagonal into 1½-inch (3.8-cm) slices. Place on the baking sheet without the slices touching and bake for 10 minutes longer. Remove and cool on wire racks. Store in an airtight tin.

CHOPPING SMALL QUANTITIES OF NUTS
Instead of using a food processor or nut chopper, put the nuts in a heavy plastic bag and crush them with a rolling pin until they are the desired size.

Anyone familiar with Jewish cooking will recognize these as mandelbrot. I don't know where my mother got the recipe, but they were part of her repertoire for quite a while. They seemed almost bland compared to the usual childhood cookies, but that is their appeal. I treasured the sweet, crunchy, adult flavor of these biscuits, and still do.

My Mother's Pre-Biscotti Biscotti   makes about 24 biscotti

3½ cups (840 mL) all-purpose flour

2 tsp. (10 mL) baking powder

¼ tsp. (1.25 mL) sea salt

3 eggs

1 cup (240 mL) vegetable oil

1 cup (240 mL) sugar

1 cup (240 mL) walnut pieces

½ cup (120 mL) granulated sugar

2 tsp. (10 mL) cinnamon

Preheat the oven to 350°F (175°C). Line a baking sheet with parchment paper.

Sift the flour, baking powder and salt together. Beat the eggs, oil and 1 cup (240 mL) sugar together until well combined. Stir in the flour mixture and walnuts. Shape into two 12- x 3-inch (30- x 7.5-cm) logs and transfer to the baking sheet. Bake for 30 minutes. Remove to a rack to cool slightly, then transfer to a cutting board and cut into 1-inch (2.5-cm) slices with a serrated knife. Transfer, cut sides up, to baking sheets and bake for 5–8 minutes longer until dry.

Combine the ½ cup (120 mL) sugar with the cinnamon. Roll the cookies in this mixture while warm and transfer to racks to cool. Store in an airtight container.

Chocolate and ginger has been a long-time favorite combination of mine. I usually satisfy my taste buds by eating chocolate-covered ginger, but these are deep, rich and chocolatey and do an excellent job.

Double Chocolate and Ginger Biscotti   makes about 45 biscotti

2²/₃ cups (640 mL) flour

1 cup (240 mL) cocoa powder

1½ tsp. (7.5 mL) baking soda

¼ tsp. (1.25 mL) sea salt

1 cup (240 mL) granulated sugar

1 cup (240 mL) light brown sugar

8 oz. (227 g) good-quality bittersweet chocolate, finely chopped

¾ cup (180 mL) unsalted butter, at room temperature

3 large eggs

1 tsp. (5 mL) pure vanilla extract

½ cup (120 mL) crystallized ginger, chopped into irregular-sized pieces from ¼ inch (.6 cm) to ½ inch (1.2 cm)

Preheat the oven to 325°F (165°C). Combine the flour, cocoa, baking soda, salt and sugars in a large bowl. Whisk until well mixed.

Place 1 cup (240 mL) of the mixture and the chocolate in the workbowl of a food processor. Pulse until the chocolate is finely ground. Mix into the dry mixture. Add the butter and mix with an electric mixer or your fingertips to a fine mealy texture.

Beat the eggs and vanilla together. Add the flour mixture along with the ginger and stir or beat until well combined. The dough will be soft.

Shape into three 15-inch (38-cm) logs and transfer to 3 parchment-lined baking sheets. The dough will spread quite a bit while baking. Bake on the middle shelf of the oven for 30–40 minutes, until the sides are firm and the tops are cracked. Place the pan on a cooling rack and let cool until firm enough to handle. Transfer to a cutting surface and cut with a serrated knife into ½-inch (1.2-cm) slices.

Reduce the oven temperature to 300°F (150°C). Return the cookies to the baking sheet and bake for 15 minutes, until dry. The biscotti will crisp as they cool. Cool completely and store between layers of waxed or parchment paper in an airtight container.

I love these crunchy, sweet and peppery biscuits. **At the David Wood Food Shop in Toronto we used to sell them in their elegant tins from the DiCamillo Bakery in Buffalo, N.Y, but they are easily made at a fraction of the cost. They are great on their own, with the Tea-Scented Fresh Goat Cheese (page 12) or with other cheese — especially a creamy Gorgonzola. I like to use a combination of black and white sesame seeds for a speckled effect.**

Biscotti di Vino   makes about 40 biscotti

2 cups (480 mL) all-purpose flour

¼ cup (60 mL) sugar

1½ tsp. (7.5 mL) baking powder

1 tsp. (5 mL) sea salt

1 tsp. (5 mL) freshly ground black pepper

½ cup (120 mL) dry red wine

½ cup (120 mL) extra virgin olive oil

1 egg white, beaten until foamy

4 Tbsp. (60 mL) lightly toasted unhulled sesame seeds

Preheat the oven to 350°F (175°C).

Stir together the flour, sugar, baking powder, salt and pepper in a large bowl. Add the wine and oil and stir with a wooden spoon just until smooth. The dough will be very stiff and a little oily.

Divide the dough into 4 pieces. Shape each piece into a 10-inch (25-cm) log. The logs will be lumpy looking. Flatten the logs slightly. Brush with egg white and sprinkle with 2 Tbsp. (30 mL) of the sesame seeds. Line 2 baking sheets with parchment paper and sprinkle the remaining sesame seeds evenly over the parchment.

Cut the logs into 1-inch (2.5-cm), slightly diagonal slices. Place the slices 1 inch (2.5 cm) apart on the baking sheets. Bake for 30–35 minutes or until lightly browned. Transfer to wire racks to cool. Store in a tightly covered container. These will keep well for 2–3 weeks.

ROLLING STIFF DOUGH INTO LOGS
When working with stiff doughs that have to be rolled into logs, roll the pieces lightly, stretching them slightly. Let them rest for a few minutes, then come back and roll them again. Continue the process until the dough is rolled to the right length. Using this slow process will prevent the dough from tearing or becoming uneven.

T Tearoom has been an inspiration for me since they invited me for a tea-tasting several years ago. I recall sampling only 27 teas, and was told that the record was 40! I've used their tea as a marinade for salmon and goat's cheese and dabbled with it in baking. This was my most successful cooking experiment and would make a fantastic Christmas cookie. You can use chai masala or any chai spice without tea leaves.

Chai Spiced Butter Balls   makes 30 cookies

2¼ cups (540 mL) all-purpose flour, sifted

½ tsp. (2.5 mL) salt

1 Tbsp. (15 mL) Herbal Spice Chai, ground

1 cup (240 mL) unsalted butter, at room temperature

¼ cup (60 mL) icing sugar, sifted

1 tsp. (5 mL) pure vanilla extract

1–1½ cups (240–360 mL) icing sugar, for rolling the cookies in

Preheat the oven to 400°F (200°C)..

Combine the flour, salt and chai with a whisk until well mixed. In a large bowl, beat the butter with an electric mixer until smooth. Gradually beat in the ¼ cup (60 mL) icing sugar and the vanilla until fluffy. Add the dry ingredients and mix only until combined. The dough will be a bit crumbly.

Roll level tablespoons of dough into balls and place 1 inch (2.5 cm) apart on parchment-lined baking sheets. Bake in the middle of the oven for 10 minutes, until lightly golden and pale brown on the bottoms. Let cool in the pan for 5 minutes on a cooling rack.

Place the icing sugar in a shallow container and roll each cookie in the sugar, covering it completely. Transfer to a rack to cool. When completely cooled, roll in the icing sugar again. Store in an airtight container between layers of waxed or parchment paper.

While I am not too fond of chocolate desserts, I do love chocolate bars, cookies, brownies and just plain chocolate. These cookies satisfy all of the above requirements. They really do put you into an altered state.

Instant Ecstasy Chocolate Cookies — makes 22 very large cookies

4 oz. (113 g) unsweetened chocolate, coarsely chopped

8 oz. (227 g) semisweet chocolate, coarsely chopped

½ cup (120 mL) unsalted butter, at room temperature

6 Tbsp. (90 mL) all-purpose flour

½ tsp. (2.5 mL) baking powder

½ tsp. (2.5 mL) sea salt

3 large eggs

1 cup (240 mL) granulated sugar

1 Tbsp. (15 mL) instant coffee powder

1 Tbsp. (15 mL) pure vanilla extract

2 cups (480 mL) pecan halves

1 cup (240 mL) whole almonds, roasted

8 oz. (227 g) large chocolate chips or chocolate chunks

Preheat the oven to 300°F (150°C).

In a heatproof bowl, combine the unsweetened chocolate, semisweet chocolate and unsalted butter. Place over a pot of simmering water, stirring occasionally until melted. Remove from the heat and cool.

Whisk the flour, baking powder and salt together. Set aside.

With an electric mixer or whisk, beat the eggs and sugar together until light and fluffy. Add the coffee powder, vanilla and cooled chocolate mixture. Add the flour mixture and mix until combined. Fold in the nuts and chocolate chips or chunks.

Scoop out the batter using a ¼-cup (60-mL) measure. Place 3 inches (7.5 cm) apart on parchment-lined baking sheets. Depending on the size of your baking sheets, you should be able to get 4–6 cookies on each sheet. Bake for 20 minutes, turning the sheets around halfway through, until the tops begin to crack. Be careful not to overbake. Let the cookies remain on the baking sheet for a minute or so to firm up, then transfer to a cooling rack.

The chocolate chunk cookie with three different chocolates — therefore, three times as good. I like to cut chocolate chunks from a good-quality block of chocolate for these cookies. Use a sharp heavy knife to chop the chocolate roughly into $1/4$- to $1/2$-inch (.6- to 1.2-cm) chunks.

Triple Chunk Chocolate Cookies   makes 30 cookies

2½ cups (600 mL) all-purpose flour

1 tsp. (5 mL) baking soda

⅛ tsp. (.5 mL) sea salt

1 cup (240 mL) unsalted butter, at room temperature

¾ cup (180 mL) granulated sugar

1 cup (240 mL) brown sugar, packed

2 large eggs

2 tsp. (10 mL) pure vanilla extract

1 cup (240 mL) bittersweet chocolate chunks

1 cup (240 mL) white chocolate chunks

1 cup (240 mL) milk chocolate chunks

1 cup (240 mL) coarsely chopped hazelnuts

Preheat oven to 300°F (150°C). Line several baking sheets with parchment paper.

Sift together the flour, baking soda and salt.

Either by hand or with an electric mixer, cream the butter until light. Beat in the sugars until fluffy. Add the eggs one at a time, beating well after each addition. Mix in the vanilla.

Incorporate the flour mixture all at once and mix thoroughly by hand. Stir in the chocolate pieces and nuts. Chill the dough until firm. (The dough may be refrigerated for three days at this point or frozen for up to a month.)

Roll the dough into balls, using about 3 Tbsp. (45 mL) per ball. Place 3 inches (7.5 cm) apart on the parchment-lined baking sheets and flatten with the palm of your hand. Bake for 10 minutes, reverse the baking sheet, and bake for 10 minutes more, or until golden brown around the edges. The cookies should remain slightly soft in the middle. Transfer to cooling racks.

A new-found fondness for the combination of cinnamon and chocolate, plus a lifelong affair with my mother's chocolate chip cookie brittle, led to this recipe. I like to use pieces of cinnamon ground coarsely in a mortar and pestle for little explosions of sweet cinnamon flavor. My pet name for this is Mayan cookie brittle.

Chocolate, Cinnamon and Pumpkin Seed Cookie Brittle makes about 24 pieces

¼ lb. (113 g) unsalted butter

½ tsp. (2.5 mL) coarsely ground cinnamon

1 oz. (28 g) unsweetened chocolate, chopped into small pieces

½ cup (120 mL) granulated sugar

¼ tsp. (1.25 mL) pure vanilla extract

1 egg

⅓ cup (80 mL) all-purpose flour

½ cup (120 mL) hulled pumpkin seeds

Preheat the oven to 375°F (190°C).

Melt the butter in a large saucepan over medium heat. Add the cinnamon. Remove from the heat, add the chocolate and stir until melted. Stir in the sugar, vanilla and egg until smooth. Stir in the flour and beat well. Immediately scrape the batter into a 10- by 15- by 1-inch (25- by 38- by 2.5-cm) jelly-roll pan lined with parchment paper. Spread the batter into a thin, even layer across the pan. Scatter the pumpkin seeds evenly over the top.

Bake for 10 minutes, or until the cookie is just set. Remove from the oven and cool on a rack for 20 minutes. Cut or break into 2 dozen rough-shaped pieces, as you would a nut brittle.

I wanted a peanut butter cookie that was rich, crumbly and smooth with an intense peanut butter taste. Through experimenting, I found that replacing some of the flour with cornstarch and using a homogenized peanut butter gave the best result. Great with a big glass of milk.

Peanut Butter Cookies   makes about 35 cookies

1 cup (240 mL) all-purpose flour

1/2 tsp. (2.5 mL) baking powder

1/2 tsp. (2.5 mL) baking soda

1/2 cup (120 mL) cornstarch

1/2 tsp. (2.5 mL) sea salt

3/4 cup (180 mL) unsalted butter

1 cup (240 mL) light brown sugar, well-packed

1/2 cup (120 mL) granulated sugar

1 large egg

1 1/2 cups (360 mL) homogenized peanut butter

Sift the flour, baking powder, baking soda, cornstarch and salt together. By hand or with an electric mixer, cream the butter. Add the sugars and beat until light and fluffy. Beat in the egg, then the peanut butter until well combined. Stir in the flour mixture by hand. Cover the dough with plastic wrap and refrigerate until firm, about half an hour or up to 2 days.

Preheat the oven to 300°F (150°C). Butter two cookie sheets or line them with parchment paper. Scoop up heaping tablespoons of the dough and roll into balls. Place about 2 inches (5 cm) apart on the cookie sheets and flatten with the back of a fork to about 1/4 inch (.6 cm). Bake for 12–14 minutes, turning the cookie sheets around halfway through to ensure even browning. Place on a cooling rack until the cookies are firm enough to remove from the pan.

These are sweet enough **to be a cookie and a handsome vehicle for butter or cheese.**

Sweet Oat Cakes   makes 35 to 40 oat cakes

2 cups (480 mL) all-purpose flour

1½ cups (360 mL) old-fashioned rolled oats

½ cup (120 mL) brown sugar

1 tsp. (5 mL) sea salt

½ tsp. (2.5 mL) baking soda

¾ cup (180 mL) unsalted butter, chilled and cut into ½-inch (1-cm) cubes

½ cup (120 mL) cold water

Preheat the oven to 350°F (175°C). In a large bowl, stir the dry ingredients together. Work in the butter with your fingertips until it is thoroughly blended. Add the water and mix just until the dough holds together.

Divide the dough into four pieces. On a floured surface, roll the dough, one piece at a time, to ⅛-inch (.5-cm) thickness. Cut into 3-inch (7.5-cm) squares and place close together on parchment-lined baking sheets. Save the scraps and reroll them.

Bake for 10–15 minutes, until golden brown. Remove from the pan and cool on wire racks. Store in an airtight container.

This is one of the oldest and most irresistible recipes I have. My mother used to make Toll House cookie brittle and I added the Skor bars when they appeared on the chocolate bar scene. We can now buy Skor bar chips, but I think the chopped up bars are so much better in this cookie.

Skor Bar Cookie Brittle   makes as many pieces as you break it into!

1 cup (240 mL) unsalted butter

1 cup (240 mL) granulated sugar

1 tsp. (5 mL) pure vanilla extract

½ tsp. (2.5 mL) sea salt

2 cups (480 mL) all-purpose flour

1 cup (240 mL) chocolate chips

4 Skor Bars, coarsely chopped

¼ cup (180 mL) finely chopped pecans or walnuts

Preheat the oven to 325°F (165°C).

With an electric mixer or by hand, cream the butter. Add the sugar and beat until light and fluffy. Beat in the vanilla and salt. Stir in the flour, then the chocolate chips, Skor Bar pieces and nuts. You'll need your hands to do this as the dough is stiff. Press evenly into a 10- by 15-inch (25- by 38-cm) jelly roll pan. Bake for 15–20 minutes, until golden brown. Cool completely on a rack. Break into pieces.

desserts

Mascarpone is the creamy mild cheese that became popular through the well-known dessert, tiramisu. Mascarpone and amaretti cookies are available in Italian delis and well-stocked supermarkets.

Baked Apples with Mascarpone and Amaretti   serves 6

6 apples

2 Tbsp. (30 mL) brown sugar

¼ tsp. (1.25 mL) cinnamon

½ cup (120 mL) water

1 cup (240 mL) mascarpone

6 amaretti cookies, crushed coarsely

Preheat the oven to 350°F (175°C). Core the apples and cut a strip from around the middle of each with a vegetable peeler. Place the apples in a baking pan that fits the apples snugly. Mix the brown sugar and cinnamon together and sprinkle into the apples. Pour the water around the apples and cover tightly. Bake for 1 hour, basting every 20 minutes, until the apples are tender.

While the apples are baking, mix the mascarpone and amaretti together.

Remove the apples from the oven and let rest for 10 minutes. Transfer to plates and fill the centers with the mascarpone mixture. Pour the syrup from the pan over the apples and serve warm.

An adult version of apples baked with cinnamon hearts, but not necessarily better.

Baked Apples with Red Wine and Cinnamon   serves 6

4 large apples

6 Tbsp. (90 mL) unsalted butter

3 Tbsp. (45 mL) brown sugar

1 Tbsp. (15 mL) all-purpose flour

1 cup (240 mL) water

2½ cups (600 mL) red wine

¾ cup (180 mL) granulated sugar

1 cinnamon stick, broken into 1-inch
    (2.5-cm) pieces

2 whole cloves

6 whole black peppercorns

4 large sprigs thyme

Preheat the oven to 350°F (175°C). Core the apples and peel a 1-inch (2.5-cm) strip of peel from the middle of each apple. Mix the butter, brown sugar and flour together with your fingertips until crumbly. Lightly butter a baking dish that will fit the apples snugly. Place the apples in the dish and fill each with the brown sugar mixture. Pour ½ cup (120 mL) of the water around the apples. Cover with a lid or tin foil and bake for 1½ hours, basting every 15 minutes until the apples are tender.

Place the red wine, sugar, cinnamon, cloves, peppercorns, thyme and the remaining water in a noncorrodible saucepan. Bring to a boil and simmer until the wine is syrupy and reduced by half. Remove the spices. Pour the spiced wine over the apples, cover, and bake for 15 minutes longer. Remove from the oven and serve warm with lightly whipped cream, if desired.

Sometimes simple is best. Use sweet blood oranges when they are in season in combination with the navel oranges and grapefruit. This is deliciously refreshing.

Orange and Pink Grapefruit Sabayon with Almond serves 4

2 medium pink grapefruit

4 large navel oranges

3 large egg yolks

¼ cup (60 mL) granulated sugar

¼ cup (60 mL) dry white wine

2 Tbsp. (30 mL) almond-flavored liqueur

1 cup (240 mL) whipping cream

Peel the grapefruit and oranges with a sharp knife, removing all the white pith. Cut between the membrane and the fruit segments to release them. Remove any seeds. Arrange the segments in a shallow baking dish that holds the fruit comfortably in one layer.

In a bowl that will fit over a pot of simmering water without touching the water, whisk the egg yolks, sugar, white wine and liqueur together until well combined. Place over a pot of simmering water and whisk constantly until thickened and light in texture, about 5 minutes. Insert the bowl in a larger bowl filled with ice and whisk frequently until cold. Whip the cream to medium peaks and fold into the chilled mixture. Cover and refrigerate for a few hours, but not overnight.

Spoon the sabayon over the orange and grapefruit segments. Serve immediately.

SEGMENTING CITRUS FRUIT
This makes the job of segmenting citrus fruits easier. With a sharp serrated knife (a bread knife works well), cut the top and bottom from the fruit. Place it firmly on a cutting board and with a gentle sawing motion, cut between the fruit and the white pith. Continue around the fruit until all the peel is removed. Remove any large sections of pith that you may have missed. Hold the fruit over a bowl and cut out the segments by cutting along each segment next to the membrane that is holding it in place. Remove the seeds. Use the juice in the recipe if required, or save it for drinking.

An updated Peach Melba, easy to make on the barbecue after you have finished grilling dinner. Serve with crème fraîche, page 291, or if you want to go all out, a spill of fresh blueberries or strawberries.

Grilled Peaches with Raspberry Purée   serves 6

2 pints (1 L) fresh raspberries

½ cup (120 mL) granulated sugar

6 ripe, juicy peaches

2 Tbsp. (30 mL) brown sugar

4 Tbsp. (60 mL) rum or brandy

To make the raspberry purée, process the raspberries and sugar until smooth in the work bowl of a food processor or blender. Press the purée through a sieve with the back of a spoon to remove the seeds. To make this by hand, place the raspberries and sugar in a large bowl and mash with a potato masher until completely mushed. Sieve as above.

Simmer the peaches in a large pot of boiling water for 20 seconds. Put the peaches in cold water to stop the cooking and remove the skins. Cut each peach in half and remove the pit.

Mix the brown sugar and rum or brandy together.

Preheat the barbecue. Grill the peaches cut side down until they are lightly marked and slightly translucent, about 3–5 minutes. Turn them over. Carefully place a spoonful of the brown sugar mixture in each hollow. Continue grilling for 3–5 minutes more. Carefully transfer the peach halves to plates. Drizzle the raspberry purée over them and serve immediately.

White-wine-poached pears with a splash of raspberry or strawberry purée make a good dessert, but the Basil Crème Anglaise adds a touch of elegance.

Pears Poached in White Wine with Basil Crème Anglaise   serves 6

2 cups (480 mL) Gewürztraminer wine

1½ cups (360 mL) granulated sugar

1 3-inch (7.5-cm) stick cinnamon

½ tsp. (2.5 mL) whole coriander seeds

peel of one lemon

6 well-shaped, slightly underripe pears
   with long stems

1 recipe Basil Crème Anglaise (see page 269)

Combine the wine, sugar, cinnamon stick, coriander seeds and lemon peel in a large noncorrodible pot that can accommodate the pears lying down. Bring to a simmer.

Carefully peel the pears, leaving the stems intact. Using a melon baller, carefully cut the cores out from the bottom. As each pear is done, drop it into the wine syrup.

When all the pears are done, add enough water to the wine syrup to make the pears float. Bring to a gentle simmer and poach gently until the pears are completely tender, about 30 minutes to 1 hour, depending on the ripeness of the pears. When they are done, transfer them carefully with a slotted spoon, stem side up, to a shallow dish. Strain the wine syrup and discard the seasonings.

Place the syrup back in the pot and bring to a boil. Continue boiling until the syrup has greatly reduced and becomes thick and sticky. Pour over the pears and cool completely. Serve in a pool of Basil Crème Anglaise.

There is much to admire in a red-wine-poached pear: its soft, rounded shape with an elegant stem, the firm but soft texture to the bite, and its hypnotic red glaze.

Pears Poached with Red Wine, Rosemary and Black Pepper   serves 6

2 cups (480 mL) dry red wine

1½ cups (360 mL) granulated sugar

1 3-inch (7.5-cm) stick cinnamon

3 whole cloves

16 whole black peppercorns

2 sprigs fresh rosemary

6 well-shaped, slightly underripe pears
   with long stems

Combine the red wine, sugar, cinnamon, cloves, peppercorns and rosemary in a large noncorrodible pot that can accommodate the pears lying down. Bring to a simmer.

Carefully peel the pears, leaving the stems intact. Using a melon baller, carefully cut the cores out from the bottom. As each pear is done, place it into the red wine syrup.

When all the pears are done, add enough water to the red wine syrup to make the pears float. Bring to a gentle simmer and poach gently until the pears are completely tender, about 30 minutes to 1 hour, depending on the ripeness of the pears. When they are done, transfer them carefully with a slotted spoon, stem side up, to a shallow dish. Strain the red wine syrup and discard the seasonings.

Place the syrup back in the pot and bring to a boil. Continue boiling until the syrup has greatly reduced and becomes thick and sticky. Pour over the pears.

Baste the pears with syrup whenever you remember to. The more basting, the more glazed and better-looking the pears will be. The pears should sit in the syrup for a minimum of 1 hour. Serve at room temperature with lightly whipped cream or crème fraîche, page 291, cascading down the side.

Eat this as is or add a scoop of vanilla ice cream. The syrup makes a good base for fruit salads. Cantaloupe and strawberry is a particularly good combination.

Fresh Pineapple with Lemon Grass and Ginger Syrup   serves 6

½ cup (120 mL) granulated sugar

20 quarter-sized slices of fresh, peeled ginger

2 stalks lemon grass, trimmed and coarse leaves discarded, cut into 2 inch (5 cm) lengths

1 cup (240 mL) water

¼ cup (60 mL) sweet white dessert wine

1 large, ripe pineapple

1 Tbsp. (15 mL) fresh mint, coarsely chopped

In a small noncorrodible pot, combine the sugar, ginger, lemon grass, water and dessert wine. Bring to a boil over high heat and boil until reduced to ⅔ cup (160 mL), about 5 minutes. Remove from the heat and cool.

Peel the pineapple. Quarter lengthwise, core and cut into ½-inch (1.2-cm) slices. Add the syrup to the pineapple and mix well. Refrigerate for up to 24 hours.

Spoon into wine glasses if desired. Sprinkle with mint and serve.

Experiment with this recipe **and use your favorite sweet dessert wine. Dessert wines made from muscat grapes are some of my favorites.**

Strawberries Steeped in Port with Mascarpone and Honey Cream serves 4

2 pints (950 mL) strawberries

1/4 cup (60 mL) port

3 Tbsp. (45 mL) granulated sugar

1/4 cup (60 mL) mascarpone cheese

2 Tbsp. (30 mL) liquid honey

1/2 cup (120 mL) whipping cream, softly whipped

Quickly wash the strawberries and dry by setting them on paper towels. Hull and cut the berries into quarters. Transfer to a bowl and add the port and sugar. Stir gently to combine and let sit at room temperature for 1/2 hour.

Whisk the mascarpone with the honey until smooth and fold in the whipped cream. Spoon the berries into four wine glasses and garnish with the mascarpone cream.

Another simple fruit dessert that is unique and delicious. Serve with gingersnap cookies.

Strawberries with Molasses Sour Cream   serves 4

2 pints (950 mL) strawberries

¼ cup (60 mL) orange juice

1 Tbsp. (15 mL) sugar

1 cup (240 mL) sour cream

¼ tsp. (1.25 mL) pure vanilla extract

4 Tbsp. (60 mL) molasses

Quickly wash and dry the strawberries. Hull and quarter them. Place in a bowl and add the orange juice and sugar. Stir gently to mix. Let stand for 10 minutes.

Mix the sour cream, vanilla and molasses together. Place the strawberries in wine glasses or dessert dishes. Drizzle the cream over the top and serve.

Yogurt Cheese with Fresh Strawberries   serves 6

2½ cups (600 mL) plain, full-fat Balkan-style yogurt

6 Tbsp. (90 mL) fragrant honey

2 pints (950 mL) fresh strawberries

Whisk the yogurt and honey in a bowl until thoroughly combined. Either line a *coeur à la crème* mold or a small basket with cheesecloth (see Ethereal Chocolate Cream, page 289). Pour the yogurt mixture into the mold and fold the excess cheesecloth over the top. Place on a plate or over a bowl to catch the drips. Cover the top with plastic wrap. Cut a small piece of cardboard to fit on top of the mold. Place on top of the yogurt with a weight on top. A small can would do nicely. Refrigerate overnight.

When ready to serve, open the top of the cheesecloth and turn the yogurt out onto a plate. Remove the cheesecloth. Hull and cut the berries in half if they are small, quarters if larger. Slice the yogurt cheese into wedges and serve with the strawberries.

Sabayon is the French version of the Italian zabaglione, a warm dessert of whipped egg yolks, sugar and marsala. We have served it over cassis sorbet for a "frozen" Kir Royale. Use any combination of summer fruits or berries.

Fresh Berries with Champagne Sabayon   serves 6

6 large egg yolks

10 Tbsp. (150 mL) granulated sugar

6 Tbsp. (90 mL) dry Champagne or sparkling wine

1 cup (240 mL) whipping cream

1 pint (475 mL) raspberries

1 pint (475 mL) strawberries

With a whisk, beat the egg yolks and sugar together in a heatproof bowl. Place the bowl over a pot of simmering water without letting the bottom of the bowl touch the water. Whisk until thick and increased in volume, 6 – 8 minutes. Remove from the pot and whisk in the Champagne. Place the bowl in a larger bowl of ice and let stand until cool, whisking occasionally. Cover and refrigerate.

When you are ready to serve, whip the cream into soft peaks and fold into the Champagne mixture. Divide the berries among 6 wine glasses and top with the sabayon.

I was about 20 when I first encountered lavender in food. I viewed my friend Judy, 5 or 6 years older than me, as a food-savvy sophisticate. To make a salad dressing, she put a few pinches of herbes de Provence in a mortar and pounded it with a clove of garlic and some salt. She added rice vinegar and French olive oil then tossed it with the salad. The sweet flavor of the lavender haunted me for days afterwards.

Lavender Crème Anglaise with Fresh Berries serves 6 to 8

4 cups (1 L) half-and-half cream

¼ cup (60 mL) granulated sugar

pinch sea salt

1 Tbsp. (15 mL) fresh lavender leaves, loosely packed

8 large egg yolks

½ pint (250 mL) fresh raspberries

½ pint (250 mL) fresh blueberries

½ pint (250 mL) fresh strawberries

½ pint (250 mL) fresh blackberries

To make the crème anglaise, place the cream, sugar, salt and lavender in a large saucepan and bring to a full rolling boil.

While waiting for the cream to boil, whisk the egg yolks together.

As soon as the cream reaches a frothy boil, remove from the heat and whisk it in a thin stream into the egg yolks. Strain through a sieve and refrigerate, whisking occasionally until cold. (Keeps for 3 days, covered and refrigerated.)

When you are ready to serve the dessert, quickly wash and drain the berries if necessary. Cut the strawberries in halves and quarters if they are large. You can arrange rows of berries on a platter, scatter them in an abstract manner or, more formally, layer them in martini or balloon wine glasses. Serve the pitcher of crème anglaise on the side.

I just love this cream. **It's the perfect accompaniment to fresh seasonal fruit.**

Balsamic Mascarpone Cream for Fresh Fruit   makes 2½ cups (600 mL), serves 4 to 6

4 Tbsp. (60 mL) cream cheese at room temperature

3 Tbsp. (45 mL) granulated sugar

5 Tbsp. (75 mL) good-quality balsamic vinegar

1 cup (240 mL) mascarpone

¾ cup (180 mL) whipping cream

fresh berries, sliced peaches, plums or pears, etc.

On low speed, whip the cream cheese and sugar. Add half of the vinegar, scraping the bowl as needed. Add the mascarpone, mixing only until smooth. On medium speed, add the cream in a steady stream along with the rest of the vinegar. Scrape the bowl well, increase the speed to high and mix until firm peaks are formed. Do not over beat as mascarpone will curdle. Chill, covered, until ready to serve with fresh fruit.

Serve this with fresh sliced peaches or strawberries, **as well as the pears poached in Gewürztraminer.**

Basil Crème Anglaise   makes 4 cups (1 L)

1 cup (240 mL) half-and-half cream

1 cup (240 mL) whipping cream

2 Tbsp. (30 mL) granulated sugar

pinch sea salt

1 3-inch (7.5-cm) piece of cinnamon stick

½ of a whole nutmeg, coarsely chopped

5 large egg yolks

½ cup (120 mL) loosely packed fresh basil leaves

Place the creams, sugar, salt, cinnamon stick and nutmeg in a large saucepan and bring to a full rolling boil.

While waiting for the mixture to boil, whisk the egg yolks together.

As soon as the cream reaches a frothy boil, remove from the heat and whisk it in a thin stream into the egg yolks. Strain through a sieve and refrigerate, whisking occasionally until cold. (The crème anglaise may be prepared up to 2 days in advance, covered and refrigerated.)

Bring a small pot of water to a boil. Add the basil leaves and stir a few times, then strain immediately through a sieve and cool under cold water. Drain and squeeze gently to remove the water.

Purée the basil and 1 cup (240 mL) of the crème anglaise in a food processor or blender. Stir the mixture into the remaining cold crème anglaise. Keep refrigerated and serve within 8 hours of making.

Wonderful with seasonal berries **but equally good with ripe peaches and plums.**

Ricotta Panna Cotta with Basil Balsamic Strawberries   serves 8

2½ tsp. (12.5 mL) gelatin

5 Tbsp. (75 mL) cold water

2 cups (480 mL) whipping cream

2/3 cup (160 mL) icing sugar

1 cup (240 mL) full-fat ricotta cheese

1 vanilla bean, slit lengthwise

1 recipe Basil Balsamic Strawberries

Basil Balsamic Strawberries
makes about 1½ cups (360 mL)

1 lb. (454 g) strawberries

2 Tbsp. (30 mL) good-quality, aged balsamic
vinegar

1 tsp. (5 mL) granulated sugar

6 large basil leaves

In a small bowl, soften the gelatin in the water. Combine 1 cup (240 mL) of the cream, icing sugar and vanilla bean in a small pot. Bring to a boil and remove from the heat. Add the gelatin and stir to dissolve. Remove the vanilla bean and scrape the seeds into the cream.

Stir in the remaining cream and ricotta. Pour into 8 4-oz. (114-mL) ramekins. Chill for at least 2 hours or up to overnight. Dip each ramekin into hot water, loosen with a knife and turn out onto individual plates. Garnish with the Basil Balsamic Strawberries.

Basil Balsamic Strawberries
Hull and cut the strawberries into quarters. Toss with the remaining ingredients.

puddings and pies

For years Uncle Leo took all the credit for our family's traditional Christmas dessert. Finally, the truth can be told! It is well worth investing in a pudding mold to make this once-a-year treat. It has a perfect, mouthwatering, sweet-and-sour flavor that is hard to resist — even when you are stuffed with turkey.

Aunt Toni's Steamed Cranberry Pudding with Eggnog Sauce   serves 8

6 Tbsp. (90 mL) unsalted butter

3/4 cup (180 mL) granulated sugar

2 large eggs

2 1/4 cups (540 mL) all-purpose flour

2 1/2 tsp. (12.5 mL) baking powder

1/4 tsp. (1.25 mL) sea salt

1/2 cup (120 mL) milk

2 cups (480 mL) cranberries, fresh or frozen

1/2 cup (120 mL) walnuts or hazelnuts, coarsely chopped

Eggnog Sauce

1 cup (240 mL) unsalted butter

1/2 cup (120 mL) granulated sugar

2 cups (480 mL) prepared eggnog

1/2 cup (120 mL) rum or brandy

Butter and flour the inside and lid of a 6-cup (1.5-L) pudding mold. Set aside.

Cream the butter and sugar until light and fluffy. Add the eggs one at a time, beating well after each addition. Sift the dry ingredients together. Add to the butter mixture alternately with the milk. Fold in the cranberries and nuts and pack into the prepared mold. Place the mold in a pot and pour boiling water into the pot to reach halfway up the side of the mold. Cover with a lid and simmer gently for 2 hours, replenishing with boiling water as necessary.

Remove the pudding from the pot, uncover and cool for 15 minutes before removing from the mold. (The pudding may be wrapped securely in foil and frozen for up to a month. Thaw and resteam for 15 minutes before serving.)

Eggnog Sauce
To make the eggnog sauce, combine the butter, sugar and eggnog in a heavy pot. Bring to a boil and cook for 5 minutes, stirring constantly. Remove from the heat. Stir in the rum or brandy.

Cut the warm pudding into slices and pass the sauce separately.

*The pudding may be made in advance **and frozen. Thaw completely and resteam in the mold for 20 minutes to heat through.***

Steamed Pumpkin Pudding with Cool Maple Sauce   serves 8

2¼ cups (540 mL) flour

1¾ tsp. (9 mL) baking powder

1½ tsp. (7.5 mL) ground cinnamon

1 tsp. (5 mL) ground dried ginger

½ tsp. (2.5 mL) ground nutmeg

¼ tsp. (1.25 mL) ground cloves

½ tsp. (2.5 mL) sea salt

¾ cup (180 mL) unsalted butter at room temperature

2 cups (480 mL) light brown sugar, packed

3 large eggs

1½ cups (360 mL) canned pumpkin purée

1 cup (240 mL) pecans, coarsely chopped

1 recipe Cool Maple Sauce

Cool Maple Sauce
makes 3 cups (720 mL)

8 large egg yolks

½ cup (120 mL) pure maple syrup

pinch sea salt

1 cup (240 mL) half-and-half cream

1 cup (240 mL) whipping cream

1 cup (240 mL) pure vanilla extract

2 Tbsp. (30 mL) walnut liqueur, optional

Generously butter a 2½-qt (2.5-L) pudding mold and lid. Prepare a large, lidded pot with boiling water and a trivet in the bottom. With a whisk, stir the flour, baking powder, cinnamon, ginger, nutmeg, cloves and salt together.

In a large bowl, beat the butter until smooth with an electric mixer. Add the brown sugar and beat until light. Beat in the eggs one at a time. Beat in the pumpkin purée until thoroughly blended. On low speed, add the dry ingredients and mix until just blended. Stir in the pecans.

Transfer to the prepared mold and smooth the top. Clip on the lid and place in the pot. The water should come halfway up the side of the mold. Cover with a lid and steam on medium heat, adding more boiling water if necessary, until a tester comes out clean, about 2 hours. Transfer the mold to a rack and cool for 10 minutes. Loosen the pudding with a small knife and turn out onto the rack. Serve with Cool Maple Sauce on the side.

Cool Maple Sauce
Also delicious over ice cream or on toast.

In a large bowl that will fit over a pot of simmering water but not touch the water, whisk the egg yolks, maple syrup and salt together until well blended. Place over the pot of simmering water and cook, whisking constantly, until the yolks thicken and increase in volume, about 8 minutes. While you are whisking, heat the creams to a simmer in a heavy pot. Whisk the hot cream into the yolk mixture and continue to whisk for 2 more minutes. Remove from the heat and add the vanilla and walnut liqueur. Cool, cover and refrigerate until ready to serve. The sauce may be prepared a day in advance.

This is what happens when croissants go to heaven. **A killer.**

Chocolate, Croissant and Almond Bread Pudding with Bourbon Whipped Cream   serves 6

4 large croissants

8 oz. (227 g) bittersweet chocolate, chopped into ½-inch (1.2-cm) chunks

4 oz. (113 g) marzipan, chopped into ¼-inch (.6-cm) chunks

5 large egg yolks

¼ cup (60 mL) granulated sugar

1 tsp. (5 mL) pure vanilla extract

2 cups (480 mL) half-and-half cream

1½ cups (360 mL) whipping cream

1 Tbsp. (15 mL) icing sugar

2 Tbsp. (30 mL) bourbon

Preheat the oven to 350°F (175°C).

Cut the croissants in half and toast them until golden brown. Tear into ½-inch (1.2-cm) pieces and place in a 9-inch-square (23-cm) deep baking dish.

Evenly distribute the chocolate and marzipan over the croissants. Beat the egg yolks, sugar and vanilla together. Heat the half-and-half cream to just below boiling and whisk it into the egg yolks. Pour the mixture over the croissants. Cover tightly with aluminum foil and place in a larger pan. Pour enough boiling water into the outer pan so that it comes halfway up the side of the baking dish. Bake for 30–35 minutes or until just set. Remove from the water bath, remove the foil and cool.

Whip the cream and icing sugar until soft peaks form. Stir in the bourbon and serve the whipped cream with the pudding.

I used to love the rich brown cakes, similar to steamed brown bread, sold in cans when I was a child. You would open both ends of the can and push the cake out. I loved to eat it thickly spread with butter. This is a grown-up version with dried pears and cranberries, but you can omit the fruit if you like it plain. Use a 3-qt. (3-L) stainless steel bowl, 2 8-cup (2-L) pudding molds or my personal preference, 2 coffee cans. See Steamers and Steaming, page 158.

Steamed Brown Bread with Dried Pears and Cranberries   serves 8

1 cup (240 mL) flour, all-purpose or whole wheat

1 cup (240 mL) rye flour

1 cup (240 mL) cornmeal

2 tsp. (10 mL) baking soda

1 tsp. (5 mL) salt

1 cup (240 mL) table molasses (not black strap or unsulphured)

2 cups (480 mL) buttermilk

3/4 cup (180 mL) finely chopped dried pears

1/2 cup (120 mL) dried cranberries

Butter the molds you have chosen. Fill half of a steamer bottom or a pot with water. If you are using a pot, place a trivet inside and bring the water to a boil.

Into a large bowl, sift the flours, cornmeal, baking soda and salt. Mix the molasses and buttermilk together, add to the dry ingredients and mix until just smooth. Stir in the pears and cranberries. Pour evenly into the prepared molds, cover tightly with tinfoil or lids and place in the steamer or pot. Cover with a lid and turn the heat down to a simmer. Replenish the water with more boiling water as necessary. Check smaller molds after 2 hours and large ones after 3 hours. A toothpick inserted in the center will come out clean when the bread is done. Remove the breads from the steamer and cool on a rack for 5 minutes before removing from the mold. Cool completely before slicing with a serrated knife.

This warm pudding is a luscious late fall dessert. If you have never had persimmons, this is a good way to start. The really ripe and fragrant ones you need for this recipe are generally less expensive than the perfect glowing orange ones available for sale in the fall.

Warm Persimmon Pudding makes 1 8-inch (23-cm) tart, serves 6 to 8

4 large, very soft persimmons

3 large eggs

1 cup (240 mL) granulated sugar

½ cup (120 mL) unsalted butter, melted

1½ cups (360 mL) all-purpose flour

1 tsp. (5 mL) baking soda

1 tsp. (5 mL) baking powder

½ tsp. (2.5 mL) ground ginger

½ tsp. (2.5 mL) ground cinnamon

¼ tsp. (1.25 mL) ground allspice

½ tsp. (2.5 mL) sea salt

2 cups (480 mL) half-and-half cream

Preheat the oven to 350°F (180°C). Butter an 8-inch (20-cm) springform pan.

To make the persimmon purée, cut the persimmons in half and scoop out the pulp. Press through a sieve and discard the seeds and fibers. You should have 2 cups (480 mL) of purée. (To quickly ripen persimmons, freeze them overnight. They will be ready to use when thawed completely.)

With a mixer or by hand, beat the eggs and sugar until well combined. Beat in the melted butter.

Sift the dry ingredients together and stir into the egg mixture. Stir in the cream, then the persimmon purée. Pour into the oiled pan and bake for about 40 minutes, or until a skewer inserted in the middle comes out clean. The pudding will sink as it cools. Serve warm with lightly whipped cream if desired.

One of the glories of summer occurs when raspberries and currants are ripe **and ready to be made into this dessert. It is so mouth-watering and easy to make that it deserves to be more popular. Bread and stewed fruit do not provoke the imagination or taste buds, but sitting overnight together transforms these simple ingredients into an exquisite dessert. I was talking to local food writer and cookbook author Noël Richardson about summer pudding. She said that it was made with gooseberries on Saturna Island where she grew up and was called Saturna Pudding. Saturna is such a romantic, even magical-sounding name, quite appropriate for this dish.**

Summer Pudding   serves 6 to 8

1 large loaf sliced white bread, one or two days old

2 cups (480 mL) red or white currants, stems removed

1 cup (240 mL) granulated sugar

3 Tbsp. (45 mL) water

2½ pints (1.2 L) raspberries (save a few for garnish)

lightly sweetened whipped cream or crème fraîche (see page 291)

Select a bowl of 2-quart (2-L) capacity in which to make the pudding. Line it with plastic wrap.

Cut the crusts from the bread and cut each slice diagonally. Line the bowl with the bread so that there are no gaps.

Combine the currants, sugar and water in a saucepan and cook over medium heat, stirring gently from time to time, until the currants start to release their juice. Add the raspberries and cook until their juice starts to run. Pour into the bread-lined mold and cover with a layer of bread. Bring the plastic wrap up over the top of the pudding, using more plastic wrap if needed to cover the top. Place a plate of about the same diameter as the bowl on top of the pudding and weight it down with a few cans or jars. Refrigerate overnight. (The pudding may be made up to 3 days in advance.)

To serve, remove the weights and plates from the pudding and open the plastic wrap. Invert the pudding onto a plate and remove the plastic wrap. Garnish with the mint sprigs and reserved raspberries. Pass a bowl of whipped cream or crème fraîche separately.

Meredith, the Fish House Pastry Chef, has done a fine job of tweaking this recipe into greatness, and it has a very large fan club. Every year we buy crateloads of Coronation Grapes that we freeze for making this pie all winter. The grapes are seedless and have a beautiful balance of sweet and sour. If you can find them — they're around in September — use them instead of the blueberries. The finishing touch is a caramelized top. We sprinkle the pie lightly with sugar and caramelize the sugar.

Okanagan Buttermilk Pie with Blueberries   makes 1 10-inch (25-cm) pie

1 tsp. (5 mL) coriander seeds

½ tsp. (2.5 mL) fennel seeds

½ cup (120 mL) whole toasted almonds, finely chopped

½ cup (120 mL) whole toasted hazelnuts, finely chopped

1 cup (240 mL) graham wafer crumbs

½ cup (120 mL) butter, melted and slightly browned

1 lb. (454 g) cream cheese, at room temperature

⅔ cup (160 mL) granulated sugar

3 eggs

1 tsp. (5 mL) pure vanilla extract

¾ cup (180 mL) buttermilk

1⅓ cups (320 mL) blueberries

To prepare the crust, heat a dry frying pan over medium heat. Add the coriander and fennel seeds and roast, shaking the pan constantly until they are lightly browned and aromatic. Cool and grind in a coffee grinder. Combine the seeds with the nuts, graham crumbs and butter. Mix well and press into 1- by 10-inch (2.5-cm by 25-cm) pie pan.

Preheat the oven to 300°F (150°C).

To prepare the filling, beat cream cheese and sugar together until smooth. Beat in the eggs one at a time, scraping down the bowl after each egg and beating until smooth. Beat in the vanilla and buttermilk.

Spread the blueberries in the pie crust and cover with the batter. Bake for 25–35 minutes, until the filling becomes golden brown around the outside edge and barely jiggles in the center. Transfer to a rack to cool completely and refrigerate for at least 4 hours before cutting.

When I plan dinners for winemakers, the first step is some playful food and wine tasting. I run back and forth from the kitchen to the table, with bits of spices, herbs, cheese, vegetables—whatever! But when it came to the porter, we had trouble. Chocolate was suggested. We tasted, sipped, froze. The chocolate and porter combined to create the flavor of chocolate-covered maraschino cherries! My friend and then sous-chef Andrew decided to use porter instead of coffee in my recipe for chocolate silk pie. It worked like a charm. If you don't want to use the porter, substitute strong black coffee instead.

Chocolate and Porter Silk Pie   makes 1 9-inch (23-cm) pie

1 recipe Chocolate Pastry

6 Tbsp. (90 mL) rich, fruity porter

1 cup (240 mL) unsalted butter

¼ cup (60 mL) granulated sugar

9 oz. (270 g) bittersweet chocolate, finely chopped

6 large egg yolks, at room temperature

¼ tsp. (1.2 mL) sea salt

1 cup (240 mL) whipping cream

Chocolate Pastry
makes 1 9-inch (23-cm) pie shell

1 cup (240 mL) all-purpose flour

½ cup (120 mL) granulated sugar

½ cup (120 mL) cocoa

¾ cup (185 mL) cold unsalted butter, cut into ½-inch (1.2-cm) cubes

1 large egg, beaten

Preheat the oven to 350°F (175°C). Press the pastry evenly into a 9-inch (23-cm) pie pan. Chill for 30 minutes. Prick with a fork and weight. Bake for 15 minutes. Remove the weights and cook for 10–15 minutes longer, until the pastry is completely dry and cooked through. Cool.

Combine the porter, butter and sugar in a saucepan. Bring to a boil and add the chocolate. Remove from the heat and whisk until the chocolate is completely melted and smooth. Scrape into a bowl. With a whisk or electric mixer, beat in the egg yolks one at a time. Mix in the salt. Cool to room temperature.

Pour half of the chocolate mixture into the cooled pie shell and refrigerate. Place the other half in the fridge as well. Stir the mixture in the bowl frequently until it is cold but not firm.

Whip the cream to soft peaks and fold into the cooled chocolate. Pile onto the pie in decorative swirls or use a pastry bag if you are feeling ambitious. Chill until set, about 4 hours. Keeps well for 4 days, refrigerated.

Chocolate Pastry
Place the flour, sugar and cocoa in the work bowl of a food processor and pulse a few times to combine. Scatter the butter on top and pulse until mealy. Pour the egg through the feed tube and pulse briefly. The dough should not come together in a ball. Turn out the pastry and gently form a loose ball. Cover and set aside at room temperature for 30 minutes before using. If you are not using the pastry immediately, wrap tightly and refrigerate for up to 5 days or freeze for up to one month.

To my taste, this leaves mincemeat in the culinary Dark Ages. **Serve it with sweetened whipped cream to which you have added a bit of rum or brandy.**

Christmas Pie   makes 1 10-inch (25-cm) pie

1 cup (240 mL) pitted prunes

1½ cups (360 mL) boiling water

⅔ cup (160 mL) Candied Kumquats

3 cups (720 mL) apples, peeled and thinly sliced

1 Tbsp. (15 mL) all-purpose flour

2 Tbsp. (30 mL) syrup from the candied kumquats

10 oz. (285 g) marzipan

4 Tbsp. (60 mL) butter

2 eggs

1 recipe Flaky Pastry (see page 292)

1 egg yolk

1 Tbsp. (15 mL) water

1 Tbsp. (15 mL) granulated sugar

Candied Kumquats
makes 2½ cups (600 mL)

1 lb. (454 g) kumquats

2 cups (480 mL) granulated sugar

1½ cups (360 mL) water

Preheat the oven to 425°F (220°C).

Pour the boiling water over the prunes, cover and let stand for 10 minutes. Drain well and coarsely chop. Combine the prunes, kumquats, apples, flour and kumquat syrup. Set aside. Place the marzipan in the work bowl of a food processor and pulse a few times. Add the butter and eggs and pulse until well combined. If you're using an electric mixer, beat the marzipan on low speed for one minute. Beat in the butter until combined, then the eggs, one at a time.

Roll out the pastry into a 15-inch (38-cm) round. Fit the pastry into the pan but do not trim the excess. Spread the marzipan mixture over the bottom of the pastry, then evenly distribute the apple mixture on top. Fold the pastry over the pie, coaxing it into elegant folds. Beat the egg yolk with the water. Brush the top of the pie with the egg yolk mixture and sprinkle with the sugar. Bake in the center of the oven for 15 minutes. Reduce the heat to 350°F (175°C) and bake for another 30–40 minutes, until the pastry is golden brown. Serve warm or at room temperature.

Candied Kumquats
Kumquats are small, oblong oranges that appear in winter. Preserved, they can be eaten skin and all; unlike oranges, the skin is not bitter. Candied kumquats can be eaten on toast or served with pork and chicken.

Cut the kumquats in half through the middle and pick out the seeds with the point of a small knife. Combine the sugar and water in a heavy saucepan. Bring to a boil and add the kumquats. Turn down to a bare simmer and cook for ½ hour, until the kumquats turn darker and become translucent. Cool. The kumquats will keep indefinitely, covered and refrigerated.

The apple version of this is the classic Tarte Tatin. **For best flavor and texture, serve it warm or at room temperature, never cold.**

Upside-Down Pear Tart   makes 1 10-inch (25-cm) tart, serves 6 to 8

2 cups (480 mL) all-purpose flour

1 Tbsp. (15 mL) granulated sugar

1/4 tsp. (1.25 mL) sea salt

3/2 cup (180 mL) unsalted butter, well chilled

1/3 cup (80 mL) ice-cold water

8 slightly underripe Bartlett pears

1/2 cup (120 mL) unsalted butter

1 cup (240 mL) sugar

Place the flour, the 1 Tbsp. (15 mL) sugar and salt in a large bowl and whisk well to combine. Cut the 3/4 cup (180 mL) butter into 1/4-inch (.6-cm) cubes and toss with the flour mixture. Add the water all at once and blend it in with your hand. Knead gently with the tips of your fingers until the dough forms a rough ball. There will be dots of butter here and there through the dough. Flatten the dough and wrap in plastic wrap. Refrigerate for 1/2 hour.

Preheat the oven to 400°F (200°C). While the pastry is chilling, peel, core and cut the pears into quarters. Have a deep 10-inch (25-cm) pie plate at hand. In a heavy frying pan melt the 1/2 cup (120 mL) butter over medium heat. Add the 1 cup (240 mL) sugar and cook, stirring frequently, until the sugar turns a deep brown. Add the pears and cook them, turning frequently. As the pears cook, they will shrink considerably and exude juice that will combine with the sugar and butter to form a syrup. Each piece of pear will become caramelized all the way through. As this happens, transfer the pieces, cut side down, to the pie plate. When all the pears are done, pour the syrup and any remaining pears into the pie pan.

On a floured surface, roll the pastry out to 1/4-inch (.6-cm) thickness. Cut a circle out of the pastry that is 1 inch (2.5 cm) larger than the top of the pie pan. Roll the pastry around the rolling pin and unroll it over the pears. Lightly tuck the edges into the pan. Place in the oven and bake for 20–30 minutes, until the pastry is golden brown. Allow the tart to cool to warm before turning it out onto a plate. Serve with lightly whipped cream or crème fraîche, page 291.

The tart is best served warm on the same day it was made. If you wish, you may bake it in advance and reheat it in a low oven.

This pie has been a staple for years and made it onto the Fish House menu when the restaurant first re-opened in 1995. When it came time to change to the fall menu, I took it off, thinking it was too summery. The servers circulated a petition, demanding the pie be put back on the menu because it was easy to sell and well loved by all who ate it. It has remained on the menu ever since, and continues to please.

Coconut Cream Pie   serves 6 to 8

1 fully baked 9-inch (23-cm) pie shell (see Flaky Pastry page 292)

2 cups (480 mL) sweetened, long-shred coconut

½ cup (120 mL) granulated sugar

2 large eggs

2 Tbsp. (30 mL) all-purpose flour

pinch sea salt

2 cups (480 mL) milk

2 Tbsp. (30 mL) unsalted butter

1 tsp. (5 mL) pure vanilla extract

1 cup (240 mL) whipping cream

Have a prebaked pie shell ready. Preheat the oven to 350°F (175°C). Spread ½ cup (120 mL) of the coconut onto a baking sheet and toast, watching carefully, until it is golden brown, about 3–5 minutes. Remove and cool. Place the remaining coconut in the freezer.

Beat the sugar, eggs, flour and salt together until smooth. Heat the milk in a large, heavy pot until just below the boiling point. Whisk the milk slowly into the egg mixture, then return it to the pot. Stir constantly over high heat with a rubber spatula until the mixture comes to a boil. Immediately remove from the heat and stir in the chilled coconut (the chilled coconut stops the cooking and prevents curdling). Scrape into a bowl and stir in the butter and vanilla. Cool completely. Cover and refrigerate until cold, or up to 3 days.

A few hours before you serve the pie, but not too early or the crust will get soggy, transfer the cold coconut mixture to the baked pie shell and smooth out the top. Whip the cream until soft peaks form and swirl it over the top of the pie. Sprinkle with the toasted coconut and refrigerate until ready to serve.

Former Fish House sous-chef Matt **gets the credit for this great dessert!**

Cornmeal Hazelnut Shortcakes with Rhubarb Mango Compote serves 8

1¼ cups (300 mL) all-purpose flour

⅓ cup (80 mL) granulated sugar

2 Tbsp. (30 mL) cornmeal

1½ tsp. (7.5 mL) baking powder

½ tsp. (2.5 mL) baking soda

¼ tsp. (1.25 mL) sea salt

⅓ cup (80 mL) finely chopped hazelnuts

2 Tbsp. (30 mL) minced candied ginger

6 Tbsp. (90 mL) unsalted butter, chilled and
cut into small cubes

¾ cup (180 mL) buttermilk

1 ripe mango, peeled and diced

1 Tbsp. (15 mL) minced candied ginger

1 recipe Rhubarb Compote

1½ cups (360 mL) whipping cream

1 Tbsp. (15 mL) granulated sugar

1 tsp. (5 mL) pure vanilla extract

Rhubarb Compote
makes about 4 cups (1 L)

2 lbs. (900 g) fresh young rhubarb with
pink stems

1½ cups (360 mL) sugar

¼ cup (60 mL) water

Preheat the oven to 350°F (175°C). In a large mixing bowl, whisk together the flour, sugar, cornmeal, baking powder and soda, salt, hazelnuts and ginger. Add the butter and cut into the flour mixture till the size of small peas. Add the buttermilk and blend quickly. Drop 16 mounds onto a nonstick baking sheet. With wet fingers or the back of a wet spoon, flatten out to ½-inch-thick (1.2-cm) rounds. Bake for 12–15 minutes until golden brown. Remove to a rack to cool.

To serve the shortcakes, mix the mango and ginger into the Rhubarb Compote. Whip the cream with the sugar and vanilla until medium-firm peaks form. Place 8 biscuits on 8 plates. Top with whipped cream and a ladleful of the compote. Seat another biscuit on top. Follow with another dollop of whipped cream and compote.

Rhubarb Compote
Serve warm, sprinkled with cinnamon, and buttered toast on the side, for an instant comfort food.

Trim the leaves and the lower end of the stalks from the rhubarb and cut into 1-inch (2.5-cm) chunks. Place in a noncorrodible saucepan with the sugar and water. Cover and set over low heat. Stew gently for at least an hour. The slower it cooks the better, as the rhubarb retains its shape. Remove from the heat and cool in a bowl. Cover and refrigerate. The compote will keep for 2 weeks.

One of the ultimate summer pleasures. One of my favorite things about it, besides eating it, is squashing the berries with my hands and watching them flow between my fingers. It is a very satisfying activity.

Strawberry Shortcake   serves 8

2¼ cups (540 mL) all-purpose flour

½ cup (120 mL) sugar

1½ tsp. (7.5 mL) baking powder

¾ tsp. (3.75 mL) baking soda

½ tsp. (2.5 mL) sea salt

6 Tbsp. (90 mL) unsalted butter, chilled

⅔ cup (160 mL) buttermilk

1 large egg yolk

½ tsp. (2.5 mL) pure vanilla extract

3 pints (1.5 L) strawberries, washed and hulled

¼ cup (60 mL) granulated sugar

3 cups (720 mL) whipping cream

2 Tbsp. (30 mL) granulated sugar

Preheat the oven to 350°F (175°C). Sift the flour, sugar, baking powder, baking soda and salt into a large bowl. Cut the butter into ½-inch (1.2-cm) cubes and toss with the flour mixture. Cut in the butter with a pastry blender or two knives until mealy. Beat the buttermilk, egg yolk and vanilla together. Combine the buttermilk with the flour mixture, stirring with a fork until just combined. Transfer the dough to a buttered and floured baking sheet and pat out evenly into a 9-inch (23-cm) circle. Bake for 15–20 minutes until golden brown. Transfer to a rack to cool.

Slice 2 cups (480 mL) of the strawberries and reserve. Lightly mash the remaining berries with a potato masher (or your hands). Stir in the sugar and set aside until you are ready to assemble the shortcake.

When the shortcake is completely cool, split it in half horizontally. Whip the cream with the sugar into soft peaks. Spread half of the mashed berries on the bottom half of the shortcake. Cover with half of the whipped cream. Gently cover with the top half of the shortcake. Spread the remaining berries and whipped cream on the top. Decorate with the reserved sliced berries. Refrigerate for at least ½ hour before serving.

muffins
and
miscellaneous

If you only make one muffin in your life, **this should be the one.**

Okanagan Apple Muffins   makes 15 muffins

½ cup (120 mL) brown sugar, firmly packed

6 Tbsp. (90 mL) all-purpose flour

¼ cup (60 mL) unsalted butter, melted

1 tsp. (5 mL) ground cinnamon

1½ cups (360 mL) brown sugar, firmly packed

⅔ cup (160 mL) vegetable oil

1 large egg

1 tsp. (5 mL) pure vanilla extract

1 cup (240 mL) water

2 tsp. (10 mL) apple cider vinegar

2½ cups (600 mL) all-purpose flour

1 tsp. (5 mL) baking soda

½ tsp. (2.5 mL) sea salt

2 cups (480 mL) peeled apple, diced into
  ½-inch (1-cm) chunks

Preheat the oven to 325°F (165°C). Butter and flour a 15-cup muffin tin, or line with paper cups.

To make the topping, combine the ½ cup (120 mL) brown sugar, 6 Tbsp. (90 mL) flour, butter and cinnamon in a bowl. Mix with your fingers until crumbly. Set aside. Beat the 1½ cups (360 mL) brown sugar, oil, egg and vanilla together in a large bowl. Combine the water and vinegar. Sift the flour, soda and salt together and blend into the oil mixture alternately with the water. Add the diced apple and mix until just combined. Spoon into the prepared muffin pan and sprinkle generously with the topping. Bake for 30 minutes, until golden brown and the top springs back when lightly touched.

Always a popular muffin **in this part of the world.**

Rhubarb and Raspberry Muffins makes 12 muffins

1 large egg

1 cup (240 mL) brown sugar

¼ cup (60 mL) unsalted butter, melted

¾ cup (180 mL) sour cream or yogurt

2 cups (480 mL) all-purpose flour

1 tsp. (5 mL) baking soda

¼ tsp. (1.25 mL) sea salt

¼ tsp. (1.25 mL) ground cinnamon

¾ cup (180 mL) diced rhubarb, fresh or frozen

¾ cup (180 mL) raspberries, fresh or frozen

Preheat the oven to 350°F (180°C). Butter and flour a 12-cup muffin tin, or line with paper cups. Beat the egg, brown sugar, melted butter and sour cream or yogurt together. Sift the flour, baking soda, salt and cinnamon together. Combine the wet and dry ingredients, mixing only until combined. Fold in the rhubarb and raspberries. Spoon into the prepared tin.

Bake for 25–30 minutes, until slightly browned and the top springs back when lightly touched.

Try sandwiching slices of this loaf **with strawberry ice cream for a deluxe ice cream sandwich.**

Blueberry Lemon Loaf   makes 2 small loaves

2 cups (480 mL) all-purpose flour

2 tsp. (10 mL) baking powder

½ tsp. (2.5 mL) sea salt

½ cup (120 mL) unsalted butter, softened

1 cup (240 mL) granulated sugar

2 large eggs

2 tsp. (10 mL) pure vanilla extract

2 Tbsp. (30 mL) finely grated lemon zest

⅔ cup (160 mL) milk

1½ cups (360 mL) blueberries, fresh or frozen

Preheat the oven to 350°F (175°C). Butter and flour two 6- by 3-inch (15- by 7.5-cm) loaf pans.

Sift the flour, baking powder and salt together. Cream the butter and sugar until light and fluffy. Add the eggs one at a time, beating well after each addition. Beat in the vanilla and lemon zest. Add half the flour mixture, beating well, then half the milk. Add the rest of the flour, then the rest of the milk. Gently fold half the blueberries into the batter.

Spoon the batter into the prepared pans. Sprinkle the rest of the berries over the tops of the loaves. Bake for 45–50 minutes, until golden brown and a toothpick inserted into the middle of the loaves comes out clean. Cool in the pans for 10 minutes, then remove to a rack to finish cooling.

Lighter than the lightest cheesecake, **with crisp flakes of chocolate that melt in your mouth, and profoundly simple in ingredients and execution, this is one of the most delicious summer desserts you can make.**

Ethereal Chocolate Cream   serves 4 to 6

2 cups (480 mL) crème fraîche (see page 291) well chilled

6 Tbsp. (90 mL) icing sugar

4 oz. (113 g) hot, melted, bittersweet chocolate

fresh berries of your choice

Whip the crème fraîche and icing sugar with a whisk until the mixture mounds lightly. Fold in the chocolate to form long streaks in the crème fraîche. It is important that the chocolate be hot to form long streaks. Do not overblend or the mixture will be uniformly chocolate and lose its charm.

Line a 2-cup (480-mL) *couer à la crème* mold or a small, shallow, clean basket (it will leave a lovely basket-weave imprint on the cream) with a piece of cheesecloth large enough to enclose the top. (Couer à la crème molds are ceramic, heart-shaped molds with drainage holes in the bottom. Most good kitchenware stores carry them.) Pour in the crème fraîche mixture and smooth the top. Bring the overhanging cheesecloth over the top. Cover with plastic wrap, place on a plate to catch the drips and refrigerate overnight.

To serve, unfold the top of the cheesecloth and center a plate over the mold. Flip the whole arrangement over and slip off the mold. Remove the cheesecloth. Surround with the fresh berries and serve immediately.

We of the Pacific Northwest love coffee. In fact, this geographic area is sometimes called latte land, a twist on a more common appellation — la la land. This is a lovely, simple dessert — refreshing and creamy at the same time.

Espresso Granita with Vanilla Ice Cream   serves 4 to 6

1 cup (240 mL) hot espresso or extremely
  strong coffee made from an espresso roast

1/2 cup (120 mL) granulated sugar

3/4 cup (180 mL) cold water

vanilla ice cream

coffee beans for garnish

To make the granita, combine the hot espresso with the sugar and stir until dissolved. Add the cold water and pour the mixture into a shallow pan that will fit in the freezer. Stir every 15 minutes with a whisk, breaking up the clumps of ice crystals until frozen.

To serve, place a scoop of vanilla ice cream in an individual dish, wine glass or martini glass. Place a scoop of granita on top. (The granita will not scoop neatly like ice cream; this is how it should be.) Garnish with a few coffee beans and serve immediately.

Crème fraîche is cultured cream, similar in flavor to sour cream, with all the properties of whipping cream. Sour cream provides the bacterial culture required. Check the container to make sure that the sour cream you are using does contain bacterial culture.

Crème Fraîche   makes 2 cups (480 mL)

½ cup (120 mL) sour cream
1½ cups (360 mL) whipping cream

Place the sour cream in a bowl and whisk briefly to loosen it up. Slowly whisk in the whipping cream. Don't whip the cream, just make sure it is thoroughly blended. Cover and keep in a warm place overnight. Transfer to a storage container and refrigerate overnight before using. Crème fraîche will keep for 3–4 weeks refrigerated and gets better with age.

Crème fraîche can be heated or reduced without breaking up (as sour cream does), or whipped like whipping cream. Because it seems to thicken more quickly than whipping cream, I prefer to use a whisk rather than an electric mixer; it gives me more control over the result.

Flaky Pastry   makes 1 9- or 10-inch (23- or 25-cm) pie or tart

2 cups (480 mL) all-purpose flour

1/2 tsp. (2.5 mL) sea salt

3/4 cup (180 mL) unsalted butter, well chilled

1/3 cup (80 mL) ice-cold water

Combine the flour and salt in a large bowl. Cut the butter into 1/2-inch (1.2-cm) cubes and place on a plate in the freezer for 5 minutes.

Toss the chilled butter with the flour. Add the water and knead gently with your fingertips until the mixture forms a shaggy ball. Do not try to incorporate the flour that remains in the bottom of the bowl. Use immediately, or wrap and refrigerate for up to 3 days.

KEEP THOSE PASTRY SCRAPS!
One of my childhood indulgences was the cinnamon pinwheels my grandmother used to make with leftover pie dough. She would fit the scraps together, slightly overlapping them, and roll them out into a long rectangle. Next, she would spread a little butter on the dough and sprinkle it with sugar and cinnamon. After rolling it up like a jelly roll, she would cut it into slices that she would bake on a cookie sheet along with the pie. I would always snatch them off the pan before they cooled, usually burning the inside of my mouth, so eager was I to gobble them down. It is still the best part of making a pie.

When this was written, I had one dog, Io. After a few months of living in Gastown, we both had the good fortune to meet Tobias, and Simone who was fostering him. The first meeting of the dogs was pleasant, but subsequent meetings blossomed into a full-blown, doggy love relationship. They played like puppies and couldn't keep their mouths off of one another. Simone had to return overseas and two families that were interested in Tobias fell through. I had been flirting with the idea of adopting Tobias. When there was no home for him and a return to the Pound was looming in his future, I knew that he had found a home with me and Io. It was one of the best decisions of my life, and they're still playing like puppies.

Before deciding to make Io's food, I asked myself: What is that kibble stuff anyway and would I like to eat extruded pellets for the rest of my life? It is convenient for humans to serve, but not the best thing for a dog to eat. The effort has paid off well. She has a beautiful, shiny black coat, bright eyes and, unlike her mother, gets loads of compliments on her good looks and healthy glow. Besides this food, Io's diet is supplemented with the occasional piece of overcooked fish. I vary the grains by using millet, barley and quinoa. Sometimes I substitute lamb for the beef. After watching her eat grass, I tried sprouting grain for part of the grain, but she enjoys eating grass more as a late night walk snack.

Io's Food   enough for 5 to 6 Dobermann pinscher-sized meals

½ lb. (227 g) raw whole grain

5 cups (1.2 L) water

8 Ester C (Vitamin C) capsules

8 Kyolic garlic pills

2 lbs. (900 g) extra-lean ground beef

1 lb. (454 g) grated raw carrots or zucchini

6 Tbsp. (90 mL) flax seed oil or essential fatty acids oil blend

Combine the grain and water in a large lidded pot. Bring to a boil, turn down to a simmer and cook for 1 hour, until the grain is very soft. Remove from the heat and cool until completely cold.

In a spice or coffee grinder, grind the Ester C and garlic pills to a powder. Combine with the ground beef, carrots or zucchini and oil. Mix well. Keep refrigerated.